Perversity and Ethics

Perversity and Ethics

William Egginton

STANFORD UNIVERSITY PRESS

Stanford, California 2006

Stanford University Press
Stanford, California
© 2006 by the Board of Trustees of the
Leland Stanford Junior University

Library of Congress Cataloging-in-Publication Data

Egginton, William.
    Perversity and ethics / William Egginton.
        p.   cm.
    Includes bibliographical references and index.
    ISBN 0-8047-5258-3 (hardcover : alk. paper) —
    ISBN 0-8047-5259-1 (pbk. : alk. paper)
    1. Ethics.   2. Good and evil.   I. Title.
BJ1034.E34   2006
170—dc22

                                                            2005021275

Printed in the United States of America
Original Printing 2005
Last figure below indicates year of this printing:
15   14   13   12   11   10   09   08   07   06

Typeset at Stanford University Press in 11/13 Adobe Garamond

Contents

Acknowledgments

I THANK the following people, without whose influence, aid, advice, and corrections the present work would have been less convincing and more speculative and had fewer insights and far more errors than it does even in its present form. In alphabetical, rather than order of appearance or importance, they are: Mary Bearden, Joan Copjec, Tim Dean, John Feneron, Christopher Fynsk, Rodolphe Gasché, Peter Gilgen, Elizabeth Grosz, Sepp Gumbrecht, Martin Hägglund, Robert Harrison, David E. Johnson, Ernesto Laclau, Carine Mardorossian, Angie Michaelis, Norris Pope, Jean-Michel Rabaté, Charles Shepherdson, Bernadette Wegenstein, and Slavoj Žižek.

Sections of Chapter 3 have appeared, in different form, in the *Journal for Cultural and Religious Theory* and *CR: the New Centennial Review*. Thanks to these journals for permission to use that material. Thanks to the University of Toronto's Robarts Library, where the last several months of research on this project were completed. Thanks, as always, to the Philosophical Reading Group at the University at Buffalo, and to my colleagues in Romance Languages and Literatures and Comparative Literature, who have inspired me in countless ways.

This book is dedicated to Berna, Xandi, and Charlie, who will always be my home.

Preface

God said, "You shall not eat of the fruit of the tree which is in the
midst of the garden, neither shall you touch it, lest you die."
—Genesis 2:17

But sweeter still than this, than these, than all,
Is first and passionate love—it stands alone,
Like Adam's recollection of his fall;
The tree of knowledge has been plucked—all's known—
And life yields nothing further to recall
Worthy of this ambrosial sin, so shown,
No doubt in fable, as the unforgiven
Fire which from Prometheus filched for us from heaven.
—Lord Byron, *Don Juan*

The story of the fall of man would seem to place the blame for that catastrophe squarely on woman's shoulders. When the serpent questions Eve's
right to cull the fruits of the world's first and most perfect orchard, she admits to knowing of God's prohibition. But we know, because the Serpent
tells Eve—and God had earlier told Adam—that the fruit of the one tree
imparts the knowledge of good and evil, knowledge that, in the purity of
her Edenic innocence, Eve cannot possible have.

As commentators new and old have noted, there is something deeply
puzzling about Eve's supposed transgression: how can she understand what
amounts to a moral prohibition, the rule against eating from the one tree,
if the knowledge required to distinguish between good and evil, between
right and wrong, is only to be had as a result of that act? This paradox
holds the key to a radical questioning of the relation between perversity
and ethics—the title of this book.

If a properly ethical act, in a formulation typical of modern ethics, is an act that is good per se, a perverse act would be not merely an evil act, but an act of evil per se. What the story of Eve's temptation reveals, however, is that the poles of ethical and perverse action, their roles as absolute motivators of behavior, are from the outset hopelessly intertwined. To do the right thing, or the wrong thing, means to be primordially inhabited by what I call the *ethical fault-line*, a rift at the core of identity that drafts the blueprint for the moral self and orients the self's desire.

Perversity and Ethics begins by considering the importance of psychoanalysis for discussions of philosophical ethics. As I explore in the first chapter, "Freud and the Banishment of Evil," psychoanalysis has commonly been received as at best irrelevant to ethical thought and at worst—because of its highly causal and apparently mechanistic understanding of the workings of human desire—a repudiation of the very idea of moral responsibility. Nevertheless, if psychoanalysis has been largely ignored by ethical thought, psychoanalytic theory has not ignored ethics. Indeed, Jacques Lacan's seminar of 1959–60, widely considered by his followers as among the most crucial in his intellectual legacy, was dedicated to what he called the *ethics of psychoanalysis*. What has been lacking, however, despite numerous and often excellent readings of the Lacanian contribution to the ethical tradition—and in particular its engagements with Kantian thought[1]—has been a sustained attempt to understand the extraordinary power and complexity of the psychoanalytic challenge to ethics in the context of contemporary ethical thought. Under the enormous influence of Slavoj Žižek's psychoanalytic engagements with philosophy and politics, it has become increasingly common among Lacanian theorists, for example, to disparage—against the idealization of the figure of the pervert among thinkers influenced by Foucault—perversion as being in no way subversive of political hegemony.[2] Equally crucial, however, is the extent to which the injunctions of modern ethical systems are themselves inevitably implicated in structures of desire that can only be described as perverse. The primordial status of the perverse moment in ethical philosophy is the central theme of this book.

In Chapter 1 I use the texts that constitute Freud's metapsychological theory—his theory of the psychosomatic foundations of human desire—to derive the notion of *institutionalization*: the process whereby the very foundation of the self coincides with the emergence of a fundamental level of drive that is directed against the moral codes and social barriers that are the self's most basic elements. The historical trajectory of these institutionalizations constitutes the book's key theoretical construct, the ethical fault-line. This concept leads in Chapter 2, "In the Beginning Was the *(Orthos) Logos*," to a discussion of Lacan's seventh seminar, which is dedicated to the ethics of psychoanalysis. At the outset of those lectures Lacan speaks of his theme as being "the universe of fault," which in French (*la faute*) signifies at once guilt or culpability—that is, the force of the law—as well as the desire to transgress that law in order to attain what lacks, that which it holds from us. It is from this multivalence that the fault-line gains its force. In this second chapter I explore Lacan's rethinking of Freud's reality principle—and of the very notion of reality inherent in it—as being primordially imbricated with laws, ethical norms, and institutions, such that abstract ideals (the good, the beautiful) are understood as affective derivatives of what Lacan calls *das Ding*, the substantial embodiment of institutionalization that simultaneously marks the innermost and outermost limits of the subject's experience of self. While Lacan carefully develops this notion as the ultimate impasse to traditional ethics, it is also the place where he turns to the possibility of another way of thinking through the ethical conundrum he has revealed. In his infamous reading of Sophocles's *Antigone*, for example, Lacan, now deeply engaged with the philosophy of Martin Heidegger, speculates that if the ethical has been repudiated in its pretensions to universally determine the good, it returns as the uncanny and ineradicable knowledge of the self's ultimate inability to be fully self-identical.

In the third chapter, "Deconstruction and the Theology of Desire," the theoretical resonances outlined in the preceding chapter between the Heideggerian notion of authenticity and Lacan's notion of the ethical as a refusal to "give way as to one's desire" will be brought into dialogue with a series of insights I will broadly refer to as deconstructive. These insights can be called deconstructive because they are united by a questioning of what Nancy describes as the "immanentism" of ethical models—according to which a core identity is assumed to exist prior to an individual's entry into relations with others. By way of an engagement with the writings of Jean-Luc Nancy and Søren Kierkegaard, I argue that psychoanalysis and deconstructive thinking converge around the affirmation of the radical impossibility of ever mediating—bringing to a close, fully understanding, or even moving beyond—what Kierkegaard calls the paradox of mediation.

That the paradox of mediation cannot be mediated means, on the one hand, that the absolute or the immediate must always be approached via history, and hence through mediation; whereas, on the other hand, the very notion of mediation necessitates an absolute or immediate that mediation keeps just beyond our grasp. The convergence of these thinkers around Kierkegaard's paradox thus signals the continual reemergence of theological questions at the heart of even the most ostensibly atheistic philosophy: the question of God, in Derrida's formulation, is an inevitable moment in the overall movement of the trace. It is, I claim, the very inevitability of the theological question that points to the agency of the ethical fault-line, for to mediate the paradox of mediation would require precisely that which the fault-line will not allow: a self-identical, nonaffected self prior to any act of mediation.

The final chapter, "Sexual Difference and the Ethics of Duplicity," turns to the question of sexual difference in its relation to the ethical fault-line. Traditional ethical thought is largely predicated on the model of an individual actor's obligations in the face of the law, society, or other people. Implicit to this model is therefore a comfortably settled sense of what constitutes the self and what constitutes the other, the inside and the outside. The initial claim in this chapter is that this implicit model is the hallmark of what I call "male" philosophy; in contrast, the positions that repudiate this model stem from what can be called "female" philosophy. These models correspond respectively to transcendentalist and immanentist[3] theories of knowledge, and the central claim in this chapter is that this difference has its basis in a cultural history in which the figure of woman has been made to carry "the burden of redemption." The modern tradition of philosophical ethics, indeed of modern philosophy in general, depends on an orientation toward the fault-line that can be described as "male" in light of Lacan's theorization of sexual difference in his later thought, because its basic move is to totalize the field of what is to be known while at the same time abstracting from that field the position of the knower. Nevertheless, while the ethical alternatives that develop in the late twentieth century, described here as the fulfillment of a "female" philosophy, would seem to offer a corrective to a deficient system of "male" ethics, there is a danger that those discourses proclaiming a resolution to the conundrum posed by the perversity of ethics will be caught in the very traps from which they believe themselves to have struggled free. Although "female" philosophy has taken center stage with the force of an epochal event, psychoanalysis and the perversity of ethics it theorizes suggest that only a subject convinced of its own essential duplicity has the chance, slight though it may be, of not falling prey to the promise of redemption, and of thereby being able to bear witness to the ethical fault-line.

Perversity and Ethics

1

Freud and the Banishment of Evil

OF THE MANY INVECTIVES hurled at psychoanalysis and its founder, Sigmund Freud, one of the most curious is the claim that psychoanalysis represents an amoral, or even immoral, practice (Wallwork ix, 2, 58). The argument is based on the notion that Freud, by founding his new practice on an essentially mechanistic, causally deterministic view of motivations, effectively banished choice, and hence moral reflection, from human behavior. Because it is regarded as the principal element of individual responsibility, the notion of intentionality is a keystone of the Western concept of justice. If one carries out a consciously intended act, then one is fully responsible for it. If, however, one's acts are determined by unseen and largely ineluctable psychological processes, then the certainty of one's intentions is brought into doubt—as is, ultimately, one's responsibility. If no one is ultimately responsible for his or her acts, then evil becomes a meaningless category. By banishing choice, the argument goes—by demonstrating that our most meritorious as well as our most shameful actions are the result of unconscious, socially, and often biologically determined impulses—Freud not only undermined the idea that humans are capable of acting for purely altruistic reasons (and hence of doing good in a stringently ethical sense[1]) but also, and perhaps more disturbingly, robbed ethical and juridical thought of the standards upon which to judge an act as evil.

If this is the extent of the moralists' complaint, however, then Freud himself is hardly to blame. Belief in physical determinism had been steadily encroaching on notions of free will for several centuries when Freud was developing his theories, and had achieved philosophical impetus in the works of Hobbes, Hume, and Locke, and even religious legitimacy in the various doctrines of predestination advanced by some Protestants in the sixteenth century. In the nineteenth century, the scientific pursuit of mechanistic causality had spread from medicine to the study of human behavior and had ultimately engendered the human sciences, of which such fields as ethnography, psychology, and of course psychoanalysis itself are among the most obvious results. If Freud's writings entailed a contribution to this movement, then, it was only insofar as his case studies purported to document specific cases of unconscious motivation and hence provided experimental support for the broader claims of the general cultural attitude.

It is nevertheless fair to say that Freud shared in this general cultural attitude and that, whatever the ultimate effects the practice he founded had on ethical thought, it was not his aim to buttress the philosophical claims of a besieged free will against the onslaught of a deterministic zeitgeist. Far from banishing evil from the consideration of human motivations, however, it is my claim that Freud reintroduced a particular notion of evil—and hence of the ethical—into the heart of human being, and did so, moreover, in a way that was as unrecognizable to his contemporaries as it has been to (some of) his followers, who have continued to act as if psychoanalysis and the psychological practices that have drawn from it are predicated on the incompatibility of ethicality and the objective evaluation of human behavior. For although the clinicians' object of study—aberrant behavior—originally derives from the sphere of moral and religious inquiry, there can be no doubt that psychology has continually been at pains to dissociate the clinical from the moral, and understandably so. Clinicians have long understood that their field must remain strictly separated from the moral order if it is to survive as a field. If evil is intentional, abnormal psychology is a sickness and, like a sickness, those who suffer from it cannot be held responsible for it. But perhaps the time has come to question this distinction—not, let it be understood, in order to reintroduce a moralizing principle into questions of psychiatry, but rather to emphasize the possibility that there can be no discussion of desire, whether normal or aberrant, that does not take place in a sphere already structured by ethics.

In the course of the following pages I argue, on the basis of an examination of those texts that form the foundation of Freud's metapsychological theory—his highly speculative theory of the microcosmic functioning of the human psyche—that Freud's thought involves precisely such a reorientation toward the ethical. I must stress again, however, that a reorientation toward the ethical has nothing to do with moral evaluation; rather, it involves the realization that there is no level of motivation that is not

somehow implicated in ethical considerations. If philosophical realism proposes that actions are founded on motivations, which are founded on descriptions, which are founded on reality—ethics overlies epistemology,
which in turn overlies ontology—Freud's discourse constitutes a curious
reversal of this hierarchy, one that resonates with other schools of twentieth-century thought such as Heideggerian phenomenology and neopragmatism. This reversal situates the ethical at the bottom of the stack, arguing that (to put it in Heideggerian terms): (a) "reality" is an
abstraction—or a "deficient mode"—of being-in-the-world; (b) being-in-
the-world incorporates a spectrum of beliefs concerning what is and ought
to be the case[2]; and therefore (c) being is in some sense always-already ethically determined.

We should not be too eager, however, to cast Freud's lot in with these
other thinkers. For one thing, it is not my claim (nor could it be) that
Freud himself was aware of, or would himself ratify, this interpretation, but
rather that on the basis of Freud's evidence and argumentation we are led
to markedly different conclusions than Freud himself arrived at. Furthermore, unlike Heideggerian and neopragmatist thought, a fundamental aspect of Freud's discovery lies in his close analysis of the relationship between desire and the ethical grounds of being—a relationship that is, in
the final analysis, at once mutually dependent and profoundly antagonistic.

ETHICS AND THE PROBLEM OF PERVERSITY

In 1845, Edgar Allan Poe published a story couched in the form of a
philosophical polemic that begins with the following words: "In the consideration of the faculties and impulses—of the *prima mobilia* of the human soul, the phrenologists have failed to make room for a propensity
which, although obviously existing as a radical, primitive, irreducible sentiment, has been equally overlooked by all the moralists who proceeded
them" (Poe 145). Poe's narrator accuses the phrenologists in question—
whose practice of determining human character on the basis of the topological analysis of the skull was then in vogue—of having corrupted the results of their research from the outset by basing them on a priori reasoning,
a form of reasoning still seeped in religious undertones:

> The intellectual or logical man, rather than the understanding or observant
> man, set himself to imagine designs—to dictate purposes to God. Having thus
> fathomed to his satisfaction the intentions of Jehovah, out of these intentions

he built his innumerable systems of mind. In the manner of phrenology, for example, we first determined, naturally enough, that it was the design of the deity that man should eat. We then assigned to man an organ of alimentiveness,
and this organ is the scourge with which the Deity compels man, will-I nill-I,
into eating. (146)

The classification of the human apparatus, in other words, does not proceed from a disinterested, scientific analysis of behavior, but rather rests on
the presumption of metaphysical *purposes*—the mouth exists to serve the
purpose of eating, and so forth—and therefore implicitly presupposes the
divine embodiment of purposefulness that empirical science is supposed to
have done away with. The problem that the phrenologists have in common
with the metaphysicians and moralists who preceded them, then, is that
their presumption of divine intent has blinded them to an empirical fact of
human existence, a phenomenon Poe refers to as *perverseness*:

> Induction, *a postiori*, would have brought phrenology to admit, as an innate
> and primitive principle of human action, a paradoxical something, which we
> may call perverseness, for want of a more characteristic term. In the sense I in-
> tend, it is, in fact, a *mobile* without motive, a motive not *motiviert*. Through its
> promptings we act without comprehensible object; or, if this shall be under-
> stood as a contradiction in terms, we may so far modify the proposition as to
> say, that through its promptings we act, for the reason that we should *not*. . . .
> I am not more certain that I breathe, than that the assurance of the wrong or
> error of any action is often the one unconquerable *force* which impels us, and
> alone impels us to its prosecution. (146–47)

Poe is correct in suggesting that not only the positivistic sciences of his own
century but also the moralists of previous centuries had overlooked the
possibility of sheer perversity as a motivation for action. He is also most
probably correct in his explanation of this omission via reference to a hidden religious agenda. Since the early days of Christianity the Church had
counted Manichaeism—the belief in a radical source of evil opposed to the
source of good that was God—among the heresies most insulting to God.
The reasoning, obviously, was that the Manichaean dualism presupposed
an ontological, if not ethical, equality between good and evil. Many of
Christian theology's attempts to theorize and explain the existence of evil
were driven by the desire to oust this pernicious belief by demonstrating
that evil could exist in a world created and ruled by a omnipotent and perfectly good God—for example, as deficiency or temporal spatial remove
from God.[3] A purely perverse motivation of the kind described by Poe
would certainly welcome comparison with a Manichaean dark-side.

In modern times, this disavowal of pure evil also found its way into Kant's ethical system, which may well have been one of those metaphysical systems Poe had in mind when penning his story. In his *Religion within the Limits of Reason Alone*, Kant explicitly denies the possibility of what he calls a diabolical evil working at the heart of human motivations, for the reason that it would require the existence of a purely malignant reason, a set of maxims in opposition to those of practical reason or duty whose only reason for existence would be opposition to the law itself (Kant, *Reason* 30).[4] Evil, for Kant, could not have its origin in such a malignant reason, for if the set of maxims determining the subjective grounds of an individual's choice were themselves evil, then that individual would not in fact be choosing evil but rather would be impelled toward evil action by his or her core of evil maxims. Such a determination would be diabolical and not human precisely because Kant defines human moral existence in terms of its freedom.

"Radical" evil, by contrast—the evil pertaining to human existence—is a form of weakness that "arises from the frailty of human nature, the lack of sufficient strength to follow out the principles it has chosen for itself" (Kant, *Reason* 32). Kant's vision of evil as a frailty of the will corresponds to the accepted views of the Christian tradition, and thus to Poe's interpretation of the banishment of perversity as having its origin in an unscientific attachment to religious presuppositions. A purely, diabolically evil act could not be attributable to a human being precisely because the human is considered an embodiment of purposefulness, of reason. Just as the members of the human body function according to a certain purpose, ordained by nature or by God, so the human being as a whole is guided by the dictates of a reason or purposefulness common to all—and therefore, while it is perfectly conceivable for a human to act for bad or selfish reasons, what is outside of the realm of comprehension is that a human might act for no reason whatsoever—*unmotiviert*, as Poe says—or, as he clarifies, because he or she *should not*. And just as the only indication we might have that an individual is acting in a moral way—that is, in obedience to the moral law—is that he or she appears to be contravening his or her own inclinations or pathological interests,[5] the only indication available that an individual is acting in complete disregard of reason would be that he or she transgresses the moral law for the sake of the transgression itself. But this would be evidence of a completely unmotivated act, and it is thus precisely this sort of action that Kant claims cannot exist.

Discovering motivation, of course, is what the practice Freud invented is all about. And if the moralists burn Freud for undermining the notion of moral choice, their motivation is of a Kantian kind. For these moralists, Freud has broken the Kantian law that ethical behavior is (a) ultimately reasonable, and (b) ultimately enabled only by a free choice.[6] Such Kantianism cannot conceive of a notion of evil of the kind advanced by Poe, an evil consisting not in our frailty in the face of moral responsibility, but in an impulse through whose prompting we act for the reason we should *not*. Poe goes on to say of this impulse: "Nor will this overwhelming tendency to do wrong for the wrong's sake, admit of analysis, or resolution into ulterior elements. It is a radical, a primitive impulse—elementary" (Poe 147). As elementary as this impulse may be, it might nonetheless admit of analysis—psychoanalysis, to be precise. This is the analysis Freud undertook in his metapsychology, and the result was the revelation that an evil thought banished was alive and well in the human soul.

EPISTEMOLOGICAL VS. ETHICAL ANALYSIS

Arnold Davidson's 1987 article "How to Do a History of Psychoanalysis: A Reading of Freud's Three Essays on the Theory of Sexuality" is noteworthy for a number of reasons, not least of which is the fact that, in it, a self-described Foucauldian (Davidson 41) uses a Foucauldian "archaeological" approach to defend psychoanalysis and its founder from a claim that had become largely associated with Michel Foucault's work. Foucault's assault on psychoanalysis is essentially an assault on a way of thinking with which psychoanalysis is clearly, for him, implicated, a way of thinking for which the power relationships determining sexuality are characterized primarily by the notion of repression. Sexuality, according to such thinking, is an inherently liberating force that some other force—ideology, morality, social conditioning, etc.—tries to control via the mechanism of repression. The critical question Foucault asks of this thesis at the outset of the *History of Sexuality* is: "Did the critical discourse that addresses itself to repression come to act as a roadblock to a power mechanism that had operated unchallenged up to that point, or is it not in fact part of the same historical network as the thing it denounces (and doubtless misrepresents) by calling it 'repression'?" (Foucault, *History* 10). Psychoanalysis, which features the concept of repression as a central tenet in its theory of the unconscious, cannot be exempted from the opprobrium implicit in such a question.

Davidson addresses this criticism by demonstrating that, despite his advancing of the repressive hypothesis, Freud's attitude toward the extant categories of sexual research was markedly different from that of his contemporaries and immediate predecessors. This difference concerns less the fact of sexuality's repression than the nature of sexuality itself or, more specifically, the sexual drive. For Davidson, Freud was writing in a world marked by a virtual "unargued unanimity" as to the nature of the sexual drive and its function:

> in the nineteenth-century psychiatric theories that preceded Freud, both a specific object and a specific aim formed part and parcel of the instinct. The nature of the sexual instinct manifested itself, as I have said, in an attraction to members of the opposite sex and in a desire for genital intercourse with them. Thus, inversion was one unnatural functional deviation of the sexual instinct, a deviation in which the natural object of this instinct did not exert its proper attraction. By claiming, in effect, that there is no natural object of the sexual instinct, that the sexual object and sexual instinct are merely soldered together, Freud dealt a conceptually devastating blow to the entire structure of nineteenth-century theories of sexual psychopathology. (Davidson 51–52)

The difference between Freud and his predecessors cannot be ascribed to a mere change in vocabulary. Freud's predecessors also used the word *Trieb*, but, Davidson argues, in their case the term is, in fact, better rendered as "instinct," as in Strachey's much criticized choice for the *Standard Edition*.[7] As Davidson puts it, "[i]t is not the introduction of a new word that signals Freud's originality but rather the fact that *Sexualtrieb* is not the same concept as that of the sexual instinct" (52). If *Trieb* is better rendered as drive, or as *pulsion* in French psychoanalytic parlance,[8] this only became historically true with Freud.

Foucault grouped Freud and the practice of psychoanalysis with those other medical and scientific practices that had obfuscated their role in the power struggle around sex. He argued that although these practices portrayed themselves as liberating sex from external, oppressive discourses, they were in fact participating in a process by which "power advanced, multiplied its relays and effects, while its target expanded, subdivided, and branched out, penetrating further into reality at the same pace" (Foucault, *History* 42). Davidson, by contrast, differentiates Freud's discourse from those of his contemporaries, arguing that, far from attributing to Freud a complacent participation in what Foucault termed "the perverse implantation," our conclusion from Freud's treatment of the perversions in his *Three Essays* ought to be "that there are no true perversions" (Davidson 58), because the very notion of perversion depends on a concept of instinct in which the aim and object of the instinct are "part and parcel" of it, a concept that Freud did away with.[9]

Although I could not be more sympathetic to Davidson's treatment of

Freud's discovery and its relationship to its historical context, my contention is somewhat different. Davidson can say that Freud demonstrated the nonexistence of the perversions because the concept of perversion was, at the time Freud was writing, utterly dependent on the notion of the sexual instinct and its naturally determined function. If the function of the instinct is no longer understood as that of driving the subject to fulfill a certain aim (the genital act) with a given object (a member of the opposite sex), then the notion of a perversion, a sickness of that function, ceases to make sense. But insofar as Freud's theory implicitly redefined the notion of the sexual drive as something with a widely variable aim and capable of different objects, it is quite plausible to read that theory not as a *renunciation* of the concept of perversion, but rather as another *redefinition*. Ultimately, Davidson's historicist project coincides with Foucault's in that both tend to view the question of perversion as an epistemological problem: the term "perversion" designates a form of sexual behavior conceived of by a community of subjects as unnatural. This conception therefore depends on a consensus regarding what *is* natural. Show that this consensus is arbitrary, historically contingent, in the service of a given power structure—perform on it, in short, a genealogy—and you will have done away with the concept and perhaps some of the harm it has caused as well.

But psychoanalytic methodology is not epistemologically oriented in the same way, and herein lies the great difference between it and the Foucauldian approach. For the epistemological approach, "perversion" can turn out to have been a category mistake, produced by "experts" unaware of the extent to which their practice is imbued with the relations of power. "It is not at all obvious," Davidson tells us, "why sadism, masochism, fetishism, and homosexuality should be treated as species of the same disease, for they appear to have no essential features in common" (49). But when we grasp the extent to which the inhabitants of a given time are embedded in a world whose fundamental elements might well include specific ideas of sexual normalcy, when we consider that intellectuals and researchers are not working in a vacuum but rather on a foundation of knowledge whose borders exceed their individual capacity to step out and choose another foundation, then it may occur to us that the "perversions" did in fact have one very important feature in common—namely, that they constituted, in the eyes of an "unargued unanimity," a kind of immoral behavior—and that this common denominator could very well be the active ingredient in their appeal. The very screen, in other words, that the epistemological approach wishes to remove from the historical phenomenon, in order that we might better see what is it we are studying, might in fact be constitutive of the phenomenon in question.

Freud radically revised existing notions of sexuality and its component drives; of this there can be no doubt. But rather than assuming that, as a result, Freud did away with our need to think about perversion and the problems it poses to the understanding of human behavior, let us hypothesize that Freud's project was a different one. If we listen to his own words, Freud did not say "there are no perversions," but rather "[n]o healthy person, it appears, can fail to make some addition that might be called perverse to the normal sexual aim; and the universality of this finding is in itself enough to show how inappropriate it is to use the word perversion as a term of reproach" (Freud, *Three Essays* 26): inappropriate as a reproach, but certainly not as a word. It is my contention that Freud's continued investigation into the perversions and into the sexual drive delved into an aspect of human being that a merely epistemological analysis fails to appreciate, and laid the grounds for a way of thinking about human motivation inextricable from notions of moral agency.

DRIVE

Let us call, as Freud did, the elementary unit of psychical motive force the "drive" (*Trieb*). Although we stress the psychical aspect, the drive is not a purely psychical entity. Rather, it is a classification bridging the psychical and the somatic; as Freud puts it, "the psychical representative of the stimuli originating from within the organism and reaching the mind, as a measure of the demand made upon the mind for work in consequence of its connection with the body" (Freud, "Instincts" 205). The model for the drive is the stimulus-response arc, which Freud describes as an organism's innate tendency to act in a way that will reduce the energy it accumulates as a result of external stimulus. An external stimulus is registered in the organism's nervous system as a specific augmentation of energy, or excitation, which the organism then seeks to discharge through a motor response. The correct motor response—most often arrived at by trial and error—will be recorded by the psychical system as the "specific action" (Freud, "Project" 318), the action that corresponds to a given stimulus in a way that reduces the excitation produced by it. The organism quickly distinguishes between stimuli it can escape in this manner and stimuli that remain more or less constant despite repeated attempts to escape. The former are experienced as external stimuli; the latter internal. The internal stimuli are what we now call drives.

Drive, then, not only lies at the border of the psychical and the somatic, it also emerges at the first moment of distinction in the organism's experiential existence. This distinction marks the organism's first attempts to define a border, an inside delimited from an outside. Just as with external stimuli, the drive is characterized by the organism's tendency to act so as to discharge the excitation accumulated by the stimulus, only in this case the excitation has a more permanent character, which is experienced by the organism as displeasure. Drive, then, has a persistence to it, a suspended nature which allows it to exist, to exert pressure, without actually accomplishing anything. While it is suspended, it is experienced as displeasure that will dissipate and hence convert to pleasure as soon as it is satisfied. Its satisfaction, therefore, corresponds with its dissipation, with its extinction. It is quite clear, however, that as long as the organism lives it is beset by drives, and hence the general state of living can be described as a state of being driven, which cannot achieve ultimate satisfaction except by extinction. This, then, is how we shall understand Thanatos, the death drive.[10]

Let me forestall any possible objections by admitting that I am, in this discussion, intentionally eschewing Freud's long and troubled struggle with the idea that there are two opposed classes of drives: life and death drives. Although the distinction appears in several different forms throughout the later part of Freud's career, his key motivation seems to have been to explain the otherwise inexplicable negativity in human behavior, which he continued to discover no matter how deep he searched for a unified source of motivation. This negativity is the focus of "Beyond the Pleasure Principle," in which Freud sets out to account for a widespread tendency, recorded by analysis, of patients to repeat inherently unpleasant experiences in their fantasies and their lives. If a distinction could be hypothesized between two primordial classes of drives, he believed, that might explain the prevalence of such otherwise obscure behavior, and might resolve the problem of our inability to "ascribe to the sexual instinct the characteristic of a compulsion to repeat which first put us on the track of the death instincts" (Freud, "Beyond" 261).

It is my contention, however, that the distinction between life and death drives is one of several instances in Freud's career (and I focus on another below) in which his desire to resolve the paradox of the drive's apparently inherent negativity led him to posit ever more outrageous and contradictory principles. For the purposes of my argument, I will merely cite one moment from his 1923 essay "The Ego and the Id," in which Freud concedes that despite the litany of distinctions he is trying to establish between them, the essential directionality of the two classes of instinct is the same: "Acting in this way, both instincts would be conservative in the strictest sense of the word, since both would be endeavoring to re-establish a state of things that was disturbed by the emergence of life" (Freud, "Ego" 40).[11] The fact that such a conservative tendency ultimately leads either class of instinct into conflict with the individual as a living organism justifies an interpretation of the death drive as the Platonic—and thus perhaps mythical—ideal of drive per se.

Within Freud's general economy of the drives there is a further distinction to be made. Some drives serve an immediately identifiable purpose in the preservation of the organism. Such drives, or needs—hunger is the classic example—Freud calls drives of self-preservation. The remaining drives, the drives that exhibit a seeming purposelessness, he calls the sexual drives. These drives, writes Freud,

> are numerous, emanate from a great variety of organic sources, act in the first instance independently of one another, and only achieve a more or less complete synthesis at a later stage. The aim which each of them strives for is the attainment of "organ pleasure"; only when synthesis is achieved do they enter the service of the reproductive function and thereupon become generally recognizable as sexual instincts. (Freud, "Instincts" 205)

The question that immediately arises is why, if the drives are not obviously and already at the service of the reproductive function, are we to refer to them as sexual drives? The sexual drives, it appears, are only termed sexual insofar as they are recognized retroactively as being components of a late-developing function, the function of sexual reproduction.[12] For the function to be realized, however, the drives must eventually conform to a specific aim (the genital act) with a given object (a member of the opposite sex). And it was Freud himself who explicitly enjoined us to consider these objects and aims not as innate to the drives, but rather, at most, as only "soldered" to them (Freud, *Three Essays* 14).

The sexual drives, then, are not innately sexual (in the sense of driving the organism to pursue reproductive relations) but are rather deemed sexual via a metonymy of sorts, in that they are recognized later as necessary components of an overarching function from which they are largely, if not completely, independent. In fact, what distinguishes these drives in their early—presexual—manifestations is precisely their independence, the fact that in the face of the perceived purposefulness or functionality of self-preservation drives, these other drives come across as fickle, detached. They are, says Freud, "distinguished by possessing the capacity to act vicariously for one another to a wide extent and by being able to change their objects readily" ("Instincts" 205). Sexual drives are thus apt to undergo a variety of vicissitudes or destinies (*Triebschicksale*), which Freud categorizes into general groups: reversal; turning-round upon the subject's self; repression; and sublimation. As the perversions involve the first two processes, we shall now turn our attention to these.

The notions of reversal and turning-round imply two previous notions: first, that a vector is involved; and second, that there is an original or primary direction to the vector such that it can be reversed. These assumptions become clear from Freud's examples—sadism/masochism and scopophilia/exhibitionism—in both of which the former term is considered the primary or original and the second the result of the reversal. The reversal in this case acts upon the aim of the drive, converting it from an experience of activity to one of passivity. If the original drive sought satisfaction in torturing or looking at an object, the reversed drive now seeks satisfaction in being tortured or being looked at. Similarly, the idea of a turning-round upon one's own self implies an original attitude in which the subject's pursuit of satisfaction involves being directed outward toward an object, an orientation that is then replaced by the perverse attitude in which the subject replaces the object with his own self, and seeks another object to take over the role of the subject.

If the reversal or turning-round of the drive is what perverts it, it would seem that the primary terms of the above pairings—sadism and scopophilia—are not in fact perversions, but rather natural or original modes of pursuing satisfaction. Indeed, Freud admits as much by distinguishing between sadism as it occurs naturally and as a perverse manifestation:

> Psychoanalysis would appear to show that the infliction of pain plays no part among the original purposive actions of the instinct. A sadistic child takes no account of whether or not he inflicts pains, nor does he intend to do so. But once the transformation into masochism has taken place, the pains are very well fitted to provide a masochistic aim. . . . When once feeling pains has become a masochistic aim, the sadistic aim of causing pains can arise also, retrogressively; for while these pains are being inflicted on other people, they are enjoyed masochistically by the subject through his identification of himself with the suffering object. (Freud, "Instincts" 207)

This original, natural sadism—like the original, natural scopophilia—constitutes a state of drivenness that has undergone no vicissitudes. Pain and humiliation are not the contents of the drive; rather, mastery is. And this is understandable, for the notion of mastery is at the heart of Freud's theory of the drives, insofar as the reduction of an excitement constitutes a kind of mastery over the stimuli of one's environment. These primordial vectors become perverse drives—and hence fulfill their potential as sexual drives—only as the result of a double reversal: first when the natural, active aim is replaced by a passive one; and second, when the still active subject seeks satisfaction by identifying with the object's passive enjoyment of his active drive.[13]

What, then, is the force that impels this reversal and turning-round of drives that exhibit a primordial directedness? Where traditional research into sexual aberrance categorized such reversals as sexual pathologies, Freud places them squarely within the realm of normal human development, because it is nothing less than the process of ego development that ensures the reversibility, if not the outright perversion, of the original drives: "the instinctual vicissitudes which consist in the instincts being turned round upon the subject's own ego and undergoing reversal from activity to passivity are dependent on the narcissistic organization of the ego and bear the stamp of that phase" (Freud, "Instincts" 210). For it is in the narcissistic phase that the ego is first constituted not as a subject but as an object, the first receptor of libidinal cathexis. This is the phase where the sexual drives first find satisfaction; but that satisfaction is not attained actively as a subject, but rather passively as an object.

Three terms from the above sentence resonate intimately with Freud's text: satisfaction (or pleasure), activity, and subject (or ego). These are the positive poles of what he refers to as the three great polarities of mental life, polarities around which the vicissitudes, and hence the essential character of the sexual drives, are fashioned:

> We may sum up by saying that the essential feature in the vicissitudes undergone by instincts lies in the subjection of the instinctual impulse to the influences of the three great polarities that dominate mental life. Of these three polarities we might describe that of activity-passivity as the biological, that of ego-external world as the real, and finally that of pleasure-unpleasure as the economic polarity. (Freud, "Instincts" 216–17)

Although these final words of Freud's "Instincts" essay are never fully explained, they carry in them the seeds for a new understanding of Freud's thought. Drives—specifically the sexual drives—undergo vicissitudes as a result of their subjection to three types of polarities in mental life. The first of these polarities, the distinction between activity and passivity, Freud characterizes as biological, in the sense of being a brute fact of physical existence. Organisms act upon the world and are acted upon by the world, and this distinction registers in the organism's psyche as a polarity. The second polarity, that of subject/object or ego/external world, he characterizes as real, in that it is a result of the subject's process of self-delimitation from external reality. We must recall, however, that this process cannot coincide exactly with the original internal/external distinction established by the experience of the inescapability of certain stimuli. For one thing, this original distinction lies at the heart of the very notion of drive as it is distinguished from stimuli, and thus cannot be something to which the drive is only later subjected. Moreover, this original "reality-ego," which Freud praises as being based on a "sound, objective criterion," is eventually replaced by a pleasure ego, "which places the characteristic of pleasure above all others" (Freud, "Instincts" 213). This pleasure ego, which is the first object of libidinal cathexis and the central element of the narcissistic stage, is created by the introjection of all that causes pleasure or reduces excitement and the rejection of all that causes displeasure or augments excitement. We might speculate, therefore, that the ego is an originally unstable, composite creation whose first experiential layer consists of the displeasurable experience of sustained drivenness as opposed to the pleasurable experience of stimulus-avoidance, and which is later converted to a reservoir of pleasurable sensations. If the original "displeasure-ego" maintained an essentially active attitude toward the stimulus-world, the "pleasure-ego" of narcissism is distinguished by its objectness—it is essentially the subject's body experienced passively as an object.

The new object, the narcissistic ego, is driven to maintain itself—its embodied experience—at the lowest possible level of excitation, and in this way instantiates the third polarity, the polarity of pleasure/displeasure. This polarity is economic insofar as it involves the regulation of quantities of excitement. But we are right to be disgruntled by the fact that this regulation of excitation was supposed to have been a characteristic of drive itself and not a mental polarity to which drive is subjected. The same could be said, to a greater or lesser extent, of each of these polarities: are they not simply characteristics of drive in it pure state, drive as active, as object-oriented, as pleasure seeking? At some point in its development, what was once a mere description of the drive's trajectory—a directionality, a vector—becomes described as a polarity, as a choice between options. The question now is: what creates this susceptibility, what brings about this choice? This process, as Freud describes it, could be called *institutionalization*.

INSTITUTIONALIZATION

It is of course the first term of each of the polarities that qualifies as an outright description of drive. Drive is (a priori, if we wish) subjective, active, and pleasure-seeking. That there are perversions, then, must not be the result of the subjection of the drive to the polarities, but rather of the fact that the polarities even exist—of the fact, in other words, that the very drivenness of existence can be conceived of as functioning in reverse, as being driven passively, toward being-an-object, toward displeasure.[14] These polarities of mental life, and hence the grounds for the drive's perversity, are the effects of institutionalization.

To grasp the notion of institutionalization and its centrality to Freud's theory, let us borrow for the moment a metaphoric pairing from Claude Lévi-Strauss. An activity or behavior that is the unadulterated expression of a biological or organic striving is called raw. Cooked, in contrast, refers to that activity or behavior that has undergone some kind of modification—for instance, as a result of conforming to social requirements. Lévi-Strauss identifies as the central theme of his eponymous work the isomorphism between nature and culture on the one hand, and continuous and discrete quantities on the other (Lévi-Strauss 28). The moment of the imposition or assumption of an external impulse leading to the modification of nature results in an interruption of a previous continuity, an interruption representing the basic unit of institutionalization. Institutionalization, in other words, is the heat that cooks the raw.

This notion of institutionalization is at the heart of Freud's distinction between the primary and secondary processes. The primary processes are concerned exclusively with the release of excitation, and hence with the pursuit of pleasure. The primary processes, in other words, describe the nature of drive. They are only primary, however, in relation to the secondary processes, which serve to constrain or interrupt the drives' hitherto uninhibited pursuit of discharge:

> We have found that one of the earliest and most important functions of the
> mental apparatus is to bind the instinctual impulses which impinge on it, to re-
> place the primary process prevailing in them by the secondary process and con-

vert their freely mobile cathectic energy into a mainly quiescent (tonic) cathexis . . . the transformation occurs on behalf of the pleasure principle; the binding is a preparatory act which introduces and assures the dominance of the pleasure principle. (Freud, "Beyond" 265–67)

The key concept in this passage is "binding" (*Bindung*). By binding, Freud means the building up of resistances such that the free passage of psychical energy between neurons is hindered. From his earliest metapsychological writings ("Project for a Scientific Psychology"), Freud described the passage of psychical energy between neurons in terms of the clearing of pathways (*Bahnungen*) due to the previous passage of energy. The more energy that passed between two neurons, the more that particular synaptic connection would be smoothed down and the lower the threshold would be for future discharges along that path. The purpose behind such a system is to facilitate the organism's repetition of specific actions—of those actions that successfully satisfied previous drives.[15]

When the energy collecting in a neuron has not yet reached the threshold level that will allow it to flow through a connection to an adjacent neuron, the energy in that neuron is considered bound, and the neuron itself cathected. According to the nature of drive, all neurons seeks to discharge the energy they have accumulated, but they can only do so to the extent that there are pathways available to conduct that energy. One function of the mental apparatus, then, is to ensure that energy can in fact accumulate, such that there remain sufficient quantities of accumulated or quiescent energy to do the work of instigating motor movements when the need arises. It does this by binding that energy, that is, by organizing constellations of neurons whose resistances are high enough to maintain a given level of energy in reserve. Although this organization must be seen in the first instance as functioning against the interests of the pleasure principle, in that it hinders the depletion of the entire system, Freud insists that it is in fact working in conjunction with the pleasure principle, serving its interests, because it is the accumulation of energy that ultimately allows for its discharge.

The processes involved in binding energy in the psychical system are the secondary processes, and they are intimately related to two concepts in Freud's thought: the ego and the reality principle. This relationship could be stated as follows: the secondary processes are those by which the ego binds the primary processes in the service of the reality principle. For example, a child in the first stages of ego-formation experiences an unpleasant accumulation of energy in its psychical system due to hunger. In the past the child has happened upon the specific action appropriate to this drive, and has satisfied the drive by feeding. According to Freud, this first satisfaction left memory traces—beaten down pathways among the synaptic connections of the interior neural network—such that the newly accumulating psychical energy is likely to flow down the same paths and cause an eventual motor response producing the same effect of satisfaction. According to the primary principle of mental functioning, however, what is most likely to happen is that the neurons in the perceptual apparatus will discharge along the same passages as those of the previous satisfaction, which means that the child will simply hallucinate the satisfaction of feeding without generating the accompanying motor discharges necessary to actually feed. The attempt at satisfaction by hallucination is abandoned when the unpleasurable stimuli continue, and the child's efforts result in disappointment. As a result, the mental apparatus is forced to form a conception of "the real circumstances in the outer world and to exert itself to alter them." A new principle of mental functioning is thus introduced in which "what was conceived of was no longer that which was pleasant but that which was real" (Freud, "Two Principles" 22). The point is that the mental apparatus must have an "idea" (a particular memory trace) of a satisfaction in order to be able to recognize and reinitiate the satisfaction sequences necessary for survival. This "idea," however, will at first be indistinguishable from the experience itself, and only the "exigencies of life" (*Not des Lebens*)—the fact that the original source of the hunger drive in question is still sending its signal—and the displeasure they produce will eventually propel the psychical system to muster up the energy needed to fulfill the specific action.

In light of the specific demands of reality, this "mustering" alters the internal organization of bound psychical energy that is the ego in its most primitive form—and alters it such as to incorporate some neural "representation" of the exigencies imposed by life. In this way, the ego brings about a modification of the pleasure principle into the reality principle:

> Moreover, the ego seeks to bring the influences of the external world to bear upon the id and its tendencies, and endeavors to substitute the reality principle for the pleasure principle which reigns unrestrictedly in the id. For the ego perception plays the part which in the id falls to instinct. The ego represents what may be called reason and commons sense, in contrast to the id, which contains the passions. (Freud, "Ego and Id" 25)

The reason or common sense represented by the ego includes, of course, not only the original life exigencies, as described in the example above, but also eventually the social constraints and demands for relinquishment of direct satisfaction that living in communities entails—the issues, in short, comprised in morality.

Institutionalization, then, which Freud imagines at the most minute neurological level as consisting in the establishment of barriers to the free flow of energy, must also and simultaneously be understood as the registration in the psyche of a certain codification or regulation of behavior—of the establishment, in other words, of the law in its most primitive sense. It is important to grasp that each moment of institutionalization is also a temporal event, because it marks a before and an after in psychical life. In a way, institutionalization is the essence of temporality, because it redirects the drive—which, as the principal motive force of the psyche, is an instantiation of pure spatiality, of a moving out into the world—along a temporal axis. Whereas the drive in its "pure" state—the mythical state of an uninstitutionalized primary process—could not know time, the drive as always-already structured by the reality principle is fundamentally a being-in-time.[16] Precisely insofar as the ego, with its taking-into-account of the exigencies of social and biological life, entails a projection into the future—a future-orientedness powered by matching the images of desires with the real possibilities of their fulfillment[17]—to the same degree the drive is an instantiation of past-orientedness, a conservative impulse striving to reestablish the conditions of a satisfaction left behind the walls of the most recent insitutionalization. As Freud writes:

> The repressed instinct never ceases to strive for complete satisfaction, which would consist in the repetition of a primary experience of satisfaction. No substitutive or reactive formations and no sublimations will suffice to remove the repressed instinct's persisting tension; and it is the difference in amount between pleasure of satisfaction which is demanded and that which is actually achieved that provides the driving factor which will permit of no halting at any position attained, but, in the poet's words, "ungebändigt immer vorwärts dringt."[18] The backward path that leads to complete satisfaction is as a rule obstructed by the resistances which maintain the repressions. (Freud, "Beyond" 249–50)

The repressions, however, must not be understood as unproblematically emerging from the organism's exterior environment. As we have just seen, the seat of this endless series of institutionalizations is the ego itself; the institutionalizations constitute the ego as such. The eternal struggle of the drive backward, against the barriers of repression, must therefore be understood as self-directed, as a striving against the fabric of one's very own self, as an urge to violate one's most sacred and dearly held beliefs.

PRIMAL MASOCHISM

Given the above conclusion, my claim would seem to be that the ego is intrinsically perverse and that the fundamental manifestation of this perversion is a masochistic one. Yet, as we have just seen, it was often Freud's position that masochism could only be understood as a reactive perversion, a reversal or turning back on itself of a more primordial, sadistic tendency of the drive.[19] Even in later years, when he became more receptive to the idea of a "primal masochism," Freud would still treat the phenomenon as a secondary effect in which the primordial destructiveness of the death instinct had intermixed with the life instinct, which was then directed outward (sadism proper), leaving a residue behind within the ego (erotogenic masochism) (Freud, "Economic" 164). Nevertheless, as we have also already seen, in some ways the notion of masochism as a more primordial perversion than sadism was already present in Freud's earlier works like "Instincts and Their Vicissitudes," in which sadism figures as a natural aspect of drive and only becomes perverted when it undergoes reversal into its masochistic form. In this scenario, the perversion of sadism proper— sexual pleasure through the infliction of pain—is the result of an identification on the part of the sadist with his suffering victim.[20] Furthermore, masochism, as I stated above, is the most paradigmatic of the perversions because it is the most paradoxical (Freud, "Economic" 159), in that it proposes at its most fundamental level an apparently contradictory pleasure in displeasure.

Although, as I have said, there are aspects of Freud's oeuvre that try to explain away the inherently paradoxical nature of masochism with reference to preexisting dualities, if we approach this problem armed with Occam's razor, we find that a single mechanism functions to explain any number of the curiosities—masochism, the flexibility of the drive as such, the strangeness of the drive's primordial aims—that drove Freud to posit a battle between two instinctual titans at the origins of life. That mechanism is, of course, institutionalization, and the resulting tendency, deeply inscribed within the economy of the drive, to *drive against* the barriers it erects.

This theory necessitates a substantial rewriting of Freud's original claims. If, for Freud, the fundamental level of masochism was the eroto-genic variety, upon which the manifest fantasies of "feminine" masochism and the overt behavior of moral masochism were based, we will again be required to subvert the hierarchy and argue that the logical content of Freud's thought demands that the primary, erotogenic variety already be a species of moral masochism. In somewhat simplified form, the theory of masochism that evolves in Freud's "Economic Problem of Masochism" involves the three levels mentioned above. An original, erotogenic masochism is manifested in boys and girls at the Oedipal stage as a desire to be sexually dominated and possessed by the father.[21] In some individuals, this perverse impulse undergoes a further sublimation into what Freud calls moral masochism, in which the subject, having constructed an overbearing superego, does everything possible to attract to himself or herself the punishment and opprobrium of society (Freud, "Economic" 169). While they are often considered the most virtuous by their fellows, such individuals may also be driven toward a life of crime, since their ultimate desire is to incur ever greater punishment (169).

Nevertheless, the entire hierarchy attains a much greater simplicity once we posit that the original or erotogenic masochism might *itself* be a kind of moral masochism, since the drive's perverse proclivity for reversal automatically takes the form of an attempt to harm the moral self.[22] Insofar as the ego's institutions are the basis of morality, and insofar as the sexual drives learn to posit satisfaction as beckoning from beyond and before those institutions, then the drives and even sexuality itself can be understood as involving, at their core, a kind of moral self-destructiveness. This interpretation is corroborated by Leo Bersani's assertion that masochism and sexuality are ultimately the same thing, and that both have at their core an experience of self-shattering (Bersani, "Rectum" 217; *Freudian Body* 38–39). To the extent that sexuality and masochism are at least isomorphic, then Freud's "feminine" masochism would simply correspond to the core sexual desires of self-annihilation and shattering, of being possessed, dominated, or even humiliated, which as a matter of convention have been bequeathed to the female gender, but are equally present in less conscious and socially acceptable forms in men. Ironically enough, Bersani actually agrees with antipornography/antisex activists like Andrea Dworkin that sex is "anticommunal, antiegalitarian, antinurturing, antiloving," but he disagrees that this is any reason to ban it or its pornographic representations (Bersani, "Rectum" 215). The phallocentrism of patriarchy and such radical feminism alike is "not primarily the denial of power to women (although it has obviously also led to that, everywhere and at all times), but above all the denial of the value of powerlessness in both men and women" (217). If this redescription and positioning of masochism at the heart of sexuality is correct, then it also explains the masochistic core at the heart of the other perversions—namely, as a tendency to subvert categories ingrained in the moral self.[23]

THE SOMATIC FOUNDATIONS OF INSTITUTIONS

If, at a more advanced and culturally elevated stage, the institutions of the ego come to represent what we could call a moral self, at a more basic level they are manifested by more visceral sensations or affects. Specific repressions involve transformations of affect, which occur through the course of a child's physical and mental development: "we have only to recall the way in which disgust emerges in childhood after having been absent to begin with—and that it is related to the activity of the secondary system" (Freud, *Interpretation* 643). Disgust, as well as shame, fear, and eventually feelings of moral disapprobation in general, are analogous affects that are ultimately conventional in nature, although they function to naturalize social constraints. They are, we may speculate, the avatars of the super-ego, and arise as somatic representatives of what are at first the commands and prohibitions received from parental authorities.

Freud's discussion of these affects and their relation to sexuality in his *Three Essays* focuses primarily on their conventional nature:

> Those who condemn the other practices (which have no doubt been common among mankind from primaeval times) as being perversions, are giving away to an unmistakable feeling of disgust, which protects them from accepting sexual aims of the kind. The limits of such disgust are, however, often purely conventional: a man who will kiss a pretty girl's lips passionately, may perhaps be disgusted at the idea of using her toothbrush, although there are no grounds for supposing that his own oral cavity, for which he feels no disgust, is any cleaner than the girl's. Here, then, our attention is drawn to the factor of disgust, which interferes with the libidinal overvaluation of the sexual object but can in turn be overridden by libido. Disgust seems to be one of the forces which have led to a restriction of the sexual aim. (Freud, *Three Essays* 17–18)

From this initial concentration on the conventional aspect of the affect of disgust in its role as a barrier to sexual enjoyment, Freud goes on to hint at

a more dynamic relationship, one in which an excess of enjoyment produced by this relationship, in which "the sexual instinct in its strength enjoys overriding this disgust" (18).

But is the pleasure a primordial one that is merely intensified by having
been pent up behind the walls of repression, or is the relation a more complex one in which the pleasure is somehow produced by the drive's original
imprisonment? In his discussion of fetishism, Freud points to

> the importance, as regards the choice of a fetish, of a coprophilic pleasure in
> smelling which has disappeared owing to repression. Both the feet and the hair
> are objects with a strong smell which have been exalted into fetishes after the
> olfactory sensation has become unpleasurable and been abandoned. Accord-
> ingly, in the perversion that corresponds to foot fetishism, it is only dirty and
> evil-smelling feet that become sexual objects. (21)

The assumption here is that many of the innate pleasures associated with
the sense of smell have undergone a culturally instigated repression, and as
a result have surfaced in a sexualized form as perversions.

Freud happened upon this notion relatively early in his career, as he en-
deavored to come up with a satisfactory explanation of the origins of repression. In a letter to Wilhelm Fliess dated November 14, 1897, Freud
writes in a state of quasi-euphoria that he believes he has at long last come
upon this explanation in man's erect stature. Whereas creatures that move
on all fours are accustomed to the proximity of their olfactory and alimen-
tative organs to the ground and to the sexual and excretory organs of other
creatures, man's erect stature has imposed a distinction of levels between
the nose and mouth and the nether regions of the body (Menninghaus
279). As Freud argues in a later essay from 1912, this lowering of the earth
with respect to the organ of smell is central to the development of aesthetic
ideal and to the incompatibility of those ideals with the coprophilic aspects
of the instincts (Freud "Most Prevalent Form" 58). The sexual instincts, in
other words, once had a natural affiliation with the sense of smell and were
joined in this sensory experience with the smell of excrement by virtue of
anatomic proximity. The civilizing process initiated by the assumption of
an erect posture eventually led to the repression of those coprophilic aspects of the sexual drive and the replacement of sexual excitement with the
affect of disgust. If and when this repression fails in modern humans, the
result is perversion as a kind of phylogenetic regression (Menninghaus
280).

This theory, along with that of the two classes of basic instincts, provides another example of Freud's reaching for a complex and highly speculative (not to say rather silly) theory in order to explain something that we may more readily account for on the basis of existing aspects of his system—albeit aspects that were not a part of that system as early as 1897. There is no need to posit a previous and natural coprophilic element to the sexual drives in order to explain such perversions as coprophilia; as we have already seen, an analogous attempt with other perversions, such as masochism, would demonstrate the futility of this approach. The allure of perversion seems to lie in a special libidinal value attained from the transgression of psychical barriers,[24] one powerful barrier being the affect of disgust corresponding to, among others, the parental mandate to avoid and hide from others the sight and smell of our own feces. Similarly, the sexual excitement of exhibitionism would consist in the transgression of the affect of shame derived from the prohibition of nakedness and so forth.[25]

We should understand the sexual pleasure of the perversions, then, not merely as a pleasure obtained at the cost of a "struggle against certain mental forces which act as resistances, and of which shame and disgust are the most prominent," but rather as a pleasure that owes itself entirely to that struggle, as the embodied experience of crossing, or imagining crossing, the limit established by a historical institutionalization. Given the theoretical elaboration of the drive throughout Freud's metapsychological theory, we can no longer accept the idea that there is anything pure or primordial about the drive; rather, the drive is the product of a process of institutionalization indispensable to the development of individual human beings. The affects that constitute the core of this institutionalization—disgust, shame, fear—can, therefore, "be regarded as historical precipitates of the external inhibitions to which the sexual instinct has been subjected during the psychogenesis of the human race" (Freud, *Three Essays* 28), but with the caveat that these sexual drives only emerged as a result of the social inhibitions placed on human activity. The drives that motivate our actions are thus conceived in a complex, dynamic relation with a core of negative affects, the very affects that form the foundation of our moral life. This relationship is essentially an antagonistic one, one founded on an unconscious promise of pleasure beyond each affect, warning, or prohibition—beyond, in short, each and every institution guiding our interactions with reality.

THE PERVERSITY OF ETHICS

Freud's explorations into the apparently universal perversity of our drives led him, unbeknownst to himself, to question the very possibility of a
systematic ethical thought. This is not only because—as moralist critiques
of psychoanalysis would have it—Freud's deterministic assumptions de-
prive the human subject of the free will necessary for ethical judgments.
Freud, as we have seen, was far from alone in harboring such presuppositions. Rather, the challenge to ethicality that emerges from a reading of his
metapsychological theory resides in what we have called institutionalization—the notion, namely, that at the most basic level desire, or drive, is always a driving-against whatever norms of behavior, sociability, acceptability have been imposed on or integrated by an individual from his or her
earliest history. If this is true, then there can be no ethical injunction that
is not at once subject to its reversal at the level of the individual's desire;
every impulse or command to do good would be counteracted by an opposite desire to do evil. It is not surprising that such a belief would have
been rejected by theology as heretical and by philosophy as impossible,
since both Christianity and philosophy of the metaphysical tradition are
indebted to an implicit equation of the good or the right with the true, or
at least with the way the world in fact *is* regardless of our inadequate attempts to grasp it. Just as falsity and error are mere deprivations of the true,
evil, for such a worldview, can only be ultimately a shadowy, deficient, mis-
informed version of the good.

The problems caused by Freud's insights, however, extend even further.
If ethicality cannot be thought outside its relation to perversity, then even
more contemporary, pragmatic, and utilitarian endeavors seem destined for
failure. For even should a given community opt for a particular political direction, in full knowledge that its choices are historically contingent and its
notions of good and of right are peculiar to it, Freud's insight promises that
rational consensus will always founder on the adverse desires its very institutionalization is bound to produce. Even Francis Fukuyama, at the conclusion of his apology for liberal capitalism and argument for its epochal
destiny as the end of history, concedes that the greatest danger for the *pax
americana* is that "if men cannot struggle on behalf of a just cause because
that just cause was victorious in an earlier generation, then they will struggle *against* the just cause. They will struggle for the sake of struggle." As a
partisan of a capitalist liberalism, he fears this tendency, because "if the

greater part of the world in which they live is characterized by peaceful and prosperous liberal democracy, then they will struggle against that peace and prosperity, and against democracy" (Fukuyama 330).

Of course, one need not invoke the perversity of ethics to explain the inevitable contestation that Fukuyama's vision would engender; the existence of incompatible cultural and religious codes is enough for that. Indeed, Freud's insight into the perversity of ethics has less to tell us about the existence of contemporary evils than about our incapacity not to be horribly, avidly drawn to them and their representations. No one, in other words, needs such a theory to understand the motivations of terrorists, but our motivations as we tune into the ubiquitous images of destruction are in some ways more troubling. The former are the purview of traditional ethical theory: very few will doubt that both those ordering suicide bombings and those ordering smart bombings feel justified in their actions, and most everyone will offer cogent arguments as to why their justification is the right one. In the heat of such a "clash of civilizations," as Huntington calls the current situation, ideologues from each side will certainly cast the conflict in Manichean terms, but the foundational, theological worldview will remain comfortably univocal: "we" are right and "they" are wrong.

What is far more difficult to explain is the urge to transgress within a given community, one itself established on apparently consensual norms. Whereas the experience of evil described above might be relegated to "historical" study, this evil, the one discarded by religious and philosophical ethics as being in some way unthinkable, is the force that, as a potentially universal aspect of human desire, now demands proper philosophical consideration. The starting point for such consideration, as we will see in the following chapters, is to avoid the pitfall of choosing between univocal and Manichean ethical spectrums, and instead grasp ethicality and institutionalization as being inextricably entangled: the discovery of institutionalization, in other words, does not banish ethicality to merely historical concerns, but rather forces us to rethink the role of the ethical in the development and determination of human desires.

In thinking through these problems, however, it will be of utmost importance to keep in view the ultimately ambiguous nature of the perversity of ethics in view. For to focus merely on the ramifications of an "evil" at the heart of ethical injunctions is to miss the point that much of what drives political change—the will to contestation, for example—depends on precisely such a negative wellspring of desire. This is not just a repetition of the well-known gesture of romanticizing transgression, so often and right-fully criticized by psychoanalytic theorists.[26] Indeed, that transgressive im-pulses are themselves irrepressibly caught up in the very ethical systems they apparently oppose is among the first conclusions one must draw from the above analysis of Freud's thought. The "pervert" thrives as much on the system whose rules he transgresses as the system relies on his transgressions for its self-justificatory rhetoric. But one must also recall that the reverse is equally implied: if perversity is inherent in the ethical, then ethical injunc-tions are inherently perverse, both because they are negatively determined by a context of inclination or interest (Kant), and because they contain and imply the desire for their own dissolution. Such would be the contribution, for instance, of these preliminary considerations for such theories of sub-ject-formation or subjectification as those proposed by Judith Butler's no-tion of performativity, or its reformulation as materialization.[27] If the force of performativity is precisely toward the formation of identities in confor-mity with socially acceptable and hence desirable models of behavior, not only does, as Butler theorizes, the iteration of such roles destabilize and re-veal their constructed nature at the very same time as it forms such identi-ties, but the very force of conformity would also contain and imply a drive to transgress and dissolve those identities. The passion of attachment en-genders, equiprimordially, the passion of detachment, or destruction.

That institutionalization produces mutually contradictory desires does not mean that the will to contestation may be automatically assumed in any situation. As Ernesto Laclau writes in criticism of Hardt and Negri's thesis in *Empire*,

> either resistance to oppression is some kind of natural and automatic mech-anism which will spontaneously operate whatever the circumstances, or it is a complex social construction which has conditions of possibility external to itself. For me the second is the correct answer. The ability and the will to re-sist are not a gift from heaven but require a set of subjective transformations that are only the product of the struggles themselves *and that can fail to take place.* (Laclau 6; emphasis in original)

In order to grasp the functioning of the perversity of ethics in this context, we have to distinguish between cases in which an individual's "objective in-terests" are served—or apparently served—by contestation, and one in which the contestation apparently takes place in disregard of those inter-ests or even against them. So, for example, if a member of an oppressor class decides to revolt against his or her family and social circle, this resistance is certainly the result of a complex series of subjective transformations that also could not have taken place; but in the final analysis the individual's desire must be seen as simultaneously ethical and perverse: ethical here describing the external perspective on his or her action; perverse describing the internal perspective, or that of his or her social circle. Richard Rorty has tried to explain such a desire—which we could also call a more generalized desire for justice—in terms of moving from a more restricted to a wider sense of loyalty: from loyalty to a smaller group to loyalty to a larger group (Rorty, "Justice"). But this redescription does not negate that a wider loyalty may entail the "betrayal" of a former, narrower loyalty, in whose confines one's sense of self has its home. Such a betrayal is hence perverse; but it is also the very definition of the ethical.[28]

It is conceivable that what is criticized from certain psychoanalytic perspectives as a romanticization of perversion may be denigrated from other, critical-theoretical perspectives as catering to anticommunitarian impulses stemming from liberal, bourgeois individualism. I think this criticism is equally invalid. As Jean-Luc Nancy has argued, both individuals and communities have been consistently conceived of in the mold of what he terms "the general horizon of our times": "immanentism" (*Inoperative* 3). I would thus like to situate the contestatory gestures that draw on the perversity of ethics within the framework of what Nancy calls the inoperative community: "the relation (the community) is, if it *is*, nothing other than what it undoes, in its very principle—and at its closure or on its limit—the autarchy of absolute immanence" (4). Immanentism in Nancy's sense is the tendency to conceive of individuals as self-contained wholes interacting with one another in a shared or common space,[29] a notion that corresponds precisely to traditional ethical models according to which, in Freudian parlance, the pleasure principle is guided by the reality principle—an immanent individual's secondary relations to others are submitted to a general rule. As with Nancy (a further discussion of his thought will usher in the engagement with deconstruction and theology in Chapter 3), the individual, as theorized in the light of a rigorously Freudian ethical thought, is "transcendent" in that reality, the community, or the "outside" in general has already cut into the individual's being in the very moment of its appearance in the world by way of a given history of institutionalizations. The shape of this cut, the line it traces through an individual's history, simultaneously marks the borders of a moral world and orients a powerful and contradictory desire in relation to those borders; it carries in its abyss both moral obligation and opprobrium, and the desire to transgress their reign. All three of these vectors—obligation, opprobrium, and transgression—are connoted by the word *fault*, which is why I call this figure the ethical fault-line. As we will see in the next chapter, this figure, which derives from Freud's theory of the drive, is the key to a Lacanian intervention into ethical philosophy.

2

In the Beginning Was the (*Orthos*) *Logos*

IN THE YEARS 1959–60, Lacan turned his attention to Freud's meta-psychological writings, most notably to the *Project for a Scientific Psychology*, *Civilization and Its Discontents*, and "Beyond the Pleasure Principle," in order to explore what he called "*l'univers de la faute*" (Lacan, *VII* 2)— the universal experience of the attraction exerted by wrong, evil, transgression, "*la faute*"—a move that resulted in perhaps the most decisive turning point in the history of his thought.[1] Lacan in the 1950s had been concerned to demonstrate that the Freudian unconscious was structured like a language, and that the tools of structural linguistics were thus a necessary complement to the Freudian technique. But his turn to the larger cultural questions posed in the metapsychological writings, accompanied by the influence of thinkers like Sartre and Heidegger,[2] led Lacan to focus increasingly on the problem of the human being's relation to its *jouissance*, or to those aspects of human existence that resist being reduced to the operations of the pleasure principle. This research led Lacan to read Freud's writings in the context of the history of ethics—of that thought, in other words, that had, from the beginning of Western culture, attempted to situate humanity on the road to happiness. Surveying the devastation of a second world war and the prospects of nuclear annihilation, Lacan at the end of the 1950s joined with a generation of intellectuals who proclaimed that the human penchant for destruction could not be accidental but must be, in some sense, an expression of the essence of modern man. But unlike many of those thinkers, he looked for his evidence and his answers in Freud,[3] and on the basis of his readings developed a radical revision of ethical thought.

As I will try to demonstrate in this chapter, the complexity that stumps most ethical theories is generated by the dynamic described in the previous chapter as the perversity of ethics. Lacan's purpose in reading Freud's metapsychological texts in conjunction with the history of ethical thought was not so much to derive from them an ethics proper to psychoanalysis, as to locate the problem of ethics within the field of human subjectivity as understood by psychoanalysis. In engaging with Aristotle, Saint Paul, Kant, Heidegger, and others, Lacan tried to show that a certain impasse that seemed to arise repeatedly in philosophy was not a problem external to thought that could somehow be dealt with, but rather was inherent in the thinking subject insofar as that subject was also a desiring subject. In the following pages I trace Lacan's thinking about this impasse through the philosophical engagements that form the seminar on ethics, in order to show, in the end, that this impasse in thought must be understood as an effect of the ethical fault-line. I then use this concept to argue for what, if anything, ethics can be in light of the apparent impasse the fault-line presents.

THE PRIMACY OF THE MAJOR PREMISE

In Aristotle's *Nichomachean Ethics*, with which Lacan begins his seminar on *The Ethics of Psychoanalysis*, the syllogistic model corresponds to a clearly definable social structure in which the minor premise, with its unreflective expression of immediate perception or desire, is seen as corresponding to the person of the slave,[4] which is in turn analogous to the lower bodily affects and passions. The major premise, on the other hand, has its analogue in the master and his law. One aim of the ethical process is to temper the slavish desires of the passions with the reasonable law of the master, an aim that, if slightly rephrased—the ethical involves the mastery of selfish or lower impulses by a selfless, higher agency—may strike many today as a satisfactory, if simplistic, description of how all traditional ethical models function. Lacan's claim is that this model of ethics and all subsequent ones based on it have failed to take into account the complexity of desire.

The gist of Lacan's reading of Aristotle's ethics can be illustrated by the following joke: a white settler is preparing for his first winter in the new world by chopping wood. One after another he stops the natives passing by to ask them about the severity of the upcoming winter, to which they answer with increasingly emphatic warnings, to which he responds with increasingly emphatic chopping. It is only after the requisite three iterations of this dialogue that he bothers to ask one of the natives how it is that natives know with such certainty how harsh the winter will be, at which point he is told that the best indicator of a winter's severity is how much wood white men chop. The point of this joke is the way it demonstrates, by undermining the often racist myth of primitive knowledge, that primitiveness itself is already a factor of the imposition of certain secondary norms or expectations.

In classical logic, when we begin with a universal law or ethical injunction (all men are mortal; chop wood according to the severity of the winter), and then later apply to it a pure observation (Socrates is a man; what natives know about the winter), we ostensibly arrive at a certain truth (Socrates is mortal) or a proper course of action (how much wood to chop). This truth is reached by subjecting the empirical evidence to the appropriate universal rule. What the absurdity of the above joke depends on, however, is that its ostensibly unadulterated minor premise (what natives know about winter) is already structured by the major premise before we even formulate the former. One only asks the question of Socrates' humanity when his humanity, with all its attributes, has become a question for us. Likewise, the "purity" of the natives' knowledge relies (in the joke) on the settler's chopping (i.e., on an element introduced by the major premise).

In fact this structure is not uncommon in the annals of humor. Consider the old Jewish joke in which an Orthodox Jew says to a reformed Jew, "How can you dare laugh about a rabbi who speaks with God every Friday evening?" "How do you know he speaks with God?," the reformed Jew asks. "Because he himself told me so." "Well, maybe he's a liar." "What an idea," laughs the Orthodox Jew. "As if God would waste his time talking to a liar."[5] In this case, the conflict between the two speakers is the result of a contradiction between the implicit syllogistic structures of their utterances. To the Orthodox Jew's report that the rabbi speaks with God, the reformed Jew applies the following logic: major premise—no one can talk to God (because he either does not exist or is unknowable); minor premise—the rabbi says he talks to God; conclusion—the rabbi is a liar. The report of the Orthodox Jew, however, is already the minor premise of another implicit syllogism, whose major premise—God would not talk to a liar—contradicts the reformed Jew's major premise precisely because it assumes that God exists and is a viable interlocutor. The reason the joke works is that we, the listeners, have already unconsciously adopted the major premise of the reformed Jew—that God really does not exist, and even if he does you certainly can't talk to Him. This is the unconscious utterance that structures our reception of the report that the rabbi says he talks to God. When the Orthodox Jew reveals that his thinking has been structured by another major premise—that God exists and that we can talk to him—this produces the uncanny effect of replacing for a moment our unquestioned assumption, our unconscious major premise, with another, thereby revealing in a flash that the purity of our reception of a report was an illusion, because our reception was already corrupted by a premise we were not aware of holding.[6]

As I noted above, Lacan begins his seminar by saying he will explore the universal experience of the attraction exerted by wrong, evil, transgression, "*la faute.*" The question of transgression is first posed about Aristotle's classical ethical formulation, a formulation in which the habits of men are supposed to be guided into conformity with the Sovereign Good through the influence of the *orthos logos*,[7] the right discourse. The problem he poses is thus: "If the rule of action is the *orthos logos*, if there can be no good action except in conformity with the latter, how is it possible that what Aristotle calls intemperance can survive? How is it possible for a subject's impulses to draw him elsewhere? How is that to be explained?" (23). Lacan's purpose in recalling Aristotle's classic formulation is to reveal a parallel between it and Freud's metapsychological models of the drive—not in order to emphasize the belatedness of Freud's reflections, but rather to demonstrate the way in which Freud's ostensibly mechanistic theories represent a sort of upheaval for the history of ethical thought.

Lacan finds what he is looking for in the third chapter of Book VII of the *Ethics* (not in the fifth chapter, as he tells his students). In this chapter, Aristotle discusses various solutions to the problem of intemperance—of how one can knowingly act wrongly—and does so by breaking actions down into syllogisms. "Beside the major premise," according to Lacan's reading,

> one must always taste what is sweet—there is a particular, concrete minor premise, i.e., this is sweet. And the principle of wrong action is to be found in the error of a particular judgment relative to the minor premise. Where is the error found? Precisely in the circumstance that the desire which is subjacent to the major premise causes the wrong judgement to be made concerning the reality of the supposed sweetness toward which the action is directed. (29–30)

The problem with this passage as it stands is that Lacan reads a section of Aristotle in which, as of yet, there is no moral error, and hence Lacan's diagnosis seems to make no sense. The error only comes in Aristotle's second, truly syllogistic example, in which the deciding subject is seen to balance two universal premises.

The syllogism Lacan cites is offered by Aristotle as an example of a fully effective actualization of moral knowledge, one in which the major and minor premises are harmonized and integrated by the deciding individual. This person believes in the universal rule that "everything sweet ought to be tasted," and encounters an object of which he judges, "this thing before me is sweet." Aristotle thus concludes that "a man who is able to taste and is not prevented is bound to act accordingly at once" (Aristotle 183). A problem, however, arises when the taster brings to bear on the issue two major premises, one, practical, forbidding the tasting of sweet things, and another, factual, recognizing the pleasantness of sweet things. Now, the introduction of the minor premise, that the object at hand is sweet, combined with the presence of *appetite*, may lead the subject, in full knowledge of the wrongfulness of his act, to taste the sweet thing. This, says Aristotle, "is the case we have been looking for, the defeat of reason in moral weakness. Thus it turns out that a morally weak man acts under the influence of some kind of reasoning and opinion, an opinion which is not intrinsically but only incidentally opposed to right reason; for it is not opinion but appetite that is opposed to right reason" (184).[8]

It is only in light of this second, altered example that we can grasp Lacan's insight. The error in judgment is due not merely to the ignorance of a universal law, but rather to the presence of what Aristotle calls *appetite* and Lacan calls *desire*. This desire, however, is not to be located on the side of the minor premise, of the empirical identification of the existence of something sweet, but is rather subjacent to, lying underneath or within, the major premise being brought to bear—not only in the knowledge of the pleasantness of sweet things, but in their prohibition as well. The *orthos logos*, in other words—the pure, self-derived truth that is meant to direct our behavior toward correct actions—is found to infect the empirical reality of a minor premise. Such empirical reality, therefore, is never an unadulterated fact lying ready-at-hand to be incorporated into an ethical order; rather, the ethical order already structures the way we encounter and select the actions and behavior that will later be submitted to that order. In a sense, the ethical order already structures and hence produces the errors it will later judge.

REALITY

As it happens, Lacan had to look hard for a passage in Aristotle that would allow him to perform such an interpretive move, and he is not shy about confessing the idiosyncrasies of his readings, as he does some fifteen years later in his *Encore* seminar.[9] The point to grasp is that Lacan does not necessarily want this reversal to be evident in Aristotle, at least not consciously evident. For it is his own reading of Freud that he intends to showcase as a veritable revolution in ethical thought, a revolution that may then be used as a lens through which to reveal the unconscious presence of the trope since the origins of practical reason. To this end Lacan draws his analogy: the major premise in Aristotelian ethics is to the minor premise as the reality principle in Freud is to the pleasure principle. "Isn't," Lacan asks, "the functioning of the apparatus that supports the reality principle in Freud strangely similar to what one finds in Aristotle?" And, indeed, this would seem an obvious enough parallel to draw:

> The reality principle or that to which the functioning of the neurotic apparatus in the end owes its efficacy appears as an apparatus that goes much further than a mere checking up; it is rather a question of rectification. It operates in the mode of detour, precaution, touching up, restraint. It corrects and compensates for that which seems to be the natural inclination of the psychic apparatus, and radically opposes it. (Lacan, *VII* 28)

On the basis of such a description one would certainly have to admit that the reality principle behaves decidedly like a moral agent, restraining, rectifying, and opposing the more primitive strivings of the pleasure principle. But, to repeat, the point of this analogy is a reversal—better yet, a deconstruction in the precise sense—of an opposition rooted in the heart of classical Freudian theory, a deconstruction that will eventually prove to be among the central and perennial elements of Lacan's thought.

To reiterate the fundamental issue: appetite, in light of a traditional interpretation, would seem to be a given, something that, if it "happens to be present" (Aristotle 184), will drive the subject to make the right or wrong choice depending on the premises involved. Lacan's reversal of this reading focuses on the "desire subjacent to the major premise" in order to assert that appetite may not be taken for granted but rather is a function of the law, of the *orthos logos*. In the analogous dynamic in Freud, appetite is represented by the pleasure principle, the primary process characterized by an inertial tendency toward the dispensation of accumulate energy. The control of the pleasure principle is exercised on what Lacan terms the "identity of perception" (Lacan, *VII* 31), in that the subject's psychic apparatus will attempt to repeat precisely the same sequence of neural discharges that produced an earlier perception of satisfaction, even if such a satisfaction is merely hallucinated. The reality principle, in contrast, consists of those secondary processes that incorporate the results of a "groping forward, a rectifying test" into the psychical architecture constituted by the neural facilitations or pathways (*Bahnungen*), permitting or favoring those discharges that are finally successful. One might say of this psychical architecture, or "backcloth of experience," that it "consists in the construction of a certain system of *Wunsch* or *Erwartung* [wish or expectation] of pleasure, defined as anticipated pleasure, and which tends for this reason to realize itself autonomously in its own sphere, theoretically without expecting anything from the outside" (31). What, then, is the sphere of this theoretical, anticipated pleasure? If the primary processes tend to be exercised toward an identity of perception, the secondary processes tend to be exercised toward an identity of *thought*, meaning that the sphere of *Wunsch* or *Erwartung*, unlike that of the primary processes, involves not perception but rather an abstraction or representation of perception.

If this reality testing is the essence of thought, then thought would appear to be associated with the reality principle, and hence—given the classical division according to which the primary processes are unconscious and the secondary conscious—with consciousness. But this is simply not the case, as we know that nothing taking place on the level of these tests is available to perception (31–32). Thought in this sense is unconscious through and through. Perhaps it is not "controlled by the pleasure principle, but it occurs in a space that as an unconscious space is to be considered as subject to the pleasure principle" (32). The processes of thought only become perceptible and available to consciousness to the extent that they become associated with words. In its most primordial form, for example, it is the cry or proto-word that gives shape and specificity to the notion of an unpleasant object. Whatever is happening in the subject's environment

> would remain obscure and unconscious if the cry did not lend it, as far as the conscious is concerned, the sign that gives it its own weight, presence, structure. It gives it as well a potentiality due to the fact that the important objects for a human subject are speaking objects, which will allow him to see revealed in the discourse of others the processes that, in fact, inhabit his own unconscious. (32)

The unconscious, then, is not simply—as Lacan is often interpreted as saying—the presence of language in the human psyche.[10] It is rather a movement of elements that is structured like a language, a movement that ultimately constitutes the phenomenon of awareness when it is translated into words used in an intersubjective context.

It is important, however, to read this passage not as the affirmation of a metaphysical, private language of the kind denied by Wittgenstein,[11] but rather as a recognition of the fact that while language is public or universal, an individual's desire is at its core pathological and hence private. The unconscious is structured like a language in that it is a function of articulation and difference, of elements that relate to one another and transfer charges and affects in ways similar to how language transfers meaning via metaphor and metonymy. While deeply indebted to language in its symbolic aspect, the unconscious is also riddled with the uncommunicable, imaginary qualities of lived experience, and hence cannot be said to be made solely of words.

The ramifications of the above analysis of thought are as follows: in the first place, the reality principle, traditionally associated with consciousness, functions at the level of the unconscious, and is only perceptible when "articulated in the terms of interhuman experience"; in the second place, the unconscious itself is to be understood as the workings of "logical components which are of the order of *logos*" (Lacan, *VII* 33), and which transfer energy in the form of "affective charges" between one another according to the dictates of the pleasure principle (i.e., in pursuit of the satisfaction produced by a former experience). Finally, the very directionality of the primary processes, and hence of the unconscious movements themselves, is determined by an architecture, by a structure that is none other than that of thought—that is, of the reality principle or secondary processes. For if the primary processes are involved in the fiction of hallucinating a foregone satisfaction, it is the secondary processes that are involved in the "process of search, of recognition and, as Freud explained later, of recovery of the object" (33). This process, the appetitive process, is thus located at the level of the secondary, not primary, process, insofar as those secondary processes in some sense logically precede or prestructure the primary processes that ostensibly precede them.

At this point it should become clear that the basic classification system we started with no longer holds together. Beginning with the difference between pleasure and reality, one may classify those processes involving perception with the former and those involving thought with the latter. However, when at the next level, the level of the experience of objects, we classify the perception of objects as conscious and the thought of objects as unconscious, we observe that we have contradicted the classical theory, for now it is the pleasure principle that has been associated with consciousness and the reality principle with the unconscious (34). So there must be another criterion of difference, one that emerges out of Lacan's deconstruction of primary and secondary processes. This new criterion is the event of language, which must be understood as establishing its domain through a series of logically retroactive effects. The event of language reveals to consciousness the processes of the unconscious, but in so doing constitutes the unconscious as that which is unknown. The unknown processes of the unconscious form the architecture of thought specific to the secondary processes or reality principle, which gives to the perceptual apparatus of the primary processes or pleasure principle the directionality that we recognize as appetite or desire. When the subject identifies pleasure using language, we enter into the realm of inquiry associated with traditional ethics, for it is then that the subject identifies his good and is invited to justify his choice of goods before the tribunal of his fellow subjects. But Lacan's inquiry demands that we approach the question of the good from still another level, for if pleasure is prestructured by reality at the level of the psychical processes (institutionalization), then this is also the case at the level of the subject's ethical discourse, and we may thus be certain that the positioning of the good in ethical thought is a functioning of something that occurs at the level of the real. This something is what Lacan calls *das Ding*.

DAS DING

The question, then, is one of reality. The reality principle has to be rethought outside the mold of what we could call the epistemological model, according to which the subject is a point of pure apperception inside the shell of his or her existence who forms images in his or her mind that more or less accurately correspond to an ultimately unknowable reality. The reality principle, in this view, would be the index of approximation, a variation of the game in which the blindfolded child uses his companions' calls of "hotter" and "colder" to locate an object or goal. Whereas the pleasure principle would regulate the instinctual discharge of energy, the reality principle would have a longer view of things, ensuring that the

effects of an immediate discharge would not, in fact, provoke further displeasure down the road; and it would manage this by means of an accurate
picture of reality.

The picture Lacan develops throughout the 1959–60 seminar entails a
powerful critique of this model. In this picture, the reality and pleasure
principles are intertwined in the same place, in the unconscious, where
perception and thought are being forged in the crucible of their own distinction. Lacan's insight in rereading Freud's *Project for a Scientific Psychology* is that reality is determined not by the accuracy of a picture, but by the
success of a specific action, Freud's *spezifische Aktion*, in producing, or reproducing, a certain satisfaction (Lacan, *VII* 41).[12] Lacan strictly follows
Freud when he emphasizes that the finding of a certain object contained in
the specific action is, and must be, a refinding, for it is the original action
that is recorded in the neural pathways. But while the refinding of this object affords a certain satisfaction, there is nonetheless something missing, a
failure of perfect repetition. And it is on the basis of this missing satisfaction that the desire supporting the subject's reality begins to take shape
(41). Reality, then, must be understood as the organization of the subject's
unconscious—of the constellation of elements that shift and transfer
charges between them according to the patterns of metonymy and metaphor, or displacement and condensation (61)—around the search for an
excess satisfaction that the successful repetition of motor actions always
fails to obtain. Does this mean that reality is a pure linguistic construction?
No, what it means is that the reference points of reality are unconsciously
determined, and that the unconscious is structured like a language.

But is it not merely a cheap assertion—one meant to tie us uncritically
to a sort of mystical Lacanian doctrine—that the satisfaction afforded by
the specific action is lacking? Is this not an example—the central example,
in fact—of the aspect of psychoanalysis so resoundingly criticized by
Deleuze and Guattari,[13] namely, that it is obsessed with lack? The provenance of Lacan's notion of lack—that it is a translation into psychoanalytic
parlance of Hegelian negativity, via Sartre, where it appears as the corner-
stone of consciousness, the "hole in being" separating the *en-soi* from the
pour-soi—is well known. I must here side strongly with Slavoj Žižek,
whose work can in many ways be described as a continuing effort to
demonstrate that, myriad philosophical endeavors notwithstanding, such
negativity is an indispensable concept for philosophy's descriptions of human being.[14] What we have in *Seminar VII* is a painstaking attempt to lo-

cate the origins and effects of this negativity in the formation of subjectivity.

Language is, of course, the source and location of the particularity of human being for Lacan. The question is to identify the specificity of our inhabitation of and by language. Throughout the time stretching from his or her birth to the beginnings of adolescence, the human child must pass from being entirely describable in terms of sensory perception to possessing the higher functions of consciousness and memory. The unconscious refers to the transitional layer between perception and consciousness, a layer or series of processes—we know there must be a process to refer to, for we are not conscious of all that our senses perceive—that takes the form of an *Aufbau* or structure (Lacan, *VII* 51). The structure in question is precisely, according to Lacan, that aspect of language necessary for the production of speech but not exhausted by its function (45): *langue*, the structure of language that remains in the unconscious and organizes its elements.

It is important to note that the structure of language need not be understood in the sense of a "mentalese" à la Jerry Fodor[15] or a deep structure à la Chomsky.[16] These theories argue for the existence of a universal, prelinguistic, mental structure that determines the actual parameters of natural languages or of the logical possibilities of thought. Lacan's notion of the unconscious as corresponding to the structure of language, in contrast, is not concerned with specifying the possible parameters of languages or thought, but rather with describing the ramifications of being a subject of language. Starting from the insight of structural linguistics that speaking subjects must implicitly master a structure (*langue*) in order to engage in acts of communication (*paroles*), Lacan theorizes that this structure should be brought to bear in analyzing the peculiarities of human desire.

The development of the capacity to use words in communication acts corresponds in theory to the development of an increasingly complex latticework of *Bahnungen*, or neural pathways, that contains the structure supporting the subject's ability to speak. The "elements" of this structure, therefore, cannot be exactly the same thing as words, although they relate to one another in analogous ways. Lacan finds what he is looking for in Freud's distinction between *Sachvorstellungen* and *Wortvorstellungen*, or thing-representations and word-representations. It is, Lacan says,

> no accident if the *Sachvorstellungen* are linked to the *Wortvorstellungen*, since it tells us that there is a relationship between thing and word. The straw of words

only appears to us as straw insofar as we have separated it from the grain of things, and it was first the straw that bore that grain.

I don't want to begin developing a theory of knowledge here, but it is obvious that the things of the human world are things in a universe structured by words, that language, symbolic processes, dominate and govern all. (Lacan, *VII* 45)

Words, in certain theories of language (e.g., Locke, Rousseau), serve the purpose of expressing our thoughts about things. It is in this way that they are like straw to the grain of things—secondary, degraded. But straw and grain are entities that owe their existence to their separation, the very separation that establishes grain as something to be valued and straw as something to be discarded. In the same way, words are bequeathed their secondary status in the very movement that establishes them and their corresponding things as separate and competing entities. The child navigating the phenomenal world while at the same time coming into consciousness through language lives time in two directions. "Objectively" he or she is moving "forward" from pure perception into language; but "subjectively," from the perspective of consciousness, he or she is looking "backwards" into the newly created annals of his or her memory, reaching for the objective existence of things independent from the knowledge he or she now has of them, a knowledge that can only be formulated in words. Things are real, but only when seen retrospectively from the vantage of an impossibly discarded knowledge through which they came into being as things in our world.

This hybrid, the word/thing, is nothing other than a discrete instance of our language/world, and it appears as a hybrid only from the perspective of a theoretical separation of language and world. In this light, we can say that a *Wortvorstellung* describes the manifestation of the language/world in consciousness,[17] while *Sachvorstellung* describes its manifestation in the unconscious. Despite these distinctions, "Sache and Wort are . . . closely linked; they form a couple. *Das Ding* is something else" (Lacan, *VII* 45). The distinction to be established, then, is not between language and the world, but rather between a language/world and something else, something produced by the fact that we are inhabitants of this language/world.

Recall that the reality principle in its revised version refers to the tendency of the unconscious to be organized around the repetition of a prior satisfaction. The pathways back to this satisfaction are inscribed in a chain of *Sachvorstellungen* that lead to a specific action that promises, in turn, a repeated satisfaction, a satisfaction of the same. But there is always something that resists the purity of this reproduction, of this incorporation into the subject's originally seamless world. This something is the "original experience of the division of reality" (52), the first experience of something other than myself, something radically, strangely, incorrigibly *other*.

To understand the emergence of otherness at a phenomenological level, we should turn to Sartre as well as to Freud's *Nebenmensch* (literally, the human nearby). If Lacan says of *das Ding* that it "is the element that is initially isolated by the subject in his experience of the *Nebenmensch* as being by its very nature alien, *Fremde* [*sic*]" (52), we find in this image an allusion to an Other that unfolds majestically in the words from *Being and Nothingness* that Sartre uses to describe the entrance of the Other into the subject's world:

> The Other is first the permanent flight of things toward a goal which I apprehend as an object at a certain distance from me but which escapes me inasmuch as it unfolds about itself its own distances. Moreover this disintegration grows by degrees; if there exists between the lawn and the Other a relation which is without distance and which creates distance, then there exists necessarily a relation between the Other and the statue which stands on a pedestal *in the middle of* the lawn, and a relation between the Other and the big chestnut trees which border the walk; there is a total space which is grouped around the Other, and this space is made *with my space*; there is a regrouping in which I take part but which escapes me, a regrouping of all the objects of my universe. (Sartre, *Being* 343)

By *Nebenmensch* we must understand the very first experience of agency, of an intentionality that escapes a world that has hitherto remained indistinguishable from the expression of our own primordially intentional interactivities with it. The Other's emergence into my world marks the first boundary, the first glimpse of an "outside" (Lacan, *VII* 52) that establishes itself from the outset as radically independent of my attempts at a repeated satisfaction, and hence in some sense as independent of that unconscious organization that supports reality itself. The emergence of the Other constitutes a regrouping of the space that until this moment was not exactly space, not as we know it now, but rather an inclusive extension of myself. Space becomes space and objects become objects through the intervention of the Other, and it is precisely this becoming-space and becoming-objectness of the world that creates the specter of a substance beyond the *Sachvorstellungen* that structure my reality, a substance that now *stands in for* that object that I can no longer even recall having lost.

The world of our experience, the Freudian world, assumes that it is this object, *das Ding*, as the absolute Other of the subject, that one is supposed to find again. It is to be found at the most as something missed. One doesn't find it, but only its pleasurable associations. It is in this state of wishing for it and waiting for it that, in the name of the pleasure principle, the optimum tension will be sought; below that there is neither perception nor effort. (*VII* 52)

Das Ding is, therefore, the product of a retroactive abstraction from the phenomenal world, the absent center supporting the desire whose tension defines the very core of our experience of reality. The reality principle comes to us from the symbolic order, but upon articulating the imaginary (sensory) material of our psyche it leaves behind something real, *das Ding*, the substance of our desire.[18]

THE LAW

It may be helpful from time to time to draw parallels between this existentially oriented side of Lacan's teaching and the semiotic model perhaps more commonly associated with Lacanian analysis. Lacan himself does so quite often in this seminar, such as when he identifies *das Ding* as "the beyond-of-the-signified" (Lacan, *VII* 54). Let us recall that Lacan's classic intervention in semiotic theory reverses the Saussurean pairing of signifier and signified, such that the signifier itself, the word in its field of structural differences, takes precedence over the signified or meaning of that word.[19] This signified is normally understood in the most naïve sense as a thought-image—an understanding propagated by Saussure's pictorial renditions—despite the fact that the vast majority of words we use on a daily basis have no imagistic correlate.[20] That the signifier takes precedence over the signified means that thought is a function of the structure of language, as opposed to language being merely its conveyor. If, as Lacan says, the signified, or meaning, is a repressed signifier (Lacan, "Agency" 149), we can locate the signified at the level of the *Sachvorstellung*, that is, at the level of the structure constituting the unconscious. *Das Ding* is then the beyond-of-the-signified in exactly the same way as it is the beyond-of-the-*Sachvorstellung*, or of thought itself.

Because *das Ding* represents a kind of beyond to every conceivable aspect of the subject's world, it only makes itself felt in the subject's world through the medium that is most alienated from the particularity of the subject's concerns, namely, the law. The law is by definition alienated from the subject's concerns precisely because of its universality, because it is a maxim intended to be applicable to all regardless of particular differences or personal interests. It is for this reason that Lacan identifies the emergence of *das Ding* in the history of philosophy with the moral philosophy of Immanuel Kant (Lacan, *VII* 55), for by defining the moral act as an act that is utterly detached from the personal interests of any given individual,[21] Kant situates the driving force of ethics squarely in the realm of the Other, in that place to which I have no access yet nonetheless attracts me with the promise of fulfilled satisfaction.

It is important to grasp the apparent contradiction: according to Kant the only way to know that I am acting in a moral way—that is, acting for the sake of duty alone—is to know that I am performing actions despite or even against my inclinations. If I am inclined to one course of action but choose another because that is what the law prescribes, only then are my actions moral; they are moral because I know that anyone else in my situation, no matter what his or her particular inclinations, ought to act in the same way. For Lacan, however, this "pure signifying system" (55) of the categorical imperative, which is meant to guarantee the universality of the law, is nothing other than the linguistic manifestation of the substance that grounds our individual desires in all their pathology, in all their particularity. How can that be? The law and desire are ostensibly at loggerheads; the purpose of any system of law or ethics is the regulation of competing individual desires. How then can it be that the law could claim such a tight affiliation with the source of all desire?

Insofar as *das Ding* refers to the negative reservoir of every failure of satisfaction bestowed by the contingencies of history and place on the emerging individual, the *Vorstellungen* that comprise the unconscious both point the way to it and strive to maintain a minimal distance from it (58). They point to it because they constitute the abstraction of satisfaction, the virtual reminders of the potential satisfaction of a repeated action; they maintain a distance from it because they are organized so as to form the borders of the individual's existence. The full satisfaction, the real original satisfaction not afforded by the various renditions of repetition, is presumed to lie in the realm of the Other, and the *Vorstellungen* are what guard that realm. But there can be no outside that is not at one and the same time radically inside, radically a part of our world; hence the Other is also a part of our psyche. This internal exterior, this outside-of-our-grasp as it is represented within our psyche (ex-timacy, as Lacan calls it),[22] must logically remain both the aim of all our desires and totally inaccessible. The *Vorstellungen* that mark the borders of that inaccessibility hold the place in the unconscious of the first prohibitions, the building blocks of the law.

The law and that which it prohibits make a simultaneous appearance on the stage of the human psyche. When Lacan affirms the incest taboo as the primordial instance of the law (66–67)—as the fundamental fulcrum on which nature and culture balance in their opposition—it is not because incest itself is the primordial desire, a desire that the beasts blissfully satisfy while mankind makes itself sick by denying it. Incest is the primordial desire because the body of the mother is both blamed and yearned for as the reservoir of a satisfaction that, in the wake of language, is believed to have once been there. Desire is not need; rather, desire is produced from the experience of a discourse giving reasons, words, for the failure of need to be satisfied. These words are the law, the prohibitions the subject uses to mask the impossibility of desire's fulfillment.

Lacan cites the Ten Commandments as a paradigmatic case of the law in order to demonstrate his contention that the law exists in order to articulate a minimal distance from *das Ding*, and therefore to structure desire as such.

> This brings us back to questioning the meaning of the ten commandments insofar as they are tied in the deepest of ways to that which regulates the distance between the subject and *das Ding*—insofar as that distance is precisely the condition of speech, insofar as the ten commandments are the condition of the existence of speech as such. . . . From another point of view, how can one not in truth see, when one merely recites them, that they are in a way the chapter and verse of our transactions at every moment of our lives? In other words, we spend our time breaking the ten commandments, and that is why society is possible. (69)

Such basic laws as the Ten Commandments are not merely the negation of those desires whose realization would prove harmful to the social body, but rather and more fundamentally are the linguistic revelation of desire as such. The value of human life—where "value" is a social manifestation of the notion of "desire for"—does not preexist the prohibition of murder but rather is dependent on it. The prohibition against lying involves the subject's relation to speech and the law in an even more fundamental way. To the extent that speech claims to represent being, speech is first and foremost a lie, a lie corresponding to the distance separating the utterance from the subject who utters it (82). The injunction not to lie therefore marks an impossible desire, the desire to be true to one's words, or for one's words to truly represent oneself. Finally, the commandment not to covet thy neighbor's possessions—his house, wife, servants, and so forth—reveals the agency of *das Ding* in a most impressive fashion, because it is exclusively the fact that these *things* are my neighbor's—the *Nebenmensch* who manifests so ominously the inaccessibility of the Other—and are thus barred from me, that drives me to covet them (83).

The law is the language that adorns the borders governed by reality, a reality itself instituted by the unconscious structure of language that is the law. The borders marked by the law are inside us and thus guard us from an outside that inhabits us as well. This *extimate* place, *das Ding*, occupies the center of the vortex of pathways and associations that make up the unconscious, and its structural connection with the law means that the most basic nature of desire, all desire, is to be drawn toward that which is prohibited, because it is prohibited.

SUBLIMATION

From the perspective of the law, *das Ding* appears as sin, transgression. Lacan cites part of the following passage from St. Paul's letter to the Romans, substituting *das Ding* for the word sin:

> While we were living in the flesh, our sinful passions, aroused by the law, were at work in our members to bear fruit for death. But now we are discharged from the law, dead to that which held us captive, so that we serve not under the old written code but in the new life of the Spirit.
>
> What then shall we say? That the law is sin? By no means! Yet, if it had not been for the law, I should not have known sin. I should not have known what it is to covet if the law had not said, "You shall not covet." (*New Oxford Annotated Bible*, Romans 7:5–7)

Although they are interdependent, sin and the law are not the same. Sin already existed and was awakened by the knowledge the law brought with it. For the law is knowledge—is spirit—but the body is "carnal, sold under sin. I do not understand my own actions. For I do not do what I want, but I do the very thing I hate." The problem Paul is trying to deal with is that he recognizes the dialectic relating sin and the law, but must at the same time defend the law as good, as not the cause of sin. He solves this problem by locating evil in the natural corruptibility of the body, the ease with which it is enslaved by physical passions. The evil of the body only resolves into sin with the advent of Spirit, or knowledge, in the shape of the law. It is the spirit that both knows and wants to act in accordance with the law, but it is the sin that dwells in the flesh that actually drives me to do what I do not want to do.

The only way out of the impasse between sin and the law is to pass through death, to "die to the law through the body of Christ," and thereby enter the new life of the Spirit. Because the law is itself caught up in the dialectic of sin, release from this life and entrance into the life of the Spirit cannot come from mere adherence to the law. What Christ provided through his sacrifice was a third way:

> But now the righteousness of God has been manifested apart from the law, although the law and the prophets bear witness to it, the righteousness of God through faith in Jesus Christ for all who believe. For there is no distinction; since all have sinned and fall short of the glory of God, they are justified by his grace as a gift. (Romans 4:21–24)

Faith, the third way between the law and sin, is distinguished by its purity, by its utter detachment from the personal interest that corrupts the body. It is quite possible to act according to the law against the wishes of the body in order to accede to a reward—eternal life—whose attraction is nevertheless measured within the economy of the pleasure principle. The justification provided by faith, in contrast, consists of grace, a "free gift" from God, and cannot be earned.

This is what Lacan means when he says that Freud and St. Paul are telling us the same thing, "namely, that what governs us on the path to our pleasure is no Sovereign Good, and that moreover, beyond a certain limit, we are in a thoroughly enigmatic position relative to that which lies within *das Ding*, because there is no ethical rule which acts as a mediator between our pleasure and its real rule" (Lacan, *VII* 95). The last phrase is the key, for "ethical rule" should be read as the law, the law that cannot mediate between the economy of pleasure and the ultimate promise of heaven, salvation. But is *das Ding* salvation? Or is it sin, and hence damnation? The conclusion to be drawn from psychoanalysis is that they are one and the same. *Das Ding* is the real motor of any and all drivenness, the ultimate location of desire, and at the same time it is that which looms behind the law's prohibitions. Because the pursuit of pleasure is structured as a lure with the promise of happiness always disappearing beyond the next obstacle strewn across our path, Christianity recognized that the ultimate goal of salvation had to be approached differently, via a bestowal utterly independent of the efforts—and hence desires—of the subject. The only way to achieve what you most desire is not to desire it, for it is desire itself that prevents you from attaining it.[23]

Žižek, paraphrasing Alain Badiou's appropriation of this Pauline doctrine of revelation to his notion of "the event," takes this "death to the law" as the opening of "another dimension," namely, that "Christian Revelation is thus an example (although probably *the* example) of how we, human beings, are not constrained to the positivity of Being; of how, from time to time, in a contingent and unpredictable way, a Truth-Event can occur that opens up to us the possibility of participating in Another Life by remaining faithful to the Truth-Event" (*Ticklish* 147). The danger to be avoided, however, is believing the way of Grace—as opposed to that of an "economy of goods"—really represents another dimension, rather than merely a kind of understanding of the intractability of one's own indebtedness to what Badiou calls Being, or "the situation."[24] In other words, the very logic of the situation is to be incessantly driven by the promise of an event that transcends the logic of one's situation. Žižek also distances himself, however, from Badiou's affirmation of a positive transcendent term, noting that it is precisely here that "Lacan parts company with St Paul and Badiou," insofar as psychoanalysis "does not already posit a 'new harmony,' a new Truth-Event; it—as it were—merely wipes the slate clean for one" (*Ticklish* 153–54). Whatever "this domain beyond the rule of law" consists of, the deciding question is whether one can actively produce it or occupy it in any way. The answer from a psychoanalytic perspective—and here I agree with Žižek that this is what marks the fundamental difference between this perspective and Badiou's—is negative.[25] As Žižek writes, "[t]he 'death drive' is thus the constitutive obverse of every emphatic assertion of Truth irreducible to the positive order of Being: the negative gesture that clears a space for creative sublimation. . . . This is the difference between Lacan and Badiou: Lacan insists on the primacy of the (negative) *act* over the (positive) establishment of a 'new harmony' via the intervention of some new Master-Signifier; while for Badiou, the different facets of negativity (ethical catastrophes) are reduced to so many versions of the 'betrayal' of (or infidelity to, or denial of) the positive Truth-Event" (Žižek, *Ticklish* 159). This is why Žižek is right in insisting that, despite his protests to the contrary, Badiou's distinction between Being and the Event is profoundly Kantian; although not because he (and here there need be no disagreement between a Kantian and a Lacanian position) posits a transcendent dimension to lived experience—he calls the emergence of a "truth" an "immanent break. 'Immanent' because a truth proceeds in the situation, and nowhere else" (Badiou, *Ethics* 42)—but rather in his faith—for psychoanalysis illusory—that this dimension can serve as the grounds for a knowledge that can distinguish right from wrong, or, to be more faithful to his own idiom, that an event that exceeds my current situation is for that very reason an eternal "truth." Ethics in Badiou's redefinition describes a fidelity to the truth of such events. An "ethics of truth," as he formulates it, consists in "that which lends consistency to the presence of some-one in the composition of the subject induced by the process of this truth" (*Ethics* 44).

Since it is certainly the case that epochal events—and it is not entirely clear what the ultimate difference might be between Badiou's "event" and what Thomas Kuhn called a paradigm shift, other than the fact that Kuhn had no ambition to associate such shifts with insights into "eternal truths" (*Ethics* 90)—may be differently valued by different observers, Badiou is of course in need of a means to determine when an event marks the emergence of a truth. He finds this distinguishing characteristic in a principle of disorganization: "the Good is, strictly speaking, the internal norm of a prolonged disorganization of life."

> On the other hand, if I "fall in love" (the word "fall" indicates disorganization in the walk of life), or if I am seized by the sleepless fury of a thought [*pensée*], or if some radical political engagement proves incompatible with every immediate principle of interest—then I find myself compelled to measure life, my life as a socialized human animal, against something other than itself. And this above all when, beyond the joyful or enthusiastic clarity of the seizing, it becomes a matter of finding out if, and how, I am to continue along the path of vital disorganization, thereby granting to this primordial disorganization a secondary and paradoxical organization, that very organization which we have called "ethical consistency." (Badiou, *Ethics* 60)

The passage is helpful in clarifying the status of Badiou's relation to Kant. For while he is at pains to stress his rejection of a transcendental realm, the disinterestedness that for Kant distinguishes ethical from nonethical acts is clearly at the core of Badiou's considerations. Then again, Badiou's language also makes evident what will become clear in Lacan's engagement with Kant, for he argues—very much aware of the Lacanian perspective—that the commitment to ethics must continue "beyond the joyful or enthusiastic clarity of the seizing" and thus admits that the moment of disinterest responds to, and is perhaps even driven by, an impassioned or radically pathological interest. Moreover, as we have seen from our discussion of drive in Freud's thought, it comes as no surprise that "disorganization" emerges as the deciding attribute of the ethical, for institutionalization dictates that drive, at its core, will always be a drive to disorganize.

Finally, then, Badiou's dedication to progress cannot be distinguished from that of any admirer of scientific (for example) revolutions: the truths that so arise are the truths of a new situation, and the dedication, commitment, or "consistency" of the geniuses and visionaries who have brought those truths about is no more meritorious per se than that of a thousand other fanatics whose innovations have been banished by history.

It comes down, then, to a confrontation with Kant. Just as for Paul an ethics of works—subject to the economy of exchange or of pleasure—is not sufficient to procure salvation, for Kant any action motivated by inclination, no matter what the consequences, fails to qualify as an ethical act. As with the truly righteous for Paul, the truly ethical for Kant corresponds to a third position beyond the dialectic of inclination and law,[26] because the power of inclination is so insidious that it is never possible to be completely sure that one is acting for the sake of duty alone (Kant, *Foundations* 23). In the end, one may only follow the categorical imperative against one's inclinations and hope that one's actions do, in fact, correspond to the dictates of a practical reason purged of pathological motivations and, hence, universal. In both cases we see the workings of the law on the border of the noumenal realm of *das Ding*.

The difference between what Lacan calls the economy of goods and the properly ethical dimension, the realm of *das Ding*, also governs the subject's relation to objects in his or her world. One's relation to a desired object will always be tinted by a certain idealization, the structure of which is characterized by the identification of the subject with an image of himself, of how he wants to be perceived by others. Idealization, in other words, involves a narcissistic projection of the subject into the space of the object. The object is desired in part because of its perceived appropriateness to the subject's ideal image. This is the classic modus operandi of the marketing industry, which understands well that selling a product is foremost a function of selling an image, a scenario in which the potential consumers see themselves. Think for a moment of the ultimate "postmodern" advertisement, one that revels in its own "subversive" reflexivity: Sprite's "Image" ads. After a typical scenario staging the centrality of "image" to a youthful subculture, an announcer's voice tells us that "image is nothing, taste is everything," hence establishing Sprite as the drink for those not interested in image or, more accurately, for those who are hiply and ironically aware of the centrality of image to their own lives. In other words, "taste" resides in the image of imagelessness.

In contrast to the narcissistic world of idealized objects, *das Ding* opens onto another realm of possible relations to objects:

> It is through this mirage relation that the notion of an object is introduced. But this object is not the same as that which is aimed at on the horizon of the instinct. Between the object as it is structured by the narcissistic relation and *das Ding*, there is a difference, and it is precisely on the slope of that difference that the problem of sublimation is situated for us. (Lacan, *VII* 98)

To make the analogy complete, if an object relation characterized primarily by identification recalls the economy of works or goods—because in these economies one's efforts are ultimately guided by a scenario in which one's self plays the central role—the relation to an object described by the term sublimation echoes the sublimity, the ungraspable nature, of the Kantian ethical act or the Pauline gift of grace.[27] In sublimation, the subject does not merely reproduce himself and his knowledge-world in the form of the object, but rather opens himself to the utter alterity of the object, to the cavernous and threatening absence of him-her-self that its being implies.[28]

This discussion of sublimation has the purpose of bringing together, in Lacan's thought, a psychoanalytic understanding of ethics with a psychoanalytic understanding of aesthetics and, in fact, ontology. Indeed, the concept of *das Ding* forms the centerpiece of a Lacanian ontology, which will become clear in its evolution into the concept of the Real. To begin with, Lacan's aesthetic theory places *das Ding* at the center of the specifically human process of creation. Any act of creation implies a break from a previous state of affairs,[29] which makes of the act a *creatio ex nihilo*, a creation out of nothing, in which the nothing corresponds retroactively to the absence of whatever was brought into being by the act of creation. This nothingness at the center of any act of creation corresponds in turn to the empty center of the unconscious that is *das Ding*, and the relation of the creating subject to *das Ding* in the act of creation is what Lacan calls sublimation, "raising the object to the dignity of the Thing" (Lacan, *VII* 112). This aesthetic dimension is visible in a wide variety of activities, some of which would not appear to involve creation at first glance. The activity of the collector is one such example, an activity that can turn an ordinary, everyday object into a work of art by sheer enumeration. As Lacan says of Jacques Prévert's matchbox collection, "the wholly gratuitous, proliferating, superfluous, and quasi absurd character of this collection pointed to its thingness as match box" (114). In fact, one could point to this as the technique par excellence of pop art, exemplified most famously by Andy

Warhol's repetitive prints of images that had achieved the status of commodities; the obsessive focus on them as commodities, via enumeration, raises them to the level of *das Ding*.

LACAN AVEC HEIDEGGER

Lacan draws philosophical support for his identification of sublimation—and hence the core aesthetic activity—with creation from Heidegger's thesis in the "The Thing," in which the philosopher speaks of the "thingness" of the vessel as lying not "in the material of which it consists, but in the void that it holds" (Heidegger, "The Thing" 169).[30] For Lacan, Heidegger is speaking at once about the first work of creation, and the creation of the first signifier:

> Today I simply want to stick to the elementary distinction as far as a vase is concerned between its use as a utensil and its signifying function. If it really is a signifier, and the first of such signifiers fashioned by the human hand, it is in its signifying essence a signifier of nothing other than of signifying as such or, in other words, of no particular signified. Heidegger situates the vase at the center of the essence of earth and sky. It unites first of all, by virtue of the act of libation, by its dual orientation—upwards in order to receive and toward the earth from which it raises something. . . . It creates the void and thereby introduces the possibility of filling it. Emptiness and fullness are introduced into a world that by itself knows not of them. (Lacan, *VII* 120)

We must understand the assertion that the vase and the first signifier both signify nothing in two profoundly related ways: a first signifier, a master signifier in Lacan's semiotic terminology, is the signifier that signifies nothing precisely because it is the signifier that stands in for the fact of signification in general. It opens the space between the world as lived-in and the world as possible reference of signification, and as such is the implicit anchoring point of all subsequent signifiers in the signifying chain.[31] In the constitution of a subject's identity, this function is served by the name of the father, the nonmeaning proper name that nevertheless serves as the anchoring point for all future statements about this particular subject. Its correlate in primary language acquisition is the first word (often some utterance like "mama," "baba," or "dada," which should not be understood as the child's trying to name the mother or father, but rather as precisely the opposite: the words for "real, existing" parents have come to be associated with those first utterances that act as signifiers), which may be repeated by the child for many months before the establishment of further signifiers and hence of the possibility of "meaning" something by it (Oller 179).

The vase signifies nothing in an analogous way, insofar as it is the most basic act of creation that then stands in for the human activity of creation in general. But, more specifically, the vase signifies nothing in a formalistic sense, in that the contours of its walls abut, contain, and in essence produce nothingness in the form of the emptiness that the vase's maker may now fill. The nothingness of the vase, in this sense, serves as a metaphor for the signifier, because it illustrates the function of the signifier to make exactly such distinctions as "empty" versus "full," "something" versus "nothing." It is the nothingness produced by the act of creation of the vase that allows for the existence of the space to be filled with drink or food, with something that may sustain life but that also may be now moved, owned, valued. The value of the substance filling that space, the value brought to it by the space itself, is a value extracted from *das Ding*, from the nothingness produced by the act of creation that is the signifier's first distinction.

Lacan's engagements with Heidegger in the 1950s[32] leave their mark in his incorporation of the Heideggerian theme of creation, as touched on in "The Thing" but elaborated more thoroughly in "The Origin of the Work of Art." In this essay Heidegger argues that the essence of the work of art lies in its having been created, but that this createdness remains essentially a feature of the work, and not a passive dependence on the artist who creates it. The createdness of the work of art has to do with the way the work, in its becoming, is a place for the occurrence of truth—truth, in Heidegger's language being "the primal conflict in which, always in some particular way, the Open is won within which everything stands and from which everything withholds itself that shows itself and withdraws itself as a being" (Heidegger, "Origin" 60–61). The fascination for Lacan in this description lies in the association of creation with "the Open," one of the terms the late Heidegger used to distinguish the nature of that being he earlier referred to as Dasein. "The Open" is the substantive form of the aspect of being that distinguishes it as human being and that affords to being "the possibility of a somewhere and of a place filled by present beings" (61). To understand Lacan's appropriation of Heidegger, we must read this "possibility of a somewhere and a place" as the space opened between the world and the human being (Heidegger himself refers to the rift [*Riss*] between "world" and "earth" [63]) by language, precisely insofar as this possible space must correspond to an expectation or wish, to a possible presence that allows for the realization of absence. For Heidegger truth and createdness come together in a work in the form of "a being such as never was before and will never come to be again," a formulation Lacan echoes in his assertion that art has the structure of *creatio ex nihilo*,[33] an act of creation from nothing but also on the borders of nothingness, a nothingness wedged between each act and the overwhelming history that asserts its claims to total determination at every turn. Art is creation; creation, in turn, marks the space or the Open that is the clearing of being; something drives the act of creation: sublimation, a relation to *das Ding*, or to the Open, that is—as the words *wish* and *expectation* connote—fundamentally driven.

Creation is a creation-out-of-nothing for Heidegger as well:

> *Art then is the becoming and happening of truth.* Does truth, then, arise out of nothing? It does indeed if by nothing is meant the mere not of that which is, and if we here think of that which is as an object present in the ordinary way, which thereafter comes to light and is challenged by the existence of the work as only presumptively a true being. Truth is never gathered from objects that are present and ordinary. Rather, the opening up of the Open, and the clearing of what is, happens only as the openness that makes its advent in thrownness is projected, sketched out. ("Origin" 71, modified translation)

Objects present in an ordinary way carry a presumption to truth that is belied by the work of art, against which they appear as "not" being. The dimension of truth is only opened out of—and at the same time creates—that nothingness by the being who, thrown into existence, encounters the world as "a clearing of what is." The rift separating the creation from nothingness is at the same time the border behind which we sense the threatening allure of *das Ding*.

But is it not dangerous to try to draw such close parallels between Lacan and Heidegger? Is not the former, after all, the thinker who, against the grain of today's anti-Cartesian zeitgeist, most obstinately retains a notion of the negative, and even of a kind of Cartesian subject-object relation? Is not the latter, by contrast, that philosopher whose work has, from the outset, provided antirepresentationalism with its primary point of reference? Furthermore, to read the openness of being in Lacanian light as the "space" opened up by language must certainly be to impose a specific notion of language, of the symbolic order, as radically other from the subject on a philosopher whose most basic thinking rejects such ruptures.

Nevertheless, while respecting their differences, a careful reading of fundamental Heideggerian texts suggest a series of parallels that cannot be ignored.[34] For example, when Heidegger describes the nonconscious, circumspect heedfulness of being-in-the-world, he uncovers a phenomenon with startling similarities to Lacan's description of unconscious properties. In his analysis of what he calls the "worldliness of the world" (*Weltlichkeit*), Heidegger is concerned to demonstrate that the natural ontology of the world, which from the Greeks on has been based on the concept of *ousia*, or presence in time as well as in space—as that which remains constant over time—lacks the character of fundamental ontology that it claims. Such a fundamental ontology would have to analyze not the world as objectively present (*vorhanden*), but the world as an existential determinant of being-in-the-world, which he calls worldliness. Rather than objectively lying at hand, objects are first encountered in-the-world as handy (*zuhanden*) objects, objects existing within a system of reference (*Verweisung*) that always situates them in terms of a what-for, a particular occasion of usage. Rather than being supported ultimately on a notion of substantial presence, the being of objects encountered depends on a circuit of referentiality that is in a state of constant churning and continued referral back to a previous context of understanding, or significance:

> For example, the thing at hand which we call a hammer has to do with hammering, and hammering has to do with fastening something, fastening something has to do with protection against bad weather. This protection "is" for the sake of providing shelter for Da-sein, that is, for the sake of a possibility of its being. *Which* relevance things at hand have is prefigured in terms of the total relevance. The total relevance which, for example, constitutes the things at hand in a workshop in their handiness is "earlier" than any single useful thing, as is the farmstead with all its utensils and neighboring lands. The total relevance, however, ultimately leads back to a what-for which *no longer* has relevance, which itself is not a being of the kind of being of things at hand within a world, but is a being whose being is defined as being-in-the-world, to whose constitution of being worldliness itself belongs. (Heidegger, *Being* 78)

The presence of an objectively present thing is replaced by the constant deferral of meaning, a deferral that returns most obviously in Derrida's notion of *différance* (Derrida, "Differance" 13),[35] but which we must also recognize at work in the Lacanian notion of signification, in which the phenomenon of meaning is a function of the signifier's constant reference back to another signifier. This sliding of the signified is responsible not only for the meaning-effect of language, but is also characteristic of the structure of the unconscious, whose subject, the self, is never presence-to-self but is rather always represented *by* a signifier *for* another signifier (Lacan, "Subversion" 316). This situation of self within an ever-churning circuit of referentiality is analogous to the being-in that, for Heidegger, characterizes the being of Dasein.

But is this circuit of referentiality to be confounded with language? Heidegger himself indicates that this is the case by using the term "signifying" (*be-deuten*, a hyphenization of the verb "to mean," "to signify," that emphasizes its radical, *deuten*, "to interpret") for the "relational character of these referential relations" (Heidegger, *Being* 81). In this way, Dasein always belongs to a significant world, a world that means and that is always already interpreted for and by Dasein. Heidegger makes clear the relation of this "significance" (*Bedeutsamkeit*) to language as follows: "But the significance with which Dasein itself is always already familiar contains the ontological condition of the possibility that Dasein, understanding and interpreting, can disclose something akin to 'significations' (*Bedeutungen*) which in turn found the possible being of words and language" (*Being* 82). Or, as the later Heidegger adds, glossing his own text: "Untrue! Language is not imposed, but is the primordial essence of truth as there (*Da*)." To put it another way, the circuit of referentiality that ultimately distinguishes Dasein as a form of being is (depending on whether one follows the early or late Heidegger) either the condition of possibility of language or language *tout court*—language, that is, as the house of Dasein's being (Heidegger, "Letter" 239).

The objection will nevertheless be made that, whatever the concrete similarities in their views of the relationship between language and being, Lacan remains trapped in a metaphysics of subjectivity that Heidegger is clearly out to dismantle, whether successfully or not. For Lacan, subjectivity is the disjunction between enunciation and utterance, an existential fact for speaking beings, whereas for Heidegger it is a conception based on a philosophical mistake owing to the uncritical acceptance of traditional ontology, which overlooks the fundamental ontological condition of Dasein as being-in-the-world—not a subject standing over-against objects, but a being absorbed in heedful circumspection for whom subjective awareness is a secondary, even deficient mode. Given such evidently antithetical positions, how can I suggest that these theories in any way coincide?

The first thing to realize is that Heidegger advanced the idea of a gap, breach, or discontinuity as the basis of subjectivity as early as in *Being and Time*. The mistake of Western philosophy is that it has confused a deficient, accidental mode of being with being itself. Whereas the normal or default state of Dasein is a heedful circumspection absorbed in taking care of things at hand, there are times when the right thing fails to show up, or is broken, or in some way distracts Dasein from the task at hand: "Similarly, when something at hand is missing whose everyday presence was so much a matter of course that we never even paid attention to it, this constitutes a *breach* in the context of references discovered in our circumspection. Circumspection comes up with emptiness and now sees for the first time what the missing thing was at hand *for* and at hand *with*" (Heidegger, *Being* 70). It is thus a breach in the normal flow of relations that underlies the phenomenon of consciousness, and hence of subjectivity conceived of on the basis of the subject-object duality. The critique of metaphysics is based on recognizing that this breach is not constitutive but rather secondary, deficient, and certainly not the worthy ground of a fundamental ontology.

If we look further into the existential analytic of Dasein, however, we find a notion of breach or discontinuity far more original and pervasive than even the one that underlies the phenomenon of subjective consciousness. In asking what attests at the ontic level to the fact of Dasein's authentic potentiality for being, Heidegger calls upon the notion of conscience and the universal affect of guilt. Feeling guilty for something, he argues, cannot be attributed to an actually existing indebtedness on the part of Dasein. Dasein, rather, is able to feel the guilt of owing, of responsibility toward, precisely because Dasein is always-already guilty. This original guilt has the character of a lack, albeit not as in the absence of an objectively present thing, but rather a lack inherent to Dasein. Insofar as Dasein's essential structure is one of care—of being always ahead of itself and already thrown into the world—Dasein is always in some sense characterized by a "not yet" in its orientation toward its own possibilities. The fact that Dasein *is* in terms of possibilities, options, and choices determines its essence as "not yet." And this constitutive, inherent "not" has its origins in the existential fact of Dasein's thrownness (*Geworfenheit*) in the world:

> Being the ground, that is existing as thrown, Da-sein constantly lags behind its possibilities. It is never existent *before* its ground, but only *from it* and *as it*. Thus being the ground means *never* to gain power over one's ownmost being from the ground up. This *not* belongs to the essential meaning of thrownness. Being the ground, it itself is a nullity of itself. Nullity by no means signifies not being objectively present or not subsisting, but means a not that constitutes this *being* of Da-sein, its thrownness. (Heidegger, *Being* 262)

This means that at an even more fundamental level than that of something like consciousness, human being is determined by negativity, a negativity that emerges in human experience as a feeling of *Angst* in the face of one's thrownness, that is, in the at first unconscious realization of the utter contingency of one's existence. Dasein must become its own ground without itself ever being able to be grounded; it must pull itself up by its own bootstraps. While every institution in the world might have an interest in making us believe that our existence is solidly grounded, according to Heidegger Dasein is at heart aware of its thrownness, and its calling to itself out of this awareness—out of this primordial guilt—is what we call conscience.[36]

In his inaugural lecture upon his return to Freiburg in 1929, "What Is Metaphysics?," Heidegger spelled out even more clearly the growing centrality of the concept of the nothing to his thought. Heidegger begins his lecture by noting that a question about metaphysics must simultaneously be a question about the whole and also a question that includes the questioner within the questioning—in other words, "from the position of the existence [*Dasein*] that questions" (Heidegger, "What Is" 82). Such a questioning cannot take the stance of modern scientific knowledge, a stance toward beings for which beings "break open and show what they are and how they are." The question of metaphysics must ask about what science excludes from its inquiries. But what science excludes is, precisely, nothing. Nothing, or the nothing (*Nichts*), must therefore become the focus of a questioning of metaphysics.

The nothing, however, is traditionally thought of as the negation of all beings. But such a definition already assumes the nothing as negated, and since negation is an act of the intellect, the nothing is thus brought under the dominion of precisely that which excludes it as a question. From the perspective of existence, on the other hand, the "not" of negation does not found the nothing, but rather is only possible because the nothing is already there. The nothing, as it were, nihilates or "nothings" ("Das Nichts selbst nichtet") [Heidegger, "Was ist" 114].

The nothing that stands at the center of the Freiburg lecture springs directly from the nullity of guilt in *Being and Time*. Like that notion, the nothing is also experienced initially in *Angst*, in the midst of which one experiences the uncanniness—literally the not-at-homeness (*das Unheimliche*)—of existence. Nevertheless, it is in this lecture that the nothing first achieves its importance as the determining element of existence:

> In the clear night of the nothing of anxiety (*Angst*) the original openness of beings as such arises: that they are beings—and not nothing. But this "and not nothing" we add in our talk is not some kind of appended clarification. Rather, it makes possible in advance the manifestedness of beings in general. The

essence of the originally nihilating nothing lies in this, that it brings Da-sein for the first time before beings as such. (Heidegger, "What Is" 90)

That beings *are* for Dasein at all is what distinguishes Dasein from beings unlike Dasein (rocks and horses are examples that he cites many years later in his "Introduction" to the lecture [Heidegger, "Introduction" 284]),[37] beings that, Heidegger assumes, are without other beings being for them. Insofar as beings are for Dasein, this is only possible because of Dasein's ontological separation from beings, through and because of which they are unconcealed. Heidegger characterizes this ontological separation as being held out into the nothing (Heidegger, "What Is" 91), and it is precisely this being held out, this projectedness into the open, that accounts for the fact that beings are for Dasein in a meaningful way; in fact, this projectedness constitutes meaning as such (Heidegger, "Introduction" 286), which, as I noted above, points to an equiprimordiality of Dasein and being in language, if not to their indistinguishability.

It should be clear at this point that the nullity (*Nichtigkeit*), as well as the nothing (*Nichts*) underlying our thrownness in the world has an immediate relationship to the Lacanian notion of *das Ding* and ultimately, therefore, to the notion of the ethical. The nullity of thrownness, which Heidegger identifies as existential guilt, is "the existential condition of the possibility of the 'morally' good and evil, that is, for morality in general and its possible factical forms" (*Being* 264). But whereas for Heidegger the nothing constitutes the metaethical ground of ethical thinking, the ethical in Lacan's thought has yet another attribute, that of being the ground of drivenness in general, and hence ultimately of desire. Both theories present a notion of the human being as held apart from total absorption in the world—whether this be thought as the separation brought about by the symbolic order or as Dasein being held out into the nothing. For Lacan, however, this insight forms the basis for a further exploration into the internal workings of desire.

KANT AVEC SADE

The relation of sublimation to ethics is nicely illustrated by a thought experiment Lacan quotes from Kant's second critique, one intended to illustrate the universality of practical reason. In Kant's scenario, a man is given the choice of entering a room and sleeping with the woman he lusts after, or of not doing so, all the while knowing that he will be executed if he chooses to do so. For Kant it is clear that no reasonable man—being aware of the consequence of his actions, and no matter how much he desires the woman in question—would entertain even for a moment such an absurd choice (Kant, *Practical* 45). In a second scenario, the same man is given the choice between betraying an honest man, with the same consequence should he refuse. In such a circumstance, according to Kant, even the most cowardly of men would at least consider the possibility of giving up his own life in order not to betray an innocent man. Kant offers this as proof that people implicitly and universally know the moral law, but Lacan reads it in another way, suggesting that while our "philosopher from Königsberg was a nice person," he was perhaps somewhat naïve about human nature: "All of which leads to the conclusion that it is not impossible for a man to sleep with a woman knowing full well that he is to be bumped off on his way out, by the gallows or anything else . . . ; it is not impossible this man coolly accepts such an eventuality on his leaving—for the pleasure of cutting up the lady concerned in small pieces, for example" (Lacan, *VII* 109). Lacan labels these two forms of transgression—sleeping with one's beloved despite the knowledge of resulting death, and sexual psychopathology—sublimation and perversion respectively, and contends that their structures are analogous.

The key to Lacan's interpretation of Kant, here and in his "Kant avec Sade," is the realization that Lacan, by moving from the register of the moral law to that of sublimation and perversion, is not merely changing the subject, but rather suggesting—scandalously—that the registers are one and the same. To see this, let us first look at how Lacan revises Kant's thought experiment at a later point in the text. This time, rather than the issue being a question of bearing false witness against an innocent man, it is one of bearing true witness against a neighbor or brother: "And what if I changed the example a little? Let us talk about true witness, about a case of conscience which is raised if I am summoned to inform on my neighbor or brother for activities which are prejudicial to the security of the state. That question is of a kind that shifts the emphasis placed on the universal rule" (190). As Alenka Zupancic has pointed out, the problem with Kant's original scenario is that we are likely to agree with his reading not because we feel the tug of a universal moral law, but because we feel the pain of the wrongly accused (54). By refusing to bear false witness in such a case, we are acting not ethically but pathologically insofar as we are guided by our sympathy for the other. Sympathy—as the root *pathos* would suggest—is

a pathological motive par excellence. It is for this reason that Lacan proposes his revision, one in which the agent would have to perform his action
against his natural sympathies.

There can be no doubt that the notion of a moral agent performing acts
against his natural sympathies evokes the specter of an even greater evil
than that of a failure to bear true witness. I am thinking of Hannah
Arendt's analysis of Eichmann's invocation of Kant in her report on his trial
in Jerusalem. As she writes at the close of the eighth chapter, aptly titled
"Duties of a Law-Abiding Citizen":

> Evil in the Third Reich had lost the quality by which most people recognized
> it—the quality of temptation. Many Germans and many Nazi's, probably an
> overwhelming majority of them, must have been tempted *not* to murder, *not* to
> rob, *not* to let their neighbors go off to their doom . . . and not to become ac-
> complices in all these crimes by benefiting from them. But, God knows, they
> had learned how to resist temptation. (150)

Nevertheless, while conforming to a degree with Kant's notion of the ethical, the insistence that an ethical act involves contradicting one's natural
sympathies—or, in Arendt's terms, learning to resist temptation—falls
short in an essential aspect. As Arendt herself points out—even while being astonished that Eichmann produced an "approximately correct definition of the categorical imperative" (Arendt 136)—Eichmann's application
of Kantian ethics was an egregiously impoverished, in that it allowed him
to substitute the will of the Führer for practical reason as the source of the
moral law (136).[38]

The fact that the stringency of Kant's ethical demands can be defended—rightfully, I believe—against the claim that they invite the sort of
evil that Eichmann's maniacal attention to duty represents—as Arendt re-
ports, he would have killed his own father had the law required it (Arendt
42)—does not, however, inure them to other, perhaps more fundamental,
associations with evil. Let us continue to quote Lacan where we last left off:

> And I who stand here right now and bear witness to the idea that there is no
> law of the good except in evil and through evil, should I bear such witness?
> This law makes my neighbor's *jouissance* the point on which, in bearing wit-
> ness in this case, the meaning of my duty is balanced. Must I go toward my
> duty of truth insofar as it preserves the authentic place of my *jouissance*, even if
> it is empty? Or must I resign myself to this lie, which, by making me substitute
> forcefully the good for the principle of my *jouissance*, commands me to blow al-
> ternately hot and cold? Either I refrain from betraying my neighbor so as to

spare my fellow man or I shelter behind my fellow man as to give up my *jouis-sance*. (Lacan, *VII* 190)

The idea that there is no law of the good except in evil is the truth to which Lacan—so he implies—feels an ethical obligation to bear witness, despite the callous disregard for his fellow man such bearing witness might seem to entail. And this is precisely the nature of the critique he levels against Kant: by hiding behind examples doctored to clothe the ethical in a sem-blance of good, Kant avoids the radical ramifications of his own thought. The ethical denotes a realm utterly separate from questions of good and evil, notions irredeemably marked by the economy of pleasure and pathol-ogy. In opposition to this economy, Lacan situates the ethical within the dimension ruled by the drive and its *jouissance*. What drives me to do my duty despite all pathological or sympathetic inclinations is my *jouissance*, which beckons to me from that place in my neighbor and myself that marks the limits of my knowledge, and the origins of our freedom. The ethical choice is not a choice that conforms with a preexisting notion of the good, which commands me to blow alternately hot and cold because it is always determined differently by different contexts. Rather, the ethical is that way we feel obliged to act over and against any notions of good versus evil, right versus wrong, that might cross our paths. But in making this claim, in forcing Kant to his logical extremes, Lacan effectively voids any difference between good and evil at the level of the ethical, which is pre-cisely what opens the door to his infamous claim that Sade is the truth of Kant.[39]

By the commutative property of logic, if Sade is the truth of Kant, then Kant is also the truth of Sade. The thesis that Lacan proffers in his essay, which was intended as a preface to *Philosophy in the Bedroom*, may be suc-cinctly (or shall we say, comprehensibly) put as follows: Kant thought there was such a thing as the law free from desire; Sade thought there was such a thing as desire free from the law; they both were wrong. To briefly reiter-ate Kant's argument: an ethical act is one not motivated by individual in-clinations, but by the universal moral law. While we cannot know the moral law—indeed to have access to the noumenal moral law would de-prive us of our freedom and hence the very possibility of morality (Kant, *Practical* 176)—the best indication that we are acting out of, as opposed to in conformity with, our duty is that our actions contradict our pathologi-cal inclinations. If what we choose to do not only is *not* what we desire or what gives us pleasure, but furthermore is exactly what we do not desire or what causes us displeasure, then the likelihood is that we have acted out of duty.

For Lacan, however, the ethical as it is here described, far from being devoid of pathological interest, is the ultimate manifestation of desire, drivenness at its purest. The fact that the moral law is noumenal, and hence offers no corresponding phenomenal object, means to Lacan only that it must exist as an object that is desired:

> One rediscovers what founds Kant's expression of the regret that, in the experience of the moral law, no intuition offers a phenomenal object.
>
> We would agree that, throughout the Critique, this object slips away, but it can be divined by the trace which is left by the implacable pursuit which Kant brings to demonstrating its elusiveness and out of which the work draws this eroticism, doubtless innocent, but perceptible, whose well-foundedness we will show in the nature of the said object. (Lacan, "Kant with Sade" 57)

Lacan wants to show that the injunction to act ethically, that is to act universally and hence nonpathologically, hides another, more profound injunction—the injunction to *jouissance.* To this end he reads the *Critique of Practical Reason* side-by-side with a text written by the Marquis de Sade only eight years after the publication of the former, one Lacan claims should be read in parts as a parody of Kant's work.

Sade's *Philosophy in the Bedroom* comes across as a parody of the second *Critique* because at its center—framed by an orgy in which a young virgin is being instructed in the ways of libertinage—Sade positions a long political pamphlet, in which the chief libertine, Dolmancé, argues for the superiority of a regime founded on what we could term the principle of universal pathology, according to which no law would prevent anyone from carrying out even the slightest of his or her desires. The "nerve of the diatribe," as Lacan calls it, would be the maxim sustaining such an (im)moral system, one that Lacan expresses in an obviously Kantian format: "I have the right of enjoyment over your body, anyone can say to me, and I will exercise this right, without any limit stopping me in the capriciousness of the exactions that I might have the taste to satiate" (Lacan, "Kant with Sade" 58). On the face of it, this parodic variant of the categorical imperative (act only in such a way that the maxim of your actions can be universalized) is patently absurd, the Kantian response being that its enactment as law results in the self-destruction of the law. For Lacan, however, such a response begs the question of an ethical maxim altogether: for if one already has a criterion for determining which maxims qualify as universal and which do not, then one is supporting one's ethics on a legality, and not vice versa. Moreover, Kant's criterion would prove to be little more than a tautology, which Lacan compares to the joke: "Long live Poland, for if there were no Poland, there would be no Poles" (57).

The accusation of tautology, however, is not simply a philosophical argument intended to dismantle Kant's theory. As Zupancic points out, Kant criticism has long been aware of the inadequacies of Kant's criterion of noncontradiction, and many critics have demonstrated the remarkable ease with which almost any maxim may be made to pass the universalizability test (Zupancic 93). Lacan's point, rather, is that the very notion of the ethical carries within itself a moment of pure tautology, such that, in the example of the depositary—whether it would be ethical for a depositary to keep a deposit from an owner who has passed away—Kant's decision that the depositary's maxim is not universalizable depends on his presupposition that there is "no deposit without a depositary equal to his charge" (Lacan, "Kant with Sade" 57). In other words, much like the dependence of Poles on Poland, the very notion of a deposit depends on depositaries fulfilling their role. The problem with this position is that the ethical choice is reduced to a question of the identity between a subject and the role he is playing, which is exactly Lacan's charge against Kant: the moral law emerges from the division of the subject by the signifier into the subject of the statement and the subject of the enunciation (59)—into the character who speaks his lines and the actor from whose body the words emerge. The fundamental model of desire or fantasy is the erasure of that difference, an erasure exactly repeated by Kant's criterion of noncontradiction in which the universalizability of a maxim presupposes the identity of subject and role. To put it glibly, Kant wants to have his difference and eat it too.[40]

The division of the subject into a moment of statement and a moment of enunciation is attested to by the very notion of duty to which Kant pays homage. If there remains something I ought to do but have not done, I am, in essence, calling to myself and cannot, in that moment, be identical to myself. I am other to myself, and the space of this otherness is marked by the moral law. A hypothetically self-identical subject would experience no call of conscience, for what he or she ought to do and what he or she does would always and simultaneously be one and the same. This is precisely why Kant insists that one can never know the moral law, which is noumenal, for in knowing it, in occupying a place of divine knowledge, one would cease to be human, cease to be capable of being moral—of being a being, to paraphrase Heidegger, for whom being moral is a question.

But if Kant himself insists upon this, then what exactly is he wrong about? Only that one could separate desire and the law in order to designate an ethical ideal in the first place. Nevertheless, if he is wrong in this assumption then so is Sade in his analogous, albeit opposite, dream of a world in which desire reigns unrestrained by the law (even though the law appear in the form of a new divinity, a supreme being of evil, or the personification of nature). What, then, of the desperation of the libertine, who in the end, parodic though the scene may be, can only exhort his followers to fornicate even when there can be no more pleasure in it, to fornicate for the sake of fornication alone?[41] Can he really be said to have abolished the law, whether within or without? No, Lacan will say: "our verdict upon the submission of Sade to the law is confirmed. Of a treatise truly about desire, there is thus little here, even nothing" (Lacan, "Kant with Sade" 75).[42]

THE ETHICS OF PSYCHOANALYSIS

It would appear that Lacan's persistent and all-important point has to do with the mutual imbrication of the law with the pathological, the interested, or desire *tout court*. The notion of mutual imbrication, however, plays a larger role in Lacan's thought and needs some elaboration. For two elements to be mutually imbricated means more than a mere mutual dependence, in which the presence of the one necessitates the presence of the other. What is at work in Lacan's notion is rather the situation or dynamic in which the presence of one element is simultaneously required and negated by the presence of the other, much like the optical illusions produced by a figure against a ground,[43] a paradox represented most obsessively by Escher in those prints depicting fields of birds (such as "Day and Night") or other creatures emerging out of the negative space created by an opposing field of similar beings. It is precisely such a relation that Lacan signifies with the figure $\diamond$,[44] the operative matheme in his formula for fantasy: "Fantasy is defined by the most general form which it receives from an algebra which we have constructed to this end, that is the formula ($\$\diamond a$), in which the stamp is read 'desire of,' to be read identically in the retrograde direction, introducing an identity which is founded on an absolute nonreciprocity" (Lacan, "Kant with Sade" 62).[45] Just as the identity of a black or white bird in Escher's print is founded on its absolute nonreciprocity with a field of birds of the opposite color, so is the subject's identity a function of the negative outline of an object, an absence whose outline is maintained by the series of imaginary relations the subject will construct in its wake, which will make up the metonymy of his or her particular desire. The subject is nothing without the absence of his or her object; the object only exists as an absence, limit, or point where the subject fades away.

The final argument of the seminar of 1959–60—the moment when Lacan seems to shift his discourse away from describing the psychical dimension of the ethical and toward a proposal for a kind of ethical stance—has to do with the possibility of at least two radically different attitudes the human being can take to this structure of fantasy, to the mutual imbrication of the law and desire. The first is the attitude that most of us adopt: namely, to persist in our quest after the object throughout our lives, all the while compromising its absolute nature through an intricate and highly particular system of exchanging one object or good for another. To paraphrase Cosmo from the movie *Moonstruck*, this choice is fine until something goes wrong—and something always goes wrong. It is the fact that something always goes wrong with desire that led Freud to claim that the purpose of psychoanalysis was to transform "hysterical misery into common unhappiness" (Breuer and Freud 305). In the practice sanctioned by the International Psychoanalytic Association, the technique of the cure would rely on a process of identification between the analysand and the analyst; but this version of psychoanalytic ethics as an ethics of identification is exactly what Lacan reacts against, claiming instead that the job of the analyst is to situate him- or herself in such a way as to maintain the greatest possible distance between the object of desire and its fulfillment in any sort of ideal for identification (Dunand 244, 246). The end of psychoanalysis, in Lacan's apparently mystical version, would be to provoke in the subject a different attitude toward the paradox of fantasy.

This second attitude has been described in various ways and has undergone various revisions from the early 1960s to the end of Lacan's teaching. These descriptions include: "realizing" one's desire; that the only thing of which one can be held guilty is "having given ground relative to one's desire"; "facing up to" one's desire; being in a "pure and simple" relation to one's desire; "recognizing the lack in the Other"; "crossing the plane" of fantasy or "piercing though" fantasy into the realm of drive.[46] What these descriptions have in common—and, indeed, the commonality of these descriptions has remained constant despite the variations—is the notion that the second attitude toward desire involves a kind of recognition or opening up to the paradox of mutual imbrication. In a sense, the normal functioning of desire manifested by the first attitude relies on a kind of disavowal of the mutual imbrication paradox, which is why Lacan says of desire (and of male desire in particular) that there is always something fetishistic (perverted) about it, because the desiring being replaces an absence or an impossibility with something potentially obtainable (Lacan, "Subversion" 320). What the subject who takes on the second attitude to desire must do is cease to disavow the paradox, see it, and experience the fact that the wild-goose chase of desire is not supported by any presence in the other—that the other is, in essence, lacking.

The realization that the other is lacking constitutes a metamorphosis on the part of the subject's desire. Desire becomes, in Lacan's later articulations, drive—the experience of which is, Lacan claims, only approachable at the level of one who has completed analysis (Lacan, *XI* 276). But what exactly is the drive, and what would the experience of it entail such that this experience becomes, for Lacan, the essence of the ethical dimension? To begin with, we must recall that Lacan first articulates the distinction between drive and desire in an article he writes in 1960 and inserts in his 1966 volume *Écrits*: "The Subversion of the Subject and the Dialectic of Desire." Nevertheless, although he does not denominate the distinction in so many terms, it is also operating in the seminar on ethics. This is what accounts for the curious fact that in the seminar on ethics Lacan refers to desire as if it were a positive thing, something to be protected, the compromising of which is the source of our guilt; whereas at the end of the above mentioned article desire appears as precisely the opposite, "a defense (*défense*), a prohibition (*défense*) against going beyond a certain limit in *jouissance*" (*Écrits* trans. 322). The reason for this apparent contradiction is that, for most of the seminar on ethics, Lacan is still envisioning both attitudes as aspects of desire, whereas beginning in the 1960s he will distinguish the two aspects as separate concepts: desire depends on a kind of unconscious perversion, in that its essence lies in the subject's assurance to himself of the existence of the Other; drive is what lies on the other side of this subjective lie, not as the substantial, pure expression of bodily enjoyment, but as the effect of signification, of the absence of the Other—of *das Ding*—on the human body. Lacan writes this experience as ($\$\lozenge$D), no longer emphasizing the relation of nonreciprocity with an object/lack, but rather a relation of nonreciprocity with the demands of language and the vortex of lack they inscribe in the unconscious.

In the same essay, Lacan describes the function of the drive by way of a distinction between two words normally translated in English as "knowledge": *connaissance* and *savoir*.[47] On the one hand, *connaissance*, which we might also translate as acquaintance, signifies the kind of direct, experiential knowledge of the world that traditional ethics supposed could provide a basis for the quest for happiness. Knowledge, in this view, would be built up on the basis of or applied to a direct acquaintance with the world; just as, in an analogous way, in Aristotle's ethical syllogisms the truth of the major premise serves to dominate or gentrify the natural inclinations of the human organism. Drive, on the other hand, far from expressing a natural or direct acquaintance with the human organism (such as a theory of instinct or genetic disposition might), operates rather at the level of discourse or the major premise that already determines the nature it seeks to effect. The drive, then, is a *savoir* that Lacan likens to a "messenger-slave" who bears, unbeknownst to him, his own death sentence tattooed on his scalp (Lacan, "Subversion" 302). It is a writing on the flesh of being that determines the most basic impulses of our existence; this incision into being that defines a being as such is nothing other than the ethical fault-line. Where desire's "perverse" attitude toward the fault-line replaces its constitutive negativity with the promised fulfillment of a lost object, analysis should provoke an attitude that does not shy away from the fault-line and its primordial undermining of being's integrity.

At the end of *Seminar VII*, Lacan describes this second attitude as a purification of desire,[48] and his literary representative for this pure desire is Antigone. Antigone's insistence on breaking the laws of the *polis* and covering Polynices' body represent for Lacan a kind of pure desire, a desire free of motivation, unreasonable or *unmotiviert*, as Poe would say.[49] Her justification invokes something that Lacan says is "of the order of the law, but which is not developed in any signifying chain or in anything else" (Lacan, *VII* 278). Jonathan Scott Lee interprets Lacan's reasoning here as the articulation of a kind of final ethical rule, one based on the irreducibility of the individual, "the uniqueness of each individual human being" (Lee 127). But while it is tempting to cull from this seminar an ethics that is commensurable with modern liberal values, I believe that is emphatically not what Lacan is up to. Lee bases his reading on this passage:

> Antigone's position represents the radical limit that affirms the unique value of his [Polynices] being without reference to any content, to whatever good or evil Polynices may have done, or to whatever he may be subjected to.
>
> The unique value involved is essentially that of language. Outside of language it is inconceivable, and the being of him who has lived cannot be detached from all he bears with him in the nature of good and evil, of destiny, of consequences for others, or of feelings for himself. That purity, that separation

of being from the characteristics of the historical drama he has lived through, is precisely the limit or the *ex nihilo* to which Antigone is attached. It is nothing more than the break that the very presence of language inaugurates in the life of man. (Lacan, *VII* 279)

The "unique value of his being" that is in question, however, cannot in the end refer to anything particularly unique to Polynices as an individual—to the fact that he is unique among individuals regardless of his particular characteristics or history—because in the next breath Lacan identifies this unique value with language, with the break inaugurated by language's presence in our lives. Rather, it is the fact that in her recounting of her actions Antigone calls forth no existing legality; she fails to take recourse even to the last and greatest of authorities to justify her desire (Lacan's translation: "For Zeus is by no means the one who proclaimed those things to me" [278]). So Lacan's reading does not stress the unique value of Antigone's brother as her brother, which would seem to be the case from such a quote as this: "this brother is something unique. And it is this alone which motivates me to oppose your edicts."[50] On the contrary, as his next words spell out, Lacan insists that her evocation of his nonreplaceability, his irreducible identity, masks a reasoning that is nothing other than tautological:

> Antigone invokes no other right than that one, a right that emerges in the language of the ineffaceable character of what is—ineffaceable, that is, from the moment when the emergent signifier freezes it like a fixed object in spite of the flood of possible transformations. What is, is, and it is so to this, to this surface, that the unshakeable, unyielding position of Antigone is fixed. (Lacan, *VII* 279)[51]

This then, is the Lacanian ethical: that the fount of desire (drive) is constitutionally beyond the law and therefore beyond communicability. This fount, so poetically evoked as the ineffaceable character of what is, frozen by the emergent signifier "like a fixed object in spite of the flood of possible transformations," is a surface, a limit without depth, a line with only one side because no unity precedes its division. This break inaugurated by the presence of language is the fault-line. It is also, I would suggest, the point of absolute affect: the place where we are affected, motivated to desire, to feel, to act; prior to, in blatant disregard of, or in transgression of whatever reasons we may or may not be able to produce.

Such absolute affect is the essential ingredient of the ethical, because without it there would be no motivation of any kind (*Triebfeder*, for

Kant[52]); but it is also, and more characteristically, an essential ingredient of aesthetic theory, since it is the aspect of representation that engages us at a somatic level.[53] To bring the two together again in schematic form, we could envisage an aesthetic experience, which might be the experience of seeing *Antigone*, in which the following would occur: identification with a character or characters results in the suspension of the theatrical frame and the momentary acceptance of the moral framework within that diegetic space; the ethical act that, in effect, demolishes that moral framework performs a kind of transmission of affect that Aristotle theorizes as catharsis. Given this scenario, it is no coincidence that the theatrical model is so central to the psychoanalytic setting, because in Lacan's description such affective transmission through a rupturing of frames is precisely what occurs in the transference situation at the moment of an effective interpretation.

> In extracting it from my experience, I told you just now that at the most sensitive and, it seems to me, significant point of the phenomenon (the transference), the subject experiences it as an abrupt perception of something which isn't very easy to define—presence.
>
> It isn't a feeling we have all the time. To be sure, we are influenced by all sorts of presences, and our world only possesses its consistency, its density, its lived stability, because, in some way, we take account of these presences, but we do not realize them as such. You really can sense that it is a feeling which I'd say we are always trying to efface from life. It wouldn't be easy to live if, at every moment, we had the feeling of presence, with all the mystery that that implies. It is a mystery from which we distance ourselves, and to which we are, in a word, inured. (Lacan, *I* 42)[54]

If, in other words, we follow this line of argumentation and strongly associate the ethical experience of absolute affect with aesthetic experience as a rupturing of a momentarily assumed representative framework, then the conclusion seems inevitable that the transference is designed precisely as an aesthetic experience, one aimed, moreover, at transmitting the effect of an encounter with the point of absolute affect that is one's desire.[55]

Let us say, then, that however often they happen, isolated experiences of presence are manifestations of absolute affect, absolute in that they cannot be made sense of, interpreted or rationalized—when one is, it is no longer absolute affect, but something relative, articulable, rational, perhaps emotional. This, it seems to me, is where to locate the work of Martha Nussbaum, who wants to locate emotional experience within the realm of reason.[56] Anger, joy, and other emotions, so the argument goes, have the structure of a judgment. I am angry because a situation is unjust; if it is revealed at a later date not to have been unjust, my judgment changes and I am no longer angry. This would be all well and good, if this were indeed the usual scenario. The usual scenario, however, is: I am angry because a situation is unjust; someone argues convincingly that the situation is not unjust; my anger grows, because my desire was somehow engaged with the perceived injustice of the situation in relative disregard of the rectitude of my judgment. Can such egoistic behavior be trained? Most certainly—but probably never entirely tamed, since the irrationality and nonjustifiability of affect is constitutive of its experience.

Nevertheless, none of this is to say that affect—which I defined earlier as the motivation to desire, to feel, to act, prior to, in blatant disregard of, or in transgression of whatever reasons we may or may not be able to produce—is somehow out of reach of reason, or outside of what Lacanians call the symbolic order. Lacanian doxa teaches that the real is that which exceeds the symbolic order, a fine definition which has had the unfortunate consequence of entitling people to speak of the real as if it were an independent realm beyond the conceptual framework of the symbolic order, a reinscription of Kantian schematism in psychoanalytic garb. Lacan, as we have seen, is a devoted reader of Kant, but the point of these readings, over and over again, is to analyze, as Derrida once put it, the philosopher's desire, not to participate in defining the limits of human knowledge.[57] We are symbolic through and through, and it is this that makes us, in Sophocles' words, *to deinotaton*, the most wondrous of all beings; this that makes us *pantaporos aporos*, having many ways open to us, and yet having no exit, no way out.[58] For an exit would be a beyond to that ineffaceable surface that marks the absolute of our desire, and although we come up with all sorts of phantasmatic renditions of what might be there, the real is the persistent absence of that fulfillment, the depthlessness of that surface and the relentless proliferation of ways, of *défilés*, that the signifier creates despite and on the surface of that impasse.

Absolute affect affects us to act, to act without reason, and yet neither the affect nor the act is pure of the stuff whose systematization forms the basis of reason. Antigone, in Lacan's reading, is bearing witness not to the unique value of the other, but rather to the Other's emptiness, to the fact that her own desire has no grounding, no justification, no reality supporting it; it cannot be exchanged for something easier or cheaper and it cannot be bartered away; it is the "pure and simple" fact that to be human is to be the victim of the cut of language, the groundlessness of demand.[59] Which is to say, ultimately, that what Antigone attests to is not merely the irreducible nature of her desire, but also and more crucially to the fact that she is always other to herself, that her desire is precisely the ineradicable trace of her ultimate lack of identity to herself. To paraphrase Heidegger, the call of conscious is Dasein calling to itself from where it *is not* (*Being* 56).

The objection could be made that his call, which Heidegger himself terms at once "unequivocal" and "unmistakeable," would seem to be the work of a perfect and perfectly private language, whose purpose is to call a fallen self back to its true, proper, own-most self (*Being* 253).[60] Is this not precisely where Derrida's admonitions concerning the problematical use of "authenticity" or "ownness" (*Eigentlichkeit*) should cause us to beware? Why, Derrida asks, "determine as *fall* the passage from one temporality to another? And why qualify temporality as authentic—or *proper* (*eigent-lich*)—and as inauthentic—or improper—when every ethical preoccupa-tion has been suspended?" (Derrida, "Ousia" 63).[61] Indeed, despite Hei-degger's refusal to consider *Being and Time* as offering what could be categorized as ethical prescriptions, and indeed despite his apparent demo-tion of ethics altogether (Heidegger, "Letter" 271), the language of authen-ticity[62] is notoriously difficult to rid of what would appear to be absurdly arbitrary ethical elements. Why indeed, as Derrida asks, should we agree to distinguish between an inauthentic temporality characterized as fallen or entangled (*verfallen*) in the world of the "They" and an authentic tempo-rality attested to by the unmistakable call of conscience and characterized by resolute being-toward-death? Is not every call already a call transmitted and hence mediated by language, and therefore irreducibly open to the possibility of not reaching its destination, of going astray?[63]

Nevertheless, the call, as Heidegger is at pains to clarify, is really not a call *in* language, which is to say it is not uttered, it always remains silent, and yet it is very much the call *of* language, namely, of the self's thrown-ness in discourse, which calls the self back from its illusory grounding in the certainty of the They (Heidegger, *Being and Time* 252). The call, then, is the impossibility of not knowing, at some level (the level of *savoir* as op-posed to *connaissance*) that, to put it in psychoanalytic terms, the Other is lacking, that there is no ultimate rationale or justification for my desire.[64] To drive the point a little further, the deconstructive critique of this "knowledge about itself" (264) is itself disingenuous, because it depends on precisely such a distinction, although never so named, between some-thing like authentic and something like inauthentic knowing.[65] What, if this were not the case, would account for the undeniable difference between the conclusions of a deconstructive reading of a philosophical text and the conclusions the text itself purports to arrive at—that is, the conclusions of what Simon Critchley refers to as the "dominant interpretation" (24) or what Derrida himself calls a "minimal consensus" on the meaning of a text (Derrida, *Limited* 146, qtd. in Critchley 24)?

As Derrida says of Lévinas in "Violence and Metaphysics":

> [a]t the heart of the desert, in the growing wasteland, this thought, which no longer fundamentally seeks to be a thought of Being and phenomenality, makes us dream of an inconceivable process of dismantling and dispossession. . . . A thought for which the entirety of the Greek logos has already erupted, and is now a quiet topsoil deposited not over bedrock, but around a more ancient volcano. A thought which, without philology and solely by remaining faithful to the immediate, but buried nudity of experience itself, seeks to liberate itself from the Greek domination of the same and the One (other names for the light of Being and of the phenomenon) as if from oppression itself—an oppression certainly comparable to none other in the world." ("Violence" 83)

In thus paraphrasing Lévinas's desire, Derrida initially appears to condone the conceivability of "an inconceivable process of dismantling and dispossession" that would underlie the "domination of the same and the One," of the Greek logos, like a more ancient volcano underlying the quiet topsoil left by more recent eruptions. Of course, Derrida invokes this distinction at the outset of the essay in order to demonstrate that Lévinas's own thought cannot really think this—that the distinction hereto alluded and hence conceived is in fact inconceivable, because "[b]y making the origin of language, meaning, and difference the relation to the infinitely other, Levinas is resigned to betraying his own intentions in his philosophical discourse," in that "nothing can so profoundly *solicit* the Greek logos—philosophy—than this irruption of the totally other; and nothing can to such an extent reawaken the logos to its origin as to its mortality, its other" ("Violence" 152). Derrida, however, can only demonstrate the impossibility of Lévinas's original distinction—that there is an experience of pure otherness underlying the dominance of the logos—at the cost of establishing another distinction, a performative distinction at the level of the reading itself, between Lévinas's intention and the betrayal of that intention as revealed by the deconstructive reading. No one is more aware of such performative distinction than Derrida himself,[66] which is why I claim in Chapter 3 that the discourses of deconstruction and psychoanalysis inevitably converge upon a zone of indistinction. Nevertheless, this performative distinction is exactly what is at stake in Heidegger's notion of authenticity: authentic being is nothing other than an "existentiell" modification (awareness) (Heidegger, *Being and Time* 247) of the condition of thrownness such that thrownness is revealed as existential, as truth. Or, to put it another way, *to be authentic is nothing other than to be duplicitous*— to engage in the performative distinction that undermines the founding distinctions of inauthentic, or metaphysical philosophy: we are all constitutively inauthentic, and authenticity is nothing other than the name of this awareness.[67] It is in the light of this reading of authenticity that we must understand what is doubtlessly an invocation of authenticity in Lacan's reading of *Antigone*, the difference being that Lacan casts the distinction in terms of one's relation to one's desire.

The place where desire is purified, the place where Antigone stands, beyond symbolic death (for that is what the realization of the mutual imbrication of law and desire entails: experiencing the utter helplessness and distress of facing up to one's own death as essential limitation [Lacan, *VII* 304]) is not a place commonly recognizable as ethical. It is a place, rather, that threatens our place—the place of culture, of interaction, of laws and decency—with the transgression of its dearest values, with the subversion of its norms, with its eventual destruction. Occupying this place, Lacan says, "Antigone chooses to be purely and simply the guardian of the being of the criminal as such" (283). From the perspective of fantasy, a figure who realizes her desire, assumed it, passed over to drive, is the personification of evil, of irrationality, of criminality, of death. The ethics of psychoanalysis, then, cannot be interpreted as an ethics in the classical sense. There is nothing there to tell us what to do because it is good or right. Rather, to be true to one's desire is to become aware of that desire's groundlessness and its imbrication with laws whose contingency undermine any notion of ultimate good or right. At the same time, the force of the law, the power of the good and the right cannot be evacuated for the purpose of some liberation of desire. The ethics of psychoanalysis, then, is not an ethics; rather, it is a story about what the ethical is, about the role the ethical plays in the constitution of subjectivity and its relation to desire. What is the ethical? It is the fault-line; the border of our being drawn within our being; the limit separating the inside from outside that is at the same time completely inside; the face of an other who invades our being and yet who remains unknown; the force of a law that defends/prohibits us from what we cannot possibly have; the fault that separates us from perfection, and that creates such an illusion as perfection in the first place.

What remains to be explored, then, is the utter irreducibility of this ethical fault-line, its insistence and resurgence in any discourse that tries to iron it out or explain it away. In the next chapter we will turn our attention in greater detail to the discourse of deconstruction, which has discovered something like this irreducibility in its persistent fascination with theology. In the final chapter we will examine the role sexual difference plays in enabling the different attitudes toward the fault-line, and the extent to which gender theory and feminism have contributed to overcoming the impasse posed by the perversity of ethics.

3

Deconstruction and the Theology of Desire

THE TOPOLOGY appropriate to ethics is the figure of a cut, a fault-line, a fault that institutes at once a sense of lack, of owing, and of obligation (*il faut*)—an impulse to act. One is affected to act, and the sense of that affect is a separation from self more primordial than the self thus separated. The operative elements of the fault-line are institutionalizations, thus guaranteeing the specificity—the pathology—of each historical trajectory an ethical orientation assumes. These institutionalizations, which conjure the contours of an absent center or reality toward which all desire flows, are not, however, mere barriers to fulfillment, but are also and at the same time the very conduits of communicability (i.e., mediation) that make community possible. It is not, in other words, that we are separated—and hence kept viable—from others by the contract of the law; rather, laws, and the very orientation of our desires along the possible routes of their violation, form the open wounds and affective vulnerabilities in which communities are grounded. The illusion, in other words, is this: were an appropriately phrased ethics finally able to formulate a universally shared notion of the good, a community could thereby emerge unsullied by antagonism, strife, or dissent. What the notion of the fault-line as the ineluctable core of ethics suggests, however, is that the very impossibility of this scenario is the only hope for community.

The notion of ethics that has emerged from the previous reading of psychoanalytic texts is at least twofold: first, the idea of institutionalization confronts traditional ethical models with the conundrum of an inherent *perversity of ethics* at the heart of all injunctions; second, the ethics of psychoanalysis, as pursued by Lacan, turns out not to be an ethics but a de-

scription of the irreducibility of this perversity in human endeavors, as well
as a redefinition of the realm of the ethical as involving none other than
this very irreducibility. Nevertheless, the claim for the irreducibility of perversity—namely, that there is no way out of the mutual imbrication of law
and desire—is far from a mere denial of transcendence. For as we have
seen in the case of the extraordinary attention Lacan pays to Kant in this
regard, the experience of a beyond—worked out as the realm of *das Ding*
in Lacan's seminar—is part and parcel of the conundrum of ethics, and to
merely deny it is to ignore its profound and unsettling force in the affairs
of desire.

In this chapter, the theoretical resonances outlined in the preceding
chapter between the Heideggerian notion of authenticity and Lacan's
motto of not giving way as to one's desire will be brought into dialogue
with a series of insights—stemming primarily from the thought of Jean-
Luc Nancy and Søren Kierkegaard, but drawing as well from that of
Jacques Derrida and Emmanuel Lévinas—I will broadly refer to here as
deconstructive, insofar as they are united by a questioning of what Nancy
describes as the "immanentism" of ethical models, in which a core identity
is assumed to exist prior to an individual's entry into relations with others.
What further—and perhaps more scandalously—unites these thinkers,
however, is the way in which their rigorous philosophical argumentation
inevitably opens onto a theological dimension. Thinking through the co-
nundrums posed by the ethical fault-line, in other words, would appear to
drive philosophy incessantly toward a confrontation with that very discourse whose death was required in order for it to take its place on the
stage of the modern world.

THE LIMITS OF LANGUAGE

In 1929 Wittgenstein gave a lecture to a Cambridge audience that can
be read today as the crucible of two trajectories in contemporary ethical
thought. Were the specter of authorial intention of any consequence, I
would be forced to admit, on the basis of what he says there and in his later
writings, that Wittgenstein himself would have certainly favored one reading over the other, and not the one whose thread I will follow here. That
said, what we can at the very least praise in Wittgenstein's genius is that
quality—which Lacan claimed as the power of the signifier itself, namely,
"to signify *something quite other* than what it says"(*Écrits* trans. 155)—that

allowed him to open, with the very words he thought would close it, the door to a world of thought he believed to be deprived of sense.

Having distinguished between the trivial and true meanings of ethical sentences by referring to their relative or absolute value—which in Kantian terms would more or less correspond to the distinction between hypothetical and categorical imperatives—Wittgenstein claims to have a kind of revelation:

> I at once see clearly, as it were in a flash of light, not only that no description that I can think of would do to describe what I mean by absolute value, but that I would reject every significant description that anybody could possibly suggest, ab initio, on the ground of its significance. That is to say, I see now that these nonsensical expressions were not nonsensical because I had not yet found the correct expressions, but that their nonsensicality was their very essence. For all I wanted to do with them was just *to go beyond* the world and that is to say beyond significant language. My whole tendency and I believe the tendency of all men who ever tried to write or talk Ethics or Religion was to run against the boundaries of language. (Wittgenstein, "Lecture" 12)

The intentionally correct interpretation, I believe, of this paragraph is the one that might have inspired such deflationist pragmatist thought as that of Richard Rorty, who claims to find in the later Wittgenstein inspiration for his program of philosophical therapy, of correcting the annoying tendency philosophers have of mistaking sloppy uses of language for big philosophical questions.[1] In this reading, properly ethical statements— statements that present themselves as absolute rather than as relying on a validity relative to an implicit goal—are philosophical chimeras, invoked because we tend to talk that way, not because there are in fact any nonrelative ethical values to which to refer.

The famous phase "to run against the boundaries of language" would, in this reading, be intended to connote futility, for the nominalism of the later Wittgenstein tended to disavow the prospect of things existing about which nothing could be said, and hence the notion that language might have any boundaries whatsoever. The other reading, nevertheless, takes more seriously such phrases as "beyond the world" and "beyond significant language"—not because of a belief in a noumenal realm free from the causal determinations of the phenomenal, or because of a conviction concerning the existence of immutable laws unconditioned by the variance of history and textuality; but rather because of a lurking suspicion that language, insofar as it is embodied in communities of communicating beings, engenders limits and limitations specific to the practice of verbal communication—and furthermore, that the existence of ethical impulses, beliefs, convictions, has everything to do with a relation, not foreign to that evoked by Wittgenstein's famous phrase, between speaking beings and those very limits.

To work with a hypothesis that may, initially, overly constrain this concept of language, against whose boundaries we purportedly run when we speak of ethics: language—in accord with another Wittgenstinian thesis concerning the impossibility of a private language[2]—may be thought of as communication. Granting the plausibility of this idea allows us to evoke another limit, one that Sheri Hoem attributes to Jean-Luc Nancy's thought about community when she writes, "For Nancy, it is the very experience of the limits of communication that allows each being to discover a certain singularity in common" (Hoem 50). The text that inspires this reading is Nancy's "The Inoperative Community," a reading of an emergent and essentially antisubjectivist notion of community in Bataille's thought that opposes to an instrumental communicational relation ("a thinking that views the subject as the negative but specular identity of the object") a being of communication, a being-communicated for which "communication as the predicament of being, as 'transcendental,' *is* above all *being-outside-itself*" (Nancy, *Inoperative* 24).[3]

The emergent community whose outlines Nancy traces in Bataille's writing refuses to be thought of as the result of a construction produced by and between subjects, insofar as the political notion of subjectivity forcibly implies a sovereignty that could then be shared in common by the members of a community. Against this classic, liberal notion, Nancy defines the being of communication—and we should recall that we are all such beings—as a being that is primordially exterior to itself, and hence always other than itself: "But these singular beings are themselves constituted by sharing, they are distributed and placed, or rather *spaced*, by the sharing that makes them *others*: other for one another, and other, infinitely other for the Subject of their fusion, which is engulfed in the sharing, in the ecstasy of the sharing: 'communicating' by not 'communing'" (*Inoperative* 25). Within this context, "limits of communication" verges on tautology, because communication would be precisely the experience of those limits that community strives to disavow through its inherent communing, a bringing-together of autonomous subjects in a sharing of sovereignty. Furthermore, those limits could not be conceived of as inhering in a community "out there," between subjects, but must rather be understood as the limits constituting beings as others, the limits of alterity within, interior alterity, interior exteriority—*extimacy*, to use Lacan's phrase.

The term extimacy (*extimité*) was coined by Lacan in the course of his seminar, but was only elaborated by his student Jacques-Alain Miller in his own seminar of 1985–86. In the English translation and condensation of that seminar, Miller writes: "Extimacy is not the contrary of intimacy. Extimacy says that the intimate is Other—like a foreign body, a parasite" ("Extimacy" 76). For the purposes of the luxuriant psychoanalytic idiom, Other and unconscious are, Miller makes clear, interchangeable, such that the extimate parasite is in fact my own unconscious, which Lacan describes as "this other to whom I am more attached than to myself, since, at the heart of my assent to my own identity, it is still he who agitates me" (*Écrits* trans. 172). The unconscious: not a hidden and repressed reserve of concrete but socially unacceptable drives, but rather a "radical heteronomy . . . gaping within man" (*Écrits* trans. 172)[4]—gaping, that is, at the very heart of my assent to my own identity. Identity, *idem-ens*, the same being or the being of sameness, requires a moment of assent, assent to sameness; but assent requires at least two parties, a partition across which unity may be established; the assent of identity occurs only at the cost of hiding, avoiding, or disavowing the heart of dissent.[5]

Beings who are singular, Nancy says, are "distributed and placed, or better spaced," and we ought to attend to this use of the notion of spacing, so frequent in Nancy's idiom, which we can figure as the constitution of being by a sharing (*partage*)—which is also both a splitting and a giving birth, insofar as a being does not exist until the world has born it, given birth to it by splitting it off from others, and hence making it other—that opens up the space of being itself. "The outside is the inside," Nancy says in another text; "it is the spacing of the dis-position of the world; it is our disposition and our co-appearance" (Nancy, *Being Singular* 13). Hegel already deconstructed the dominance of dispositions (*Anlagen*) over circumstances in the well-known section on phrenology in the *Phenomenology of Spirit*, saying that "an *original* being of Spirit is equally well to be spoken of as a being that does not exist *qua being*." (Hegel, *Spirit* 204). To distinguish an original moment of being that might only secondarily be overrun by contingent circumstances, in other words, is a spurious move that attempts to posit being where there is in fact none. But this "non-Being of Being, its meaning, is its dis-position," because "it is absolute antecedence, where the 'with' is always already given; in another sense, it does not 'underlie' or preexist the different positions; it is their simultaneity" (Nancy,

Being Singular 92). The point to grasp, then, is not merely that the antecedent being attributed to dispositions is spurious, but rather that this supposition of absolute antecedence is always present in the form of the with, of the simultaneous coappearance of our self with others—a connotation not foreign to the German *Anlage*, which prefixes *Lage* (literally how something lies) with *an*, the indicator of proximity, but also the prefix of total nouminality, as in Kant's *Ding an sich*.[6] Dis-positions, rather than ultimate guarantors of inner selfhood, are thus the movement of the limits of interiority that spaces beings in the world along with other beings; individuality is found in the coming into being of this space that is inseparable from the "with" marking our coappearance with others: ego *cum*, e(r)go sum (Nancy, *Being Singular* 31).

Spacing is thus the movement of the with, which in typography has its own mark, the one that creates a space where previously there was none: the hyphen, "a mark of union and also a mark of division, a mark of sharing that effaces itself, leaving each term to its isolation and its being-with-the-others" (Nancy, *Being Singular* 37). Returning to a sentence quoted above—"communication as the predicament of being, as 'transcendental,' *is* above all *being-outside-itself*"—we can note that, in addition to the climactic *being-outside-itself*, one word, "is," is emphasized, as if to cause the reader to pause, to read "communication . . . is," before fulfilling the further predication that, in addition to being, it is *being-outside-itself*. Communication is. And furthermore, it is *being-outside-itself*. But insofar as communication is, then being equals communication, or the experiencing of being's own interior/exterior limit, a convergence expressed poetically in a sentence from Juan García Ponce's *De ánima* in which the third person singular of the Spanish verb to be, *es*, is, impossibly, hyphenated (García Ponce 10, cited in Johnson, "Marking" 65). This "hyphenization of being," in David E. Johnson's words, "marks the vanishing limit of language's touching of language, a touching of 'itself' that opens and closes the space for (the) itself" ("Marking" 66). But the place where language touches itself, or where being touches itself, is at once the limit of language and of communication, the place of interior alterity, "the place in which language ex-poses itself to itself, communicates itself to itself and, thus, loses the 'itself'" (66). Furthermore, this mark, by marking the disjunction between word and voice, becomes for Johnson the mark of the ethical, "in so far as ethics has historically depended on the voice, on the call, of conscience" (66).

The hyphenization of being marks the origin of the ethical insofar as the ethical is characterized by a running against the limits of language, or of communication; and if, as we have seen, communication is already the experience of its own limits, then there is something inherently ethical about communication, insofar as communication is understood as being-outside-itself, "infinite exposure" (Nancy, *Birth* 155), singularity. With both Kant and Heidegger, the voice or call of conscience originates in the self, in Dasein, such that ethics would seem to entail a speaking-to-oneself or difference-to-oneself already inherent in the individual's (nonindivisible) identity.[7] As Nancy states in *The Birth to Presence*, "[t]he subject contains its difference from itself. The subject not only has this difference, it *is* this difference. If the subject did not differ from itself, it would not be what it is: a subject *relating* itself to itself. A = A signifies that A *in itself* is its difference from itself, and that it derives its equality, its being-equal to itself, only from this difference" (11).[8] The sign of equality is here the redoubling, the remarking, of the hyphenization of being; hence identity is nothing other than a remarking of interior alterity, of the extimacy of being. But in this redoubling a movement occurs, an affecting; a distinction emerges in which that which was redoubled is affected, or becomes affect. This is the pure A, the simple A, that can only be so seen in retrospect, but from that perspective can be recognized as the soul. This soul is pure affection, what Nancy calls "the possession of alteration as a property" (Nancy, *Birth* 18), and which we can recognize as the pure remainder of all prior distinctions, the unchanging that enables (and is itself a product of) alteration and is the ultimate ground of its experience: "the soul *is* affected, it is in that it is affected—by its identity" (29).[9]

Compare Nancy's use of "soul" with the following passage from Lévinas:

> The soul, reified as some-thing, is, phenomenologically, what shows itself in the nonreified face; it shows itself in expression and, in this appearing, has the structure of the glimmer [*la pointe*] of someone. That which Descartes makes a substance . . . , that from which Leibniz makes a monad, that which Plato posits as the soul contemplating the Ideas, that which Spinoza thinks as a mode of thought, is described phenomenologically as *face*. Without this phenomenology one is pushed toward a reification of the soul, whereas here a problem other than to be or not to be is posed, a problem prior to that question. (Lévinas, *God* 12)

Where Nancy sees soul as an inevitable outcome or product of affection, and therefore not a thing that could be understood to precede the movement of that affection, Lévinas situates soul as something ultimately irreducible and prior to all reification, in the phenomenological experience of the encounter with another person.

It makes sense to interrogate further Lévinas's position in this regard, especially as he is widely considered the essential point of departure for so-called postmodern ethics.[10] Lévinas is often understood as having given the lie to his former teacher Heidegger, insofar as Heidegger's thought refused a place of importance for ethics. But whereas Lévinas conceived of his claim for ethics as a kind of first philosophy as a reversal of Heidegger, I consider precisely Heidegger's thought to be where this priority is most in evidence, whereas Lévinas's various attempts to formulate an explicit ethics have the paradoxical effect of burying the true ethical dimension, that of the fault-line, in the grave of an ontological stability, as we will see.

As Tina Chanter thoroughly documents, Lévinas's criticism of Heidegger evolves considerably throughout his career. It is particularly telling that the stated reason for his criticism changes profoundly from his earliest to his later writings. As Chanter writes:

> if the early Levinas criticizes Heidegger for allowing the present instant, and subjectivity, to dissipate into the other, or time, through the movement of ecstasies, the later Levinas criticizes him for reducing the other to the self, negating the alterity of the future by incorporating death into Dasein's understanding of its ownmost-potentiality-for-being, and thereby totalizing the different ecstases in a way that not only eradicates the specificity of the instant, but also reestablishes the primacy of subjectivity over otherness. (33)

Put into simple terms, the earlier Lévinas criticizes Heidegger for undermining subjectivity, and the later Lévinas criticizes him for reinforcing subjectivity at the expense of otherness.

In his earlier work, for instance, Lévinas writes, "The *here* that belongs to consciousness, the place of its sleep and of its escape into itself, is radically different from the *Da* involved in Heidegger's *Dasein*. The latter already implies the world. The *here* we are starting with, the *here* of position, precedes every act of understanding, every horizon, and all time" (qtd. in Chanter 150). I can only agree here with Lévinas's assessment of the difference between his *here* and Heidegger's *Da*, as Heidegger's entire thought is aimed at disrupting the notion of any element of subjectivity that would "precede every act of understanding, every horizon, and all time." On the contrary, Dasein is nothing other than understanding, horizon, and time, and Lévinas's defense of some kernel of existence that transcends these variables, "a time that is not yet time" (Chanter 151), is a remnant of precisely what Heidegger's thought seeks to undermine.

The later Lévinas, in contrast, speaks of "the risk of occupying—from the *Da* of my *Dasein*—the place of an Other and, thus, in the concrete, of exiling him, dooming him to a miserable condition in some 'third' or 'fourth' world, bringing him death" (qtd. in Chanter 152). But we cannot help but notice that, in order for this criticism to work, Lévinas has had to reverse his reading of Dasein's *Da*; whereas before it (correctly) indicated the extent to which Dasein is always outside of itself, already implying the world, now it refers to precisely the opposite: that within me that goes out and occupies the other, bringing violence and death along with it.

This apparent contradiction, however, is readily explained when we realize that what is distasteful for Lévinas in Heidegger's philosophy (as opposed to his politics, for which Lévinas had every right to be enraged) is the same in each complaint; merely its position has changed. What is distasteful, that is, is the violence done to, the unsettling of, some position of tranquility, peace, sovereignty. At first that position is a pretemporal, phenomenological consciousness; later it is the Other whose place Dasein occupies and to whom Dasein brings death. But here I must agree emphatically with Martin Hägglund, for whom Lévinas's Other, in the peace of its absoluteness, becomes indistinguishable from the absolutely same: "Apparently unaware of the inconsistency, Levinas thus criticizes the philosophy of identity, totality, and monadic being by invoking an absolute that reinstates these ideals. Indeed, Levinas speaks of the wholly Other instead of the wholly Same. But this makes no essential difference since these two extremes—as Derrida maintains in 'Violence and Metaphysics'—invert into each other and at bottom are founded on the same ideal."

Heidegger, in contrast, with the notion of ecstatic unity developed in *Being and Time* and the idea of original temporality expounded in *Kant and the Problem of Metaphysics*, is consistent in his theorization of a subject that is through and through finite, at odds with itself, for whom other people and the otherness of death are constitutive elements of its being. For otherness to inhabit me from the outset—and this is the point of Heidegger's insistence on such terms as *Jemeinigkeit*—means that there cannot be a wholly Other to serve as guarantee for the consistency my self only appears to lack; rather, this radical inconsistency, this interior otherness, this death that is my own-most potentiality, this is all there is. Therefore, if Lévinas apparently could not decide whether to differ with Heidegger because he undermined the integrity of the self or to differ from him because he undermined the integrity of the other, that is probably because Heidegger consistently did both.[11]

Nancy, like Lévinas, uses the notion of "soul," but to Nancy, who is close to Heidegger in this regard, soul is the core of identity only insofar as identity is understood not as an immobile origin, point of fixity, but rather as ever-moving, ever-becoming process: identification. The soul is determined, but not externally: "this determination is not imprinted on it by an alien force, but . . . takes place only as the perturbance of substance by the other—which is itself" (Nancy, *Birth* 30). If we return momentarily to Hegel's idiom, which is in many places the origin of Nancy's own reflection, we find that the substance that is always perturbed by the self that is the other, that is split asunder, is precisely the ethical substance, and that the primary form of its sundering is sexual difference. When the individual acts, he or she shatters the tranquility of the ethical substance—the "pure," "immediate" being of embedded cultural identity, for example; the simple, unquestioning knowledge of what is right—and irrevocably engenders a split between two possible laws, "for as simple ethical consciousness, it has turned towards one law, but turned its back on the other and violates the latter by its deed. . . . [T]he action itself is this splitting into two, this explicit self-affirmation and the establishing over against itself of an alien eternal reality; that there is such a reality, this stems from the action itself and results from it" (Hegel, *Spirit* 282). The emergence of guilt in the aftermath of the disturbance of ethical substance—and indeed we recognize it as substance only in its disturbance—results from the fact that while the individual in his or her act is faced with two opposing laws and must choose and completely identify with one, the laws are in essence linked to one another, such that betrayal of the one is at the same time betrayal of the other, and hence of the self. Guilt is what arises from this betrayal.

The manifest existence of two laws emerges for Hegel in the existence of two sexes, and he identifies men with human law and women with divine law.[12] Nancy makes a similar move, albeit without giving specific sexual content to one or the other side of the split: "The trembling of the soul is not indifferent to the difference between the sexes. It *is* this difference, or an even more archaic but still sexual difference—or it is the difference of love, insofar as this difference imparts the soul, neither man nor woman, but either one in the other, and makes the soul tremble: transits the soul, entrances it" (Nancy, *Birth* 30). To clarify, ethical substance is unified substance as always-already divided; it is the very division of substance that allows the appearance of unity of substance in the first place. At the social level the primary paradigm of the process of division that begins for Hegel at the level of sensory perception is the division of the world into sexes and concomitant sex roles and identities; in other words, sexual difference is one and perhaps the primary name for the limits of language that constitute the ethical fault-line. Identity is born or imparted on the edge of this divide, and hence soul, a singular point of identity—interiority—is born of and carries with it this "impartation" (the giving of self through the division into self and other) at every moment of its existence, it *is* its existence.

THE HEART OF THE THING

I want to draw a connection, an analogy of sorts, between this soul that emerges from the division or impartation of identity, that point of relative immobility or affection, and another immobility that Nancy locates at the *heart* of language: "*Immobile in truth*: there, the thing restrains the word from speaking at the very moment it speaks, and the two do not surrender to the expressive mimesis that Hegel wanted to see in them." Here Nancy seems to give back to Kant what Hegel wanted to take from him, the possibility of some thing that is unattainable by knowledge and hence not subject to the endless chain of causality binding the phenomenal world. "There is certainly a thing at the heart of the word," he adds, but then goes on to caution, "but that implies no kind of 'meta-speech' but rather a nonspeech of the words themselves, which is always immobile in them, even in speech" (Nancy, *Birth* 168).

In his seminar of 1973–74, Lacan made passing and not entirely flattering reference to Nancy, albeit as one of the authors of a small book about his own work that Lacan urged on his followers as an example of how to read him. The book, *The Title of the Letter*, which was written by Nancy with Philippe Lacoue-Labarthe, is an extended reading and critique of Lacan's influential address and article from 1957, "L'instance de la lettre dans l'inconcient ou la raison depuis Freud" ["The Agency of the Letter in the Unconscious or Reason Since Freud"] (*Écrits* trans. 146–78). In referencing its authors, Lacan rather petulantly points out to his seminar students that his critics have ultimately misread him, or curtailed their reading, by failing to realize that the impasse to which they trace his argument is not merely an impasse in his argument, but an impasse per se: "It is as if it were precisely upon reaching the impasse to which my discourse is designed to lead them that they considered their work done, declaring themselves—or rather declaring me, which amounts to the same thing given their conclusions—confounded" (Lacan, *XX* 65–66).

Is there something to Lacan's complaint? Nancy and Lacoue-Labarthe argue in their text that Lacan's exploration of the movements of signification comes to a halt at a certain point, one that is at the same time a center and an origin, and a guarantee of systematicity. This point is the bar separating the signifier from the signified in Lacan's rewriting of Saussure's formula for signification: "the bar is *foundational* or *originary*. It is the *archê* of a system which, while systematizing the division, the lack, or the hole in the places of origin, has nevertheless maintained its own 'archaic' value of systematicity—that is, of origin and center—without questioning it further" (Nancy and Lacoue-Labarthe 112). The unifying, almost absolute nature of the knowledge with which Lacan can articulate this center and origin comes from an authority that inserts itself in various forms from outside the text of signification, of movement, of what Lacan calls metonymy. This outside may take the form of a master or teacher, like Freud or Hegel or Heidegger, depending on where one finds oneself in Lacan's argument; or it may appear in the shape of an invocation of analytic experience. Regardless of its shape or form, though, the function of this reference is to put a halt to the dissemination of meaning by recourse to something escaping that movement. That this something speaks in the name of or from the position of *being* makes of Lacan's discourse an ontology, albeit a negative ontology, "since its center is designated and its circumference delineated by a hole" (126).[13] Being must reemerge here because Lacan's ontology is ultimately an "onto-theo-semio-logy," due to his privileging of metaphor over metonymy, his linking of the former to desire (and hence to the lack of being) and the latter to "the question of being" itself (*Écrits* trans. 175)—a formulation that gives his critics cause to wonder if the question to which "*metaphor* is linked is nothing other than the *presence* of being" (Nancy and Lacoue-Labarthe 140), despite the emphasis on its character as lack, as hole.[14]

Although Nancy and Lacoue-Labarthe permitted the book to be republished in France as recently as 1990, with its English translation appearing in 1992, and indeed reiterated their essential support of its thesis in the preface to the 1990 edition, one cannot help but wonder whether the philosophical and academic-political environment of the day might be at least partially responsible for an apparent animosity whose relevance now, some thirty years later and some twenty years after the death of Lacan, might be diminished.[15] That environment was pushed along by a heady revolutionary fervor that targeted the powerful intellectual institutions that codified discourse in France at that time, as well as the structuralist claims to systematicity they proffered. Resistance to Lacan, and recourse to deconstructive strategies to implement that resistance, went hand in hand with this zeitgeist. Nevertheless, a series of concerns and formulations appears to emerge in Nancy's more recent writings that can be convincingly read as sustaining and pursuing Lacan's fascination with the impasse of signification, rather than rejecting it outright.[16]

The key to understanding Lacan's use of the term "being," which so disturbed Nancy in his earlier consideration of Lacan's teaching, is to grasp that being is not the thing that puts signification to rest; rather, signification reaches impasses or limits—and these *are* being. As if invoking the very hyphenization that Nancy discusses years later, Lacan stipulates that the " 'being' referred to is that which appears in a lightening moment in the void of the verb 'to be' and I said that it poses its question for the subject" (*Écrits* trans. 168). The verb "to be," then, attests to a void, or gaping, that opens up at its heart, and that poses a question for the subject; or rather, as Lacan specifies, it poses a question *with* the subject as one might write *with* a pen or "Aristotle's man thought *with* his soul" (*Écrits* trans. 168), suggesting that this void in being entails a with or an along-side, a relation to something that manifests itself as essential to human being—as soul, as subject—and that is revealed in the quasi-instrumental function of facilitating a questioning that emerges from that void, the questioning of identity, of the nature of that "A" to which I am equal, of *what, how, why,* and most fundamentally *that* I am.

If we return to Descartes, as Lacan does in "The Agency of the Letter," the effect of this reversal or change in perspective is to see the I of thought not as apodictically founding the I of being, but rather to grasp the being of "I am" as the very shuddering or trembling of the spacing, the void opened up by the act of enunciation, the question not "of knowing whether I speak of myself in a way that conforms to what I am, but rather of knowing whether I am the same as that of which I speak" (*Écrits* trans. 165).[17] Whereas metonymy is the movement of thought that endlessly pushes the fulfillment of desire into a subject's future, metaphor marks and holds open the space of the subject itself, the space of sense, which in French designates meaning without losing its connotation of direction, orientedness, and hence movement and the spacing it entails.[18] Metaphor, replacing one word with another, manifests in its purest form the void at the heart of being, because it is the very equivalence of nonequivalence itself that is the condition of possibility of saying that something "is" something, or that I . . . am.[19] It is a crossing of the very spacing of being that language engenders, a crossing that is "creative or poetic, in other words, which is the advent of the signification in question" (*Écrits* trans. 164), but that itself resists signification, or rather, whatever new signification emerges will always remit us to a moment of stoppage, of immobility, at the border of the void in being.

This void is the impasse in question; it is the "abyss opened up at the thought that a thought should make itself heard in the abyss" (*Écrits* trans. 170); and it is thus the very fault-line separating the abyss from the thought emerging there. Lacan gives this impasse or fault-line a new name only several years after the delivery of his talk, the "Agency of the Letter," a name that ties this conception explicitly into a history of epistemological and ethical thought: *das Ding*, which he designates as "the beyond-of-the-signified" (Lacan, *VII* 54). As the utter beyond of that which is signified, which is meant, *das Ding* is the abyss from which thought emerges and against which it distinguishes itself as thought, as well as the residue of immobility against which the incessant sliding of thought drives; it marks the limits of language against which we run when, for example, we speak of ethics, of absolute and themselves unjustifiable justifications.

To return to the quotation from Nancy that initiated our excursus into Lacan's text, "[t]here is certainly a thing at the heart of the word, but that implies no kind of 'meta-speech' but rather a non-speech of the words themselves, which is always immobile in them, even in speech" (Nancy, *Birth* 168).[20] Just as a meta-language would be the place from which what is articulated in language has its external and eternal guarantee, its foundation in extra-linguistic truth, and just as Lacan himself disavowed the existence of such a place and baptized the limits of our ability to speak from such a place as the very boundaries of *das Ding*, so does Nancy locate at the heart, at the vortex, of language or speech an immobile place of nonspeech, a "black hole" in meaning: "At the heart of things, where this heart is identically the heart of words and the heart of thought—a black hole from which nothing escapes, no light, a hole of absolute gravity—truth absolutely halts all movement of the concept and, with its gravity, impedes all momentum, all succession of sentences, all motion, all impulse of intelligence" (168). The heart of things is what Kant had called the *Ding an sich*: literally, the thing *at* itself, at a point of no remove or no mediation from itself, and hence the point of utter unknowability for we who can only think the thing via a conceptual apparatus, only know it through a sensual apparatus—a hole from which nothing escapes. The gravity of the heart of things is emitted by its truth, that which halts the movement of the concept, as the flash of metaphor halts the slippage of the signifier. This slippage in thought is akin to what Lacan, following Freud, referred to as the movement of the *Sachvorstellungen*—thing representations, analogous to what Nancy calls "thing-words"—that slide along the pathways of the reality principle to the vortex of *das Ding*: " 'To think,' in the sense of setting the activity of discourse into motion, is to lead discourse itself toward the moment of this gravity, toward this 'black hole' that it designates as its most characteristic limit, and toward which, finally, it cannot help precipitating itself in one way or another (stupidly or clairvoyantly, arrogantly or confidently)" (168–69).

This black hole is discourse's or thought's most characteristic limit, a limit that can only be understood as the "thing in its presence" precisely insofar as it is the point at which discourse, in its duplicity and its reflexivity, solidifies into a massive, nonsignifying singularity: "thought without reflexivity, without intentionality, without '*adequatio rei et intellectus*' " (Nancy, *Birth* 169). Point of "distinct indistinction," this "heart-thing" is the dual vanishing point of thing and thought; Kantian thing-in-itself and point of pure apperception wrapped around in a non-Euclidean space and revealed as one; the subject now extended out from, around, and back into that place, that hyphen, like a doughnut, the torus whose topology Lacan claimed as that proper to subjectivity (Lacan, "Of Structure" 193).[21] The wrapping around of this spectrum of knowledge, a first projecting of the thought of being into Riemannian space,[22] was the work of Hegel, to whom Nancy attributes this notion of the unity of thinghood and essence; it is the revelation or "relevation"[23] of propositional knowledge (which would leave the spectrum in flat, abstract space) as speculative, dialectical knowledge (which curves that space around, allows its furthest edges to touch)—the world is no longer framed by the knower and the thing to be known; rather, that ultimate exterior/ultimate interior point are one, itself framed by the fabric of the world.

LIKE A ONE-SIDED LINE

I will pause here to explore this borrowing from the language of topology, in order to avoid the appearance of obscurantist meddling in scientific discourse that provides the critics of poststructuralism with fodder for their ridicule. Indeed, one of the glaring examples of the poststructualist dissemination of fashionable nonsense for Sokal and Bricmont was Lacan's frequent recourse to topology in his work in the early 1960s. For example, in reference to the above-noted mention of the torus, the two-dimensional plane corresponding to the surface of a doughnut or inner-tube, the authors ridicule Lacan's claim that it is "exactly the structure of the neurotic," commenting in parentheses "(whatever that means)" and then taking him to task for denying that his use of the term was to be understood analogically (Sokal and Bricmont 20). What they fail to grasp is that Lacan's denial of the topology's analogous status was a continuation of a line of argumentation that they left unquoted (perhaps finding it equally incomprehensible, insofar as, like the rest of the thought they criticize, they fail to comprehend it), in which Lacan discusses the possibility of two things being the same (itself a respected question in the history of metaphysics): "The sameness is not in *things* but in the *mark* which makes it possible to add things with no consideration as to their differences" (Lacan, "Of Structure" 192). This argument is akin to the old *reductio* of correspondence theories of truth: if the truth of a sentence depends on its correspondence with reality, how do I test this correspondence? By holding the sentence in one hand and the reality in the other? If the torus is the structure of subjectivity (or neurosis, which amounts to the same thing for our purposes), it cannot be so by analogy, for that would imply the existence of the analogon, that example of subjectivity or neurosis one can hold in one's hand and compare with a torus.

The torus is one of a series of figures that become important for Lacan in the early 1960s as examples of spaces that undo the differentiation between sides of a place, or between the inside and outside of a three-dimensional figure. A torus, unlike a Moebius strip or especially a Klein bottle, is not a terribly complicated shape. To understand its virtue as a symbolization of subjectivity let us return briefly to Miller's elaboration of the concept of extimacy. In his seminar, Miller diagrams this concept as a pair of concentric circles, and then points out that in order to grasp the concept we must imagine that the inside and outside circumference are in fact the same. On the two-dimensional surface of the page it is clearly not possible for these two distinct lines to be the same, but should a dimension be added, and the two-dimensional figure now be seen as the shadow of a three-dimensional torus, then the space inhabiting the middle of the figure, which had before been separated by the body of the figure from that space surrounding it, is now revealed to be one and the same as the latter, and hence the interior and exterior lines are themselves one line.

Analogously (because in this case we are working with two symbolizations), the Moebius strip is a two-dimensional plane curved in three dimensions in such a way that it has only one side; close this one-sided plane and you have a Klein bottle, an object whose inside and outside touch on one and the same surface. Commenting on his diagram of a Moebius strip, in which a line has been drawn along the surface until it meets itself, Lacan says, "[y]ou can see that the line in this instance may be considered either as one or as two lines. This diagram can be considered the basis of a sort of essential inscription at the origin, in the knot which constitutes the subject" (Lacan, "Of Structure" 192). Like the mark in the sentence quoted above, such a line is a "unitary trait" (*trait unaire*) that constitutes the sameness in different things, but also the difference that makes the thing what it is—a thing—in the first place: "In order that the 'thing' which is sought be here in you, it is necessary that the first trait be rubbed out because the trait itself is a modification. It is the taking away of all difference, and in this case, without the trait, the first thing is simply lost" (192).

To return to the figure of the torus, the hole at its center is represented, its place held, by a trait, a signifier, a metaphor. What lies on the other side of this trait is a thing, but the only access to the thing is via the trait. The subject tries to attain the thing by repeating the "specific action" that originally gave it satisfaction; it demands that same satisfaction, which it does not attain. This circuit of "local demand" (Nasio 154) is repeated, with the result that a difference is always produced at the heart of the identity it accedes to: "[t]he trait, I insist, is identical, but it assures the difference only of identity—not by the effect of sameness or difference but by the difference of identity" (Lacan, "Of Structure" 192). The difference of identity is precisely a line that is both one and two, in that it joins and divides an inside and outside that are at the same time indistinguishable.

How can we understand this *trait unaire* that provokes an apparent need in Lacan's thought for a topology of paradoxical spaces? In the seminar on ethics, Lacan speaks of *das Ding* as lying at the center

> only in the sense that it is excluded. That is to say, in reality *das Ding* has to be posited as exterior, as the prehistoric Other that it is impossible to forget—the Other whose primacy of position Freud affirms in the form of something *entfremdet*, something strange to me, although it is at the heart of me, something that on the level of the unconscious only a representation can represent. (Lacan, *VII* 71)

In a topographical analysis, therefore, *das Ding* would occupy the space at the center of the torus, which is simultaneously the space outside the structure, and the very skin of the torus would be defined by a line that is both singular and plural. It seems from within the world to mark its borders: beginning and end, the outsides of knowledge and the inside of intimate experience. But the world is all, it has no borders, only a singular mark lying at its heart, the hyphenization of being, the difference of identity; and we only need recall that this singular mark is a logical derivation of the structure of signification, which strives to represent all[24] but cannot, because to do so would imply occupying a place that is itself not part of the all that is to be represented. Signification, therefore, opens up a hole in being, a "loss in reality, yet nothing can do that, since by status reality is as full as possible" (Lacan, "Of Structure" 193). The perception of something that exceeds the boundaries of reality is thus the effect of inhabiting a world, a universe whose experience is organized around a gaping cut in the fabric of being, the border (there is only one) of which is nothing other than the stopping point of signification itself, its breakdown, its immobility.

In a world of signification, this heart is a point of at-itself-ness—is, according to Nancy, the stopping point of the motion of dialecticity, the *an sich* being the only nondialectical words in Hegel's vocabulary (Gasché, "Horizon" 144).[25] The idea is not that, "objectively speaking," there is a point at which the notional movement of knowledge comes to an absolute halt, but rather that precisely because there is no such absolutely external place of judgment, judgment is "infinite" and self-incorporating and hence necessarily produces its own absolute limits that are experienced, depending on the moment, as either an absolute inside or an absolute outside.[26] Within the realm of movement, of thought, the identity of a thing is determined always in relation to other things, things that come before and after it, its causes (the French *chose* being an etymological progeny of *causa*); at the heart of things, however, at the limit or focal point at which the movement that is the world of my knowledge has its moment, this logic of exchange and equivalence disappears: "nothing takes the place of this thing here (especially not a monument). It is the very incidence, or the accident, or the occasion of the coincidence; its fall, its flight, its case, its *clinamen*, its *kairos*, its *Ereignis*" (Nancy, *Birth* 187). Incident, accident, even the occident share the medieval Latin root of *cadere*, to fall, an etymological provenance claimed by the case (Ger. *der Fall*)[27] that is or so happens to have befallen, a family heritage emphasizing the event-like nature of that which is. The paradox of the immobility at the heart of things is that it is at once profoundly immobile and radically, singularly ephemeral. It is immobile because it does not owe its essence to the eternal chain of events leading back to the prime mover; it is ephemeral because it coincides with its essence in a pure and singular moment Nancy calls *Ereignis, clinamen,* and *kairos: Ereignis*—an eventess that is at the same time an appropriation, a coming into being as a radical relation, a coming into my being, here and now, inclined toward me; *clinamen*—not bias in motion between immobile poles, but absolute bias, bias per se, primordial dissymmetry; *kairos*—unique temporal unity, pregnant with messianic possibility.[28]

My heart is what is most intimate, central, inalienable; it is at the same time the border of pure alienation, an open wound being devoured by an other whose existence is as indistinguishable from that act of incorporation and separation as is my own. The heart is immobile and intimate, and at the same time radically inclined and voracious. It is therefore no surprise that the vision that so moved the poet Dante Alighieri's world that it initiated for him a new life, the *Vita nuova*, was of a naked woman resting in the arms of the god of love, who, announcing to the poet that the flaming object he holds in his hand is the poet's heart [E ne l'una de le mani mi parea che questi tenesse una cosa la quale ardesse tutta, e pareami che mi dicesse queste parole: 'Vide cor tuum'] (Dante 16), proceeds to force her to devour it; his heart literally belongs to her, his other, embraced in the arms of the deity who represents more than any other the giving to another that is radically constitutive of a self. It seems appropriate that this vision should combine almost irrepressible desire with horror or anguish: the beauty of Beatrice's nudity is barely concealed, draped only in a cloth that Dante describes not as *rosso*, red, but as *sanguigno*, the color of blood, making of the border of her body an open wound abutting the other, the exposed vulnerability at the core of the self.

This very heart, interior and exterior, is figured by the poet at the end of the *libello* as the source of an unruly desire, which must be opposed and controlled by the intellectual soul (thought) of reason [L'una parte chiamo cuore, ciò è l'appetito; l'altra chiamo anima, ciò è la ragione] (Dante 192). This heart he calls appetite (of which Lacan's *petit a* is a quasi-anagram), an inclination that his reason only puts to rest by recalling that initial vision—by recalling, in other words, that the heart is another's, not in the banal sense of everyday love lyrics, but in the radically constitutive sense of being made-unmade by that other. The heart is the permanent and immobile horizon of utmost vulnerability against which the world of sense guards, and toward which it incessantly drives.[29]

Is this not, perhaps, what it means to say that one's heart belongs to another? That the core of self-identity only comes into being through a revelation of its strangeness? "My heart," writes Nancy in *L'intrus*, "was becoming my own stranger: foreign precisely because it was inside. The strangeness could not have come from outside without having first surged up from inside" (Nancy, *L'intrus* 17). Nancy conceives of the strangeness of this interior alien body, in his case a transplanted heart that his own body was striving to reject, as an ultimate barrier to spirit, to knowing: "The mind here runs up against an object that is null: nothing to know, nothing to understand, nothing to feel: the intrusion on thought of a body strange to thought" (17). Thought and its metastases, consciousness, the "I," a sense of self, are the result of the encounter with such a strange body, which is to say that the selves who speak for us, and through whom we experience the world, are produced by a kind of accident, failure, a tripping over or running into some obstacle, before which there was quite simply no sense of either the obstacle or the self: "Until now, it had been a stranger by dint of its not being sensible, even present. Then it fails, and the strangeness brings me back to myself. 'I' am because I am sick. ('Sick' is not the exact term: it is not infected, it is rusty, stiff, blocked)" (17–18).

Nancy's implicit interlocutor in this passage is the Heidegger of *Being and Time*, for whom the making-itself-known of the world depends on a disturbance in the order of reference, the result of "bumping into things that are unusable":

> But in a *disturbance of reference*—in being unusable for . . . —the reference becomes explicit. It does not yet become explicit as an ontological structure, but ontically for our circumspection which gets annoyed by the damaged tool. This circumspect noticing of the reference to the particular what-for makes the what-for visible and with it the context of the work, the whole "workshop" as that in which taking care of useful things appears not as a totality never seen before, but as a totality that has continually been seen beforehand in our circumspection. But with this totality world makes itself known. (Heidegger, *Being and Time* 70)

The encounter with something that fails to fulfill its function (an expectation) within the chain of reference constituting average everydayness is what brings Dasein's context into sight; makes, in other words, the subject aware of its environs; produces, in the language of metaphysics, consciousness. The moment of failure or blockage draws a boundary between the world that makes itself known and the world that does not make itself known, which is Heidegger's rewriting of the distinction between the phenomenal world and the world of things as they are in themselves: "When the world does not make itself known, that is the condition for the possibility of what is at hand not emerging from its inconspicuousness. And this is the constitution of the phenomenal structure of the being-in-itself of these beings" (70). Thought, self, and the "I" are what emerge on this side of that border; the heart, then, can only have been what was there, or can be approached only as a limit, one against which we run as we "exscribe" our very existence on its walls (Nancy, *Birth* 339).

What becomes clear in Nancy's appropriation of this unsettling of the traditional metaphysical hierarchy, in which the "I" sits at the origin and pure point of apperception, is precisely the profound similarity between this "sickness"—the encounter with the obstacle of otherness that brings to a sudden halt mere, immersed being-in-the-world—and Lacan's notion from the later 1950s of the function of metaphor as marking the ultimate point at which the chain of elements constitutive of meaning hinges on the abyss of being. "Who, 'I'?" Nancy asks. "It is precisely the question, the old question: what is this subject of enunciation, always stranger to the subject of the utterance, for which it is necessarily the intruder and therefore necessarily the motor, the clutch, or the heart?" (Nancy, *L'intrus* 13). The heart, then, is the abyss from which thought thinks; the being that language attempts to pin down through its metaphoric function of stoppage; the subject of the enunciation always proffering up its reality to the subject of the utterance, haplessly chasing after its own being. But it is from this sickness or stoppage that thought, self, and the "I" emerge, are imparted into existence by detachment/contact with the heart that is the innermost and most radical experience of nonself.

PHILOSOPHY AND THE NAMES OF GOD

What began as a discussion of the ethical in the work of Jean-Luc Nancy has brought us at last to what can only be termed a theological level of concern. As Nancy puts it, the question of the being of God "will perhaps turn out to have been the necessary but unanswerable question in which the god set about withdrawing." It is a question to which he ventures that "God is not predicable," going on to add, in parentheses, "(This places us instantaneously at a peak of philosophical saturation, in a Hegelian reabsorption of predication: subject and predicate have here, in God, merged with one another)" (Nancy, *Inoperative* 110–11). If God defies predication, God becomes coterminous with being itself, becomes "the very fact of his being." But the problem with this answer, a problem that arises from the nature of the question itself, is that predication inevitably reemerges, and statements about God become functional equivalents of statements about desire, the subject (or its absence), history, community, a potentially end-less litany of what Nancy calls "the names of a generalized and multiplied difference" (113). But this litany cannot help but lead us into error:

> In baptizing our abysses with the name of God, we are guilty of at least two er-rors or two incoherencies: we fill in the abysses by attributing a bottom to them, and we blaspheme (in the true sense of the word) the name of God by making it the name of some*thing*. On the other hand, the most subtle—and most theological—error would doubtless consist in *believing* that the infinite cannot provide a bottom and that naming a person is not naming a sort of "thing." (113)

Indeed, this is the "sin" for which Nancy implicitly takes Lévinas to task, in that by calling God "infinite" because he is unthematizable (113),[30] Lév-inas inevitably thematizes him, as, in fact, does any act of naming. Such a sin is exactly what Žižek finds objectionable in what he calls "one of the most deplorable aspects of the postmodern era," namely, "the return of the religious dimension in all its different guises" (*Fragile* 1). When Žižek goes on to implicate in this "onslaught of obscurantism" the "emerging religious sensitivity within deconstructionism itself," it seems clear that what he has in mind is the impact that Lévinas's work has had on such thinkers as Nancy and Derrida.[31] Nevertheless, keeping in mind Nancy's own vehe-ment rejection of "the sickening traffic [that] has grown up around a so-called return of the spiritual and of the religious" (Nancy, *Inoperative* 121), it is not a stretch to claim that Nancy's thought concerning the religious engages similar rather than opposed concerns to those of Žižek, namely, a refusal of the "obscurantist" gesture according to which the abyss of the unknown, "all the obscure confines of our experience," is baptized as the divine (142).[32] For Nancy, the history of the West has been characterized by the forced choice between this gesture and the opposing denunciation of such beliefs as superstition, a denunciation that has the effect of elevating its enunciator to precisely the place of divinity left behind by the departing God. The challenge is to leave that place nameless, and hence the space open:

> Space is everywhere open, there is no place wherein to receive either the mys-tery or the splendor of a god. It is granted us to see the limitless openness of that space, it falls to our age to know—with a knowledge more acute than the

most penetrating science, more luminous than any consciousness—how we are
delivered up to that gaping naked face. It reveals to us nothing but us—*neither
gods nor men*—and that too is a joy. (148–49)

It is not, therefore, a question of saying something on the order of "at the
heart of things, in the abyss of thought, is God," a claim that would merely
imitate the innumerable other divine baptisms that do nothing other than
stand ephemerally guard by the gates of an ever receding limit to human
knowledge. Precisely insofar as that limit, that horizon, reinscribes and re-
inforces a teleological and metaphysical certainty regarding the nature of
knowledge and of humankind's place in the world, this limit needs to be
thought otherwise: not a border between two identifiable worlds—between gods and men—but the opening of a space whose border must be
figured as a kind of historical event horizon. Like the sidereal entity that inspires this metaphor, such a border is simultaneously absolute and utterly
porous; a line that seems to have only one side; an immobile heart bor-
dered by a horizon of pure becoming, a *clinamen*.

Although both Nancy and Žižek denounce the use of religious language
to approximate this horizon, they have also both come forward as apolo-
gists or defenders of at least one religious tradition: Christianity. In both
cases, however, what is being defended is not so much a particular doctrine
as a historical and epochal structure related to modern, Western thought.
This structure is, for Žižek, characterized by the internal paradox between
the eternal truth Christianity purports to represent and the precisely historical, even contingent nature of its manifestation, namely, the incarnation. Whereas previous religious forms tended to "emphasize the insuffi-
ciency of every temporal finite object . . . Christianity, on the other hand,
offers Christ as a mortal-temporal individual, and insists that belief in the
temporal Event of Incarnation is the only path to *eternal* truth and salvation" (Žižek, *Fragile* 96). The key term here is "event," which Žižek links
to the Kantian notion of the act as the point where "eternity intervenes in
time" (93),[33] which is to say the moment of freedom, at which the endless
causal chain of the phenomenal world is cut by something that itself has no
cause, that is unconditioned. The revolutionary potential of Christianity—
that it opens the way for a transvaluation of traditional thought and values—is its implicit subordination of eternity to temporality, and hence of
essence to existence.

Better yet, rather than merely reversing a traditional hierarchy, perhaps
Christianity instantiates something more radical: namely, the deconstruction of the very order giving rise to that hierarchy, in which eternity is re-

vealed to be not the primordial backdrop to human temporality but rather itself the name given to the event, the gap, that intervenes in the world and thereby creates temporality—and thus sense—as, in Žižek's words, "the series/succession of failed attempts to grasp it" (*Fragile* 95). This, it seems to me, is one way to grasp Nancy's (admittedly bizarre) claim that deconstruction is Christian:

> Christianity is itself, essentially, the movement of its own distension, because it represents the constitution of a subject in opening and in distension from itself. Clearly then, one must then say that deconstruction, which is not possible except through this distension, is itself Christian. It is Christian because Christianity is, from its origin, deconstructive, because it relates in the first place to its own origin as to a play, to an interval, a beating, an opening in the origin. (Nancy, "Déconstruction" 512–13)[34]

How do we make sense of this? The opening in the origin of Christianity is precisely that between the historical substance of man and the eternal substance of God, between the historical moment of a message and the eternal truth it announces. In this sense, each of the three Christian doctrines Nancy analyzes—faith, sin, incarnation—participates in this primordial distension that makes of Christianity one epochal manifestation of deconstruction. Faith, in his reading, consists of a relation to the Name of God precisely insofar as God is not present in any demonstrable way (515); it is "adherence to the infinity of sense." Sin, for its part, is not an act but an "original condition of historicity, of development" (517), insofar as it is the "clutch" (embrayeur) and motor of history, the original imbalance that drives humanity toward the redemption that has been announced; sin is the "indebtedness of existence as such" (518), a condition to which Nancy suggests Heidegger's existential category of guilt might be subordinate.[35] Finally, as the living God, "the Son is the visibility of the Invisible, not in the sense of a god who would appear, but in the sense of an announcement of presence." The life of the living God "presents the person to/in him- or herself in the infinite dimension from him- or herself to him- or herself" [présente la personne à elle-même dans la dimension infinie d'elle-même à elle-même] (519).[36] What is common in all of this is, again, the opening that Nancy says is the very structure of sense itself, "[t]he *Open as such*, the Open of the annunciation [*annonce*], of the project, of history and faith, that, through the living God, is revealed at the heart of Christianity" (519).

FAITH AND THE APORIA OF KNOWLEDGE

For Nancy, as for Žižek, it would appear that the paradox peculiar to one religion constitutes the heart of an epochal thought. In its doctrines of faith, of sin, and of the incarnation, what Christianity reveals is the outline of an opening at the heart of being: faith—the category of "an intimacy that lacks itself, that escapes from itself"; sin—the original imbalance, the indebtedness of existence to others, to those who are not here—like the subject of enunciation it is the clutch (*embrayeur*), as well as the heart, of history, of sense; the living God—attesting to a gap (*béance*) that opens at the heart of identity, the infinite distance from self lying at the heart of the in-itself. For Søren Kierkegaard, this same essence of Christianity might have been captured in the questions posed by his narrator in the introduction to his *Concluding Unscientific Postscript*: "Can a historical point of departure be given for an eternal consciousness; how can such a point of departure be of more than historical interest; can an eternal happiness be built on historical knowledge?" (Kierkegaard, *Concluding* 15). For this narrator, the contradiction between Christianity's temporal and eternal axes, between "world historical" or objective being and lived or subjective existence, creates a challenge for the person of faith that will ultimately become the essence of faith itself.

In the *Philosophical Fragments*, this tension emerges as the incommensurability between the historical and the eternal, between the mediate and the immediate. Although it may sound anti-intuitive to draw a parallel between the eternal and the immediate, the two are in Kierkegaard's view inseparable, as both concepts rely on a negation of time or change, a negation of mediation. The historical, then, is the realm of existence—and indeed "everything that has come into existence is *eo ipso* historical," because by coming into existence it has undergone the kind of change that is incompatible with necessity and hence with the eternal (Kierkegaard, *Fragments* 93). But the historical is also incapable of being grasped in its immediacy: "The historical cannot be given immediately to the senses, since the *elusiveness* of coming into existence is involved in it. The immediate impression of a natural phenomenon or of an event is not the impression of the historical, for the *coming into existence* involved cannot be sensed immediately, but only the immediate presence" (100). Coming into existence is elusive and uncertain because our knowledge of any such moment is intrinsically mediated insofar as it must come to us via a medium, its transmission through time via language, for example. Whereas Kierkegaard argues that sensory perception is immediate and hence incorrigible, as Descartes also held,[37] the moment we take the coming into existence (origin, historical truth) of an object of our sense-certainty as the object of our inquiry, the certainty of our immediate perceptions gives way inexorably to the uncertainty of mediation and, *pace* Hegel, there can be no dialectical synthesis of this contradiction.

It is clear, however, that this limitation applies to more than mere historical knowledge. Since the issue with historicity is mediation, it would seem now impossible to transmit the certainty of sense perception to anything outside the ken of sense perception, and hence impossible to have *communicable* certainty about anything whatsoever. For there to be any such thing as knowledge at all,

> the organ of the historical must have a structure analogous with the historical itself; it must comprise a corresponding somewhat by which it may repeatedly negate in its certainty the uncertainty that corresponds to the uncertainty of coming into existence. . . . Now faith has precisely the required character, for in the certainty of belief [Danish: *Tro*, faith or belief] there is always present a negated uncertainty, in every way corresponding to the uncertainty of coming into existence. (Kierkegaard, *Fragments* 100–101)

The final phrase of this sentence is subject to (at least) two readings, and the choice between the two determines radically different understandings of Kierkegaard's thought. The first reading—call it onto-theological—emphasizes faith as the certainty in and through which the uncertainty of historical coming into being is always present as negated; the second reading—call it deconstructive—emphasizes the certainty of faith as nothing other than the constant presence of the uncertainty of historical coming into being as negated.[38] According to the first reading, the uncertainty of the historical is avoided by faith; according to the second, the uncertainty of the historical produces faith and consequently faith, as a product of uncertainty, underlies all knowledge. Faith, in this second, deconstructive reading, is the aporia of knowledge, the fundamental point of undecidabilty between certainty and uncertainty; it is the name for the knowledge that no knowledge will ever close the gap between the historical and the eternal, between the contingent and the necessary, between the mediate and the immediate.[39]

The conclusion we might initially draw from this second reading is that Kierkegaard's thought leads one not to a theology but to an atheism, insofar as the immediate or eternal can be said not to exist except as an effect of the mediate or historical—hence Sartre's claim that, in David Wood's paraphrase, becoming a Christian and becoming an atheist are structurally equivalent.[40] This conclusion draws further support from Kierkegaard himself, who argues in the *Concluding Unscientific Postscript* that "the eternity of abstraction" is only gained at the cost of "disregarding existence" (313). Nevertheless, such a denial of the immediate as implied by atheism is also impossible, because its logical conclusion (by mere process of elimination) would be to render certain the historical and mediate, practically a contradiction in terms. It would seem, then, that the aporetic structure of faith points to a further aporia between theology and atheism.

Returning to the *Fragments*, "what is this unknown something with which the Reason collides when inspired by its paradoxical passion, with the result of unsettling even man's knowledge of himself? It is the Unknown. It is not a human being, in so far as we know what man is; nor is it any other known thing. So let us call this unknown something: *the God*. It is nothing more than a name we assign to it" (Kierkegaard, *Fragments* 49).[41] The god, then, is what we may call the unknown—not, let us add, the unknown as something positively unknowable, but rather the unknown as the beyond of a constitutive and internal barrier to knowing itself—and faith is what we call the knowledge, the fatally fallible certainty, that no knowledge will ever bridge the gap, pierce the barrier, and render the unknowable transparent.

ETHICS AND ANXIETY

Given this argument, which resembles a negative theology,[42] it would appear that the question of faith is relegated to purely epistemological status, a necessary offshoot of the inherent limitations of the human mind. To draw such a conclusion, however, would be to miss entirely the point of Kierkegaard's irreducible importance for contemporary thought, an importance that derives from his status as thinker of ethics. This claim might seem disingenuous, given that perhaps Kierkegaard's greatest claim to fame is his demotion of the ethical way of life (and before it the aesthetic) in the face of a third, religious mode. But it is precisely the qualities he attributes to the religious, as opposed to the ethical, that point the way to the emergence not of a new ethics, but of another way of thinking about the ethical and its relation to the epochal soul of the Judeo-Christian west.

To begin to trace the emergence of this notion, I will refer to the reading of Genesis with which Kierkegaard begins his study *The Concept of Dread*. What attracts Kierkegaard to this founding text of the Judeo-Christian tradition is the clues it might hold concerning the origin of sin and evil and the nature of temptation. And what he finds there is a profound paradox lying at the heart of Western ethics.

To pick up the story where it most concerns us, God had only just made man and woman. They were fresh, innocent, and like the beasts they knew no shame. And yet Adam and Eve were not entirely like beasts. Unlike the beasts, they could speak. And insofar as they could speak, there were rules to follow. Or, at least, there was one rule. The first time we hear of the existence of a rule, it is in the words of the Serpent, as it asks of Eve, "[d]id God say, 'You shall eat of any tree in the garden'?" Her reply: "God said, 'You shall not eat of the fruit of the tree which is in the midst of the garden, neither shall you touch it, lest you die" (New Oxford Bible, Genesis 2:17).

The story of how Eve is tempted to break this rule, cedes to temptation, and convinces Adam to do the same is supposed to account for how a creature—mankind—created by a perfect and good being arrived at its present situation, so far from all that is perfect and good. This demotion is supposed to have occurred at one fell moment, when one individual was given a choice—and chose poorly. Thus was born sin, thus was born death, thus was born suffering. But let us reflect upon the moment of that choice. A choice is determined as moral by its situation within a moral framework according to which a limit is inscribed within the range of possible options. Choices falling within the limit are morally permissible; those falling outside it are not. Eve's moral framework was provided by the one rule, the prohibition to eat from the tree located at the center of the garden. But is there not another element necessary for making a moral choice? Is it not assumed that one understands the difference between right and wrong, between good and evil? Indeed, in U.S. jurisprudence, while ignorance of the law is not sufficient to exonerate its violator, the ability to distinguish between right and wrong is a necessary condition for criminal liability. For Eve, however, this fundamental knowledge is only available by way of transgression. For it is only the tree, the Serpent tells her, that will give her the knowledge of good and evil, and indeed God later corroborates the Serpent's testimony. This, then, is the paradox of the fall: To have fallen, mankind must have been morally responsible, meaning it must have had knowledge of good and evil; and yet to have such knowledge, to really know what evil is and how it differs from good, mankind must already have fallen.[43]

How are we to reconcile the text of Genesis with the traditional belief that, insofar as the fall is what brings distance between man and God, far from lacking knowledge of good and evil, prelapsarian humans must have had a perfect and all-encompassing knowledge?[44] In fact, there is no contradiction between these two points, because knowledge of good and evil is knowledge that depends on a distinction been perfection and some deprivation of perfection. The knowledge "gained" by eating of the tree, therefore, is not an addition to human knowledge but rather a fundamental subtraction: prior to the fall human being was characterized by perfect transparency; after the fall, by knowledge of good *and* evil, hence opacity, distinction, choice, and desire. Nevertheless, it is clear that the seeds of this knowledge preceded the capture of the knowledge itself, since an Eve inhabiting a perfectly transparent world would not have had any choice to make.

While the founding text of Judeo-Christian culture may nominally account for the presence of evil in God's creation, we cannot fail to note that it is equally and at the same time a parable concerning the nature of desire. Here, among the first written words of a nascent tradition, desire is described not as a natural striving or instinctual extension of human being, but as a dark, conflicted, perhaps even perverse drive, entangled in a troubled relationship with knowledge and prohibition. Without knowledge, Eve could not have been tempted, and could not have sinned. Is it not, then, the knowledge itself and its founding distinction between good and evil that brings with it the desire to transgress in the first place? Is not, in other words, the knowledge of what is good, of what is desirable, coterminous with a drive to contravene, undo, and transgress that very good?

If this is the case, it certainly presents a problem for the philosophical tradition of ethics, a tradition that has been characterized largely by what we might call a kind of ethical realism. In ethical realism thinkers are first compelled to divine an intrinsic nature to mankind, and then on the basis of that nature proceed to derive an ultimate good and a series of prescriptions concerning the attainment of that good. If human nature were also inhabited by a drive to contravene its own sovereign good, this would constitute the breakdown of ethical systems per se, for systems organized around the attainment of the good would ultimately founder on the paradoxical contradiction of their own ends. Such, in short, is the paradox that

Kierkegaard discovers at the heart of Genesis—the paradox, in fact, inherent in the genesis of institutions, insofar as institutionalization presupposes the establishment of a system of prohibitions that is coterminous with the system of knowledge necessary for recognizing those prohibitions. If it is a paradox for a particular religio-ethical order, in other words, it would seem just as much to be a universal paradox of human sociality.

Kierkegaard's approach to the problem is not to attempt to undo the paradox, but rather to disclose what the paradox bears witness to, which is the need to question a fundamental presupposition concerning the original nature of the human, namely, the *innocence* that was lost in the fall: "Innocence is ignorance. This is by no means the pure being of immediacy, but it is ignorance. The fact that ignorance regarded from without seems as though designed to become knowledge is entirely irrelevant to ignorance" (Kierkegaard, *Dread* 34). Innocence, in other words, is ignorance experienced from inside, ignorance ignorant of the knowledge of which it is ignorant, but which nevertheless must exist for there to be ignorance of it. Our mistake is to take for the beginning, the origin, a moment of immediacy or "a perfection one ought to wish to recover" (34), and then to think the original innocence in terms of this immediacy. But when we think, on the contrary, of innocence as ignorance, we see that it is only conceivable within the context of a preceding knowledge that determines it with regard to that knowledge as something unknown. Innocence is the illusion of immediacy that carries within it the kernel of its constitutive mediation; Eve can only be innocent of transgressing the law insofar as her ignorance implies a more fundamental knowledge of good and evil that determines, unbeknownst to her, her desires.

The result of this redefinition of innocence as ignorance is that the bliss we proverbially associate with the latter must be replaced by another experience, namely, dread or anxiety (*angest*). Because the ignorance of innocence is always ignorance of a more fundamental knowledge against which it is defined, the innocent, insofar as his or her existence is concerned, exists in a state of anxiety or apprehensiveness (Chamberlain and Rée 178), an openness to apprehending what is not yet or not necessarily present; an attunement, in other words, to the ever-present *possibility* that at any given moment something other than what is the case now may arise.[45] This anxiety is an apprehensiveness about everything, or indeed about nothing: "But what effect does nothing produce? It begets dread. This is the profound secret of innocence, that at the same time it is dread. Dreamingly the spirit projects its own reality, but this reality is nothing, but this innocence constantly sees nothing outside of it" (Kierkegaard, *Concept* 38, translation modified). The possibility of its own actuality being something other than what it is, a possibility due directly to its ignorance, translates for spirit into a distinction, and hence a knowledge, between actual being and its endless alternatives, a knowledge—inherent in and inseparable from innocence—that is the ground, not the consequence, of sin. The original sinner, in other words, "is none other than innocence itself" (Chamberlain and Rée 178) insofar as it is not immediacy but the ignorance of *constitutive mediation* or, in other words, the fault-line. As regards Genesis, what this reasoning suggests is that the source of the absurd prohibition could not have been external to humankind—could not, in other words, have issued from a God "out there"; possibility, rather, and the sin to which it gives birth, have their origin in language. For "the imperfection of the account, the doubt how it could have occurred to anyone to say to Adam what he cannot understand, is eliminated when one reflects that the speaker is language, and that hence it is Adam himself who speaks" (Kierkegaard, *Concept* 43).[46]

If the ground of sin is ultimately the anxiety that emerges from the knowledge of endless possibility, how is it that sin manifests itself as temptation, as attraction, and not merely as repulsion? "The nature of original sin has often been considered," Kierkegaard writes in his journal, "and yet the principle category has been missing—it is *dread*, that is what really determines it; for dread is a desire for what one fears, a sympathetic antipathy" (Kierkegaard, *Journals* 105). Anxiety is a desire for what one fears because the infinite possibility that is its source threatens the sinner with the eradication of his or her being, while at the same time the sinner sees, in the specter of possibility itself, the shadow of a knowledge not subject to mediation, knowledge of the eternal, the true, the immobile mark determining forever the contours of good and evil.

INFINITE RESPONSIBILITY

The suggestion that sin derives from possibility, which in turn derives from language, presents us with the specter of a sin, and hence a guilt, that is not only original but is also inescapable and infinite. An ethical theory based on such a notion could apparently only produce a concept of responsibility impoverished in its radicality; for if one's responsibility is infinite and infinitely distributed, the impulse to act in any given situation runs the risk of being severely diminished, not to say obliterated. In claiming, for example, that Abraham's willingness to sacrifice his only son illustrates "the most common and everyday experience of responsibility," Derrida derives from another of Kierkegaard's biblical encounters a similar conclusion, namely, that our responsibility for others is infinite:

> The simple concepts of alterity and of singularity constitute the concept of duty as much as that of responsibility. As a result, the concepts of responsibility, of decision, or of duty, are condemned *apriori* to paradox, scandal, and aporia. . . . As soon as I enter into a relation with the other, with the gaze, look, request, love, command, or call of the other, I know that I can respond only by sacrificing ethics, that is, by sacrificing whatever obliges me also to respond in the same way, in the same instant, to all the others. (Derrida, "Whom" 162–63)

The point of Kierkegaard's reading of Genesis 22 is that when Abraham raises his knife to kill Isaac, he abandons the ethical way of life—the order of social ties, familial relations, and interpersonal, universal responsibility—and enters the religious mode, in which one disregards all ethical commands in favor of one's obedience to the absolute other in its incomprehensible absurdity. Derrida's strategy here is to argue that the sacrifice of the ethical is inherent in the very notion of ethical responsibility, because following our responsibility to a given other in one instance necessarily implies neglecting the same responsibility we have to an infinite number of others. The religious, the moment of faith over and above ethical duty, is the aporia of duty in that it marks the point at which the ethical, as the field in which action finds its justification, runs inexorably into the vanishing point of all justification: your acts will all involve a choice; you will try to justify your choices; yet you will eventually act in such a way that there will be no justification for having chosen one way rather than another. "Abraham's hyper ethical sacrifice" bears witness to the underlying moment of unjustifiability in ethics' desire to ground all action in justification.

David Wood has argued that Derrida overstates his point: "If I am walking down the street and interrupt my daily round to help someone bleeding in a ditch I am not 'sacrificing' any other" (Wood 66). The fact that I am on this street and not any other, he adds, is simply a fact of contingency. It is precisely here, however, that we must stress an aspect crucial to both Derrida's and Kierkegaard's demotion of the ethical: what Wood calls contingency, "an essential condition of any life," is the fact of possibility—the fact, as Kierkegaard says in the *Fragments*, "of the suffering of actuality, in which possibilities . . . are shown to be nothing the moment they become actual, since possibilities are *annihilated* by actuality" (Kierkegaard, *Fragments,* trans. Swenson 162). Were the ethical to be properly thought in the exclusive terms of universal, communicable, justificatory practices, the fact of infinite possibility (hence contingency) would constitute a paralytic stumbling block for the system. What Kierkegaard, and through him Derrida, demonstrates is that the very insertion into an ethical system—that is, a system of universally communicable, institutionalized rules of behavior—produces an excess, a noncommunicable, unjustifiable pure act.[47]

For Kierkegaard, the marker of this pure act is faith: "the man who is educated by possibility . . . knows no finite evasion by which he might escape. Now the dread of possibility holds him as its prey, until, it can deliver him saved into the hands of faith. In no other place does he find repose, for every other point of rest is mere chatter, even though in men's eyes it is shrewdness" (Kierkegaard, *Dread* 141, translation modified).[48] Faith is presented here as a salvation from the anxiety of possibility, but it is clear that is has a specific character, for it is contrasted with other resting places that provide no rest, no evasion, insofar as they are "finite" and "mere chatter." What this negative description of those other places tells us is that faith as a resting place from the anxiety of possibility is first, nonfinite, and second, not mere chatter, by which I think we must understand the following: our tendency is to evade the paralysis of infinite responsibility, the anxiety of possibility, by searching for a finite duty within the bounds of the ethical, that is, within the realm of what can be communicated as duty. This means that we intrinsically believe that doing what we ought to do, when such duty is communicable in terms of justificatory practices, saves us from the abyss of anxiety. What Kierkegaard suggests, on the contrary, is that doing so will do absolutely nothing to free us from our self-imposed paralysis because it absolutely fails to confront the radical source of existential anxiety, namely, the fathomless unjustifiability and noncommunicability of our desire.[49]

It is here that Abraham's sacrifice enters the picture. Abraham is not, for Kierkegaard, a model for how we should act; indeed, he could not be such a model, for insofar as we, with the clarity of hindsight from the pedestal of dogma, look back on his action and hold it up as a model, we deprive the act of the very absurdity and unjustifiability that make it a unique act in the first place: "We leave out the distress, the anxiety, the paradox" that Abraham was faced with when making his choice (Kierkegaard, *Fear* 65). What Abraham indicates, for Kierkegaard, is that the aporetic structure of the particular individual's existence within the universal, hence within the ethical realm, "cannot be mediated, for all mediation takes place only by virtue of the universal; it is and remains for all eternity a paradox, impervious to thought. And yet faith is this paradox, or else . . . faith has never existed simply because it has always existed, or else Abraham is lost" (56).

The repetition of this final phrase throughout the essay invites us to pause and consider its importance. Abraham only is, only exists for us, because faith is this paradox. The alternative is that faith is not this paradox and is therefore something else, namely, something subject to mediation by the universal, in which case it has always existed (been communicated, made an example of) and hence has, in fact, never *existed*—has never, that is, come into being as a pure act in its noncommunicability and unjustifiability. What is crucial about Abraham's act is not the horrible nature of God's command but, as Derrida has also stressed, that it cannot be put into words, cannot be explained, either to Abraham's family or to us, else faith has never existed and Abraham is lost. The act is so horrible precisely in that it remains incomprehensible, so that an ethical thinker like Kant is forced to say, when faced with it, that the only thing one can be certain of is that the apparition is not God, "for if the voice commands him to do something contrary to the moral law, then no matter how majestic the apparition may be, and no matter how it may seem to surpass the whole of nature, he must consider it an illusion" (Kant, *Conflict* 115).

KIERKEGAARD AND KANT

What, then, in ethical terms, is the status of this act? If it is an illustration of another mode of being, one that outstrips the ethical, is it not then de facto an example to be followed? Is there not an implicit ethics in this "hyper-ethical" act? To address this question it may be of use to place Kierkegaard's notion of the religious way of being alongside the Kantian notion of the ethical: are the two in radical opposition, as Kierkegaard might seem to imply through his terminology; or do they share a similar fundamental structure? It is certainly not unreasonable to claim to discern profound similarities between Kant's and Kierkegaard's thought. As Paul Ricoeur has pointed out, not only can Kierkegaard be convincingly classified within the post-Hegelian "return to Kant" of post-1840 Germany, a more crucial resonance emerges from the fact that "the philosophical function of 'paradox' in Kierkegaard is closely parallel to that of 'limits' in Kant" (Ricoeur 16).[50] Indeed, as far as the Kantian ethical and the Kierkegaardian religious are concerned, the similarity would lie in the notion that the source of the impulse to act (in an ethical or religious way) comes from beyond a limit that functions as a kind of absolute in relation to normal action. Normal or nonethical action for Kant consists of actions that one undertakes according to one's inclinations, which are pathological in that the will is passively determined and therefore not free. For an action to be free, and hence unconditioned, its source of motivation must come from beyond the realm of inclination. But the individual's knowledge that his or her actions are truly unconditioned remains at all times a negative knowledge: only when our actions contradict our desires do we have evidence that we are acting out of duty, but even then Kant gives us to understand that we cannot be entirely sure that we are acting out of duty as opposed to merely in conformity with it.[51] At the very least, the source of our motivation must remain veiled in secrecy to others if not also to ourselves, for were we to act in an ethical way while communicating as much to others, the possibility would clearly arise that our real motivation was the desire to be admired for our actions, an obviously pathological motivation.[52]

It would seem, then, that in the case of Kant's ethical theory, the source of truly ethical motivation is marked by an epistemological limit. Which makes sense, because the freedom that must be the source of ethical action is precisely what lies beyond the ken of human knowledge, which is limited to the phenomenal realm in which freedom is only felt as an effect.[53] In a similar vein we can note that Kierkegaard's notion of the religious departure from the ethical has precisely this character of relation to an epistemological limit. What ultimately sets Abraham's action apart from any possible reconciliation with the realm of ethical, and hence universal, justification, is that Abraham cannot speak. "The relief provided by speaking is that it translates me into the universal" (Kierkegaard, *Fear* 113), says Kierkegaard, and that is precisely what Abraham cannot do. For Abraham's act to be properly religious, an act of faith, a "hyper-ethical" act, it must remain noncommunicable and unjustifiable. In this way, Kierkegaard's religious and Kant's ethical can be said to be structural analogues: for both define the source of the highest form of action as emerging from beyond an absolute limit, a limit marked only by its inaccessibility to human knowledge.

This argument, of course, overlooks a fundamental distinction, one that both philosophers would instantly point out: whereas, as Derrida notes, "Kant explains that to act morally is to act 'out of duty' and not 'by conforming to duty' . . . Kierkegaard sees acting 'out of duty,' in the universalizable sense of the law, as a dereliction of one's absolute duty" (Derrida,

"Whom" 159). The key to this distinction is Kant's own insistence on the universality of reason. His assumption that humans share an identical core of reason allows him to argue that the renunciation of self-serving interests translates automatically into actions that are in conformity with reason. Kierkegaard's implicit critique is that insofar as duty is determined as a function of universality, then "the ethical is the temptation" (Kierkegaard, *Fear* 115; also qtd. in Derrida, "Whom" 157), an inclination, namely, to turn away in horror from the utterly incommunicable nature of the real ethical—now termed religious—impulse. Kant, in other words, gets it right when he figures the ethical as an impulse emerging from beyond the limits of knowledge; he fails when he falls short of realizing the implications of this insight, and tries, impossibly, to make this impulse into an index of universality.

If such a characterization is accurate, then it would seem to open Kierkegaard to a series of attacks from a politico-ethical perspective. Richard Rorty, for example, has included Kierkegaard along with Nietzsche and Heidegger as thinkers who are fine for reading in the privacy of one's home, but are recipes for disaster once applied to social situations.[54] Lévinas finds that the sort of existence advanced by Kierkegaard, one "whose inwardness exceeds exteriority and cannot be contained by it . . . participates in the violence of the modern world, with its cult of Passion and Fury" (Lévinas, "Existence" 30). Indeed, as we discussed in Chapter 2, Hannah Arendt famously criticized Eichmann's misappropriation of Kantian ethics by saying, "[m]any Germans and many Nazi's, probably an overwhelming majority of them, must have been tempted *not* to murder, *not* to rob, *not* to let their neighbors go off to their doom . . . and not to become accomplices in all these crimes by benefiting from them. But, God knows, they had learned how to resist temptation" (Arendt 150). Is it not then at least as pertinent to say of Kierkegaard—who here seems to praise turning one's back on all familial and social ties in order to commit the most atrocious act of violence—that his is a philosophy of the most irresponsible sort?

In the case of Kant, as Arendt makes clear, Eichmann misreads him egregiously, placing at the source of the will not, as Kant insists, pure universality condensed into the formula of the categorical imperative, but rather the entirely pathological inclination of one man, the Führer. In a similar way, the politico-ethical critique of Kierkegaard introduces a term that is anathema to Kierkegaard's purpose and, indeed, exactly the issue he is trying to exclude: to say that Kierkegaard is *justifying* the worst excesses of human violence is to forget that what Kierkegaard underlines in his analysis of Abraham is precisely that nothing can justify his action. Indeed, what Kierkegaard is presenting here is precisely an intensification of Arendt's critique. Arendt, as it were, let Kant off the hook: she has Eichmann misreading Kant by putting the Führer in the place of the will. According to Kierkegaard, however, that will always be a potentiality, not to say a necessity, as long as the ethical order is thought of as being universal, and hence communicable; the religious, and hence the true ethical, is radically incommunicable and will always be perceived as horror from the universal or the social.[55]

To the extent that Kierkegaard can be read as condoning Abraham's act from the comfort of hindsight, he is guilty of precisely the same error. Thus, when he says of Abraham, "[a]nd yet what did he achieve? He remained true to his love. But anyone who loves God needs no tears, no admiration; he forgets the suffering in the love. Indeed, so completely has he forgotten it that there would not be the slightest trace of his suffering left if God himself did not remember it, for he sees in secret, and recognizes distress and counts the tears and forgets nothing" (Kierkegaard, *Fear* 120), the secret is out and Abraham is justified; but then Kierkegaard is lost.[56] So we must hold Kierkegaard to a much more difficult truth, one to which he himself attests: "The tragic hero, who is the favorite of ethics, is the purely human; him I can understand, and all his undertakings are out in the open. If I go further, I always run up against the paradox, the divine and the demonic, for silence is both" (Kierkegaard, *Fear* 88).[57]

OF WHICH WE CANNOT SPEAK

From the depth of his mistrust, Lévinas's greatest praise for Kierkegaard is reserved for his perception of "an impossibility within the very *capacity to speak* that was the achievement of totalizing thought" (Lévinas, "Existence" 28). By betraying this impossibility and speaking of Abraham's act as though to justify it before the court of posterity, Kierkegaard contradicts his own insight and repeats the fundamental error of Kantian ethics, painting over the highest moment of human pathological ecstasy with the speech of universal reason.[58] It is only a reading that ignores this contradiction that will, in the end, embrace the onto-theological interpretation of faith and thus dismiss Kierkegaard as a merely religious thinker, a dismissal that seems, in such contradictory moments, to be in harmony with Kierkegaard's own understanding of his work.[59]

What we learn if we stay attuned to the driving force of Kierkegaard's thought, on the contrary, is that, in Paul Ricoeur's words, "singularity is constantly regenerated at the margins of discourse" (21), and that this singularity, which is the heart of existence, is the "indivisible remainder" (Žižek, *Indivisible*) of the paradox that the paradox of mediation "cannot be mediated" (Kierkegaard, *Fear* 56). Singularity—and here we have to assimilate the term to its current use by thinkers such as Jean-Luc Nancy—is just this: that existence is mediation; that mediation cannot be thought outside of a relation with the immediate; and that this paradoxical relation itself is incapable of mediation, hence universalization, into communicable, justificatory practices. In David Wood's words, "If the self is a relation that relates itself to itself through the medium of its relation to the infinite [immediate], then this self-relation will never cease to be problematic" (Wood 72).

If the problematic nature of this singularity is, as I have implicitly been arguing, at the heart of the distension that Nancy claimed was simultaneously deconstructive and Christian, to find the same problematic inscribed at the heart of one of modernity's prototypical discourses, namely psychoanalysis, might point in the direction of another epochal reconciliation. If, in other words, with the return of the religious in philosophy we are standing at the brink of the zone of indistinction between philosophy and religion, is it not also the case that the "Christianization of deconstruction" discloses the outline of yet another zone of indistinction, namely, that bridging the long-embattled discourses of deconstruction and psychoanalysis?

This is the convergence I have tried to demonstrate in this chapter, by examining how deconstruction and psychoanalysis share an openness or sensitivity to the very impasse of knowledge that is attested to by the resurgence of the theological in philosophical discourse. In this light, the deconstructive insight that animates the philosophical reading of Kierkegaard's text cannot fail to find there, in the resistance to mediation that the paradox of mediation poses, the aporetic grounding of the distinction each "practice"—deconstruction, psychoanalysis—holds dear. For, to put it in simple terms, if deconstruction has always emphasized the unlimited nature of mediation, its endless dissemination, and reproached psychoanalysis for the pretension with which it authorizes certain endpoints to this cascade;[60] and if psychoanalysis has insisted on the inexorability of the signifying cut, of the real as that which always returns to the same place, all the while shrugging off deconstruction as being lost in flights of fantasy[61]—then Kierkegaard's refrain, that the paradox of mediation cannot be mediated, discloses that in their very opposition each discourse displays the truth of the other. For the paradox of mediation is precisely that it is endless, pure dissemination, despite its dependence on the immediate; and yet it is precisely this paradox that is the ultimate endpoint, the grounding cut, the abyss that cannot, under any circumstances, be mediated.[62]

This is why we should not be surprised by the curious digressions Kierkegaard presents in the context of Johannes de Silencio's various attempts to reconstruct Abraham's experience in ways that make sense, or could be communicable. In each case a brief paragraph is inserted in which the narrator implicitly compares that attempt to a different strategy for weaning a child from the breast. Thus the Abraham who claims to Isaac, in raising his hand to slay him, that this is his own desire and not God's—for "it is better that he believes me a monster than that he should lose faith in you"—is juxtaposed to the mother who blackens her breast, to which the narrator adds, "[h]ow fortunate the one who did not need more terrible means to wean the child" (Kierkegaard, *Fear* 11). And so the refrain continues after each example, leaving no doubt that what is at issue is nothing other than the fundamental inadequacy of each method of weaning to fully account for, cover up, justify, or universalize what for the child is an incomprehensibly terrible experience of loss. In the same way, Johannes de Silencio's various versions of Abraham can never entirely account for and hence communicate the reason for his act.

Is it not precisely here, however, where the deconstructivist critic will pounce, triumphantly pointing to the reductive tendencies of the psychoanalytically inclined, who will always, no matter the particularities of the case at hand, locate the origin of the drive for meaning in the mother's body or in some part, such as the original lost object, the breast?[63] To the contrary: here the crucial move is precisely the opposite one—the impossibility of completely weaning the child, the persistence of a traumatic remainder to any process of separation, and so forth, is not the *meaning* of Johannes de Silencio's text, nor it is the answer or explanation to the impossibility of communicating Abraham's speech. For the child is a victim not of "nature" *but of deconstruction*. It is not the breast or the mother's body he or she misses, but rather the assurance of an ultimate explanation, the solidity of signification, an answer that will ground his or her endless quest for self-knowledge.[64] The traumatic kernel at the heart of our fantasy constructions, the impossible real that always returns, all of these psychoanalytic formulations that make deconstructivists apoplectic are nothing other than failed attempts to signify the traumatic truth that is nothing other than deconstruction itself, the truth that Kierkegaard found at the heart of Christianity, the truth around which modernity is distended to the point of breaking—the truth, namely, that the paradox of mediation can never be mediated. This paradox—which can be rephrased as holding that there is no desire prior to its institutionalization, and that this primordial institutionalization is radically resistant to any attempt to rationalize, control, or institutionalize it—is the truth of the ethical.

4

Sexual Difference and the Ethics of Duplicity

THE NOTION OF FAULT traces a line, the fault-line formed by the history of those institutionalizations that, in marking the limits of acceptability and desirability, give shape to the self and the drives that undergird it. Historical and socially defined, the fault-line is relentlessly pathological, born of the residues of the choices and chances that particularize a life, while simultaneously defining the very essence of pathology: *pathos*, passion that is at once pleasure and suffering. The fault-line separates and hence binds what we want and what we cannot want, what we dream will complete us and what we fear will deprive us of our very existence. It is the border that defines our selves, distinguishing us from otherness and hence constituting our identity, while simultaneously withholding that very otherness in whose grasp lies the elusive promise of our fulfillment. This fault-line is a topological characterization of the ethical as it has come to the fore in the previous three chapters: as drivenness and the somatic foundations of institutionalization; as the reality principle and the force of *das Ding*; and as the theological impasse that emerges in such atheisms as psychoanalysis and deconstruction alike. There remains, however, another realm whose relation to the ethical fault-line has yet to be elucidated.

Just as the clinical phenomenon of perversion has been largely associated with men,[1] the perversity of ethics and the impasse it provokes imply a series of philosophical presuppositions whose subjective structure is, from a psychoanalytic perspective, decidedly male. If this is the case, it suggests at least the possibility that an ethics based on another, perhaps female subjective structure, could provide a viable alternative to a tradition many argue is demonstrably bankrupt. In a certain, obvious sense, this is the ethical claim of feminisms in general, regardless of their attitude toward psycho-analysis. In a more specific sense, feminist thinkers have often been the forerunners in embracing an alternative ethical tradition that raises, for ex-ample, the respect for otherness above respect for such concepts as duty, the law, the right, or the greatest good. In his reading of *Antigone*, as we saw in Chapter 2, Lacan at times seemed to be suggesting as much, and in the early 1970s he returned to the themes of his seminar on ethics in order to delve into the problem of sexual difference.

In the pages that follow I will present a theory about sexual difference that derives from the one Lacan developed in the 1970s.[2] I will attempt to show not only how this theory contains within it a cultural history of sex-ual difference, but also how much of contemporary gender studies, from the thinkers least likely to be familiar with Lacanian works to the more the-oretically sophisticated critiques of his ideas, are all imbued, to some ex-tent, with the content of that thought. The point, however, is neither to praise nor bury Lacan but to acknowledge in the words of his acolytes as much as his detractors the existence of a common thread of sexual differ-ence pointing to a bifurcation in thought at the most fundamental level, one that touches or underlies our orientation in the world, the way the world discloses itself—in Heidegger's parlance, the way it "worlds."

Philosophy, I will argue, can be broadly divided between those thoughts or aspects of thought that have seen only one of these orientations and those thoughts or aspects of thought that have recognized another way—and perhaps opted for it. We will call these orientations "male" philosophy and "female" philosophy, respectively; and the fact that the vast majority of history's philosophers have been anatomically male goes a long way, but perhaps not the whole way, to explaining why male philosophy has for so long held sway. The factor that distinguishes male from female philosophy is their relation to, and their orientation regarding the fault-line. To be "man" or to be "woman"[3] is, more than a fact of nature or an imposition of culture, a sort of "choice" on which our very subjectivity, our very ability to choose, has always been founded. The aim of this chapter is to explore the ethical possibilities suggested by the distinction between male and fe-male philosophy, and to argue for the import of female philosophy in thinking the fundamental impasse of ethics.[4] But it is also this chapter's task to sound a note of caution; for to claim a solution to the perversity of ethics is to claim to have bridged the ethical fault-line, which has been the fantasy, as inevitable as it is insatiable, of all ethical systems to date.

NATURE, NURTURE, NIETZSCHE?

Perhaps the first temptation we need to avoid is that of falling into the tired dilemma of determining whether sexual difference is a natural (and hence essential) attribute or one imposed by cultural, and hence contingent, circumstances. Although Freud's "pseudoscience" was often aligned (or maligned) by its detractors with the side of biological determinism because of Freud's notorious claim that "anatomy is destiny" (McElvaine 19), contemporary psychoanalysis in its Lacanian and object-relations form, and insofar as it has been appropriated by feminism, has increasingly been seen as relying on and promoting the premises of cultural determinism (Nadeau 109, 115). This latter belief has accompanied the growing backlash of science against its perceived attackers in the humanistic disciplines and social sciences, who, it is claimed, are willing to do away with both the notion of objective truth and the value of material evidence in order to shore up a set of political goals that would be better served by retaining those notions and values.[5] The defenders of science feel besieged on both sides: religious conservatives and "liberal" intellectuals have unwittingly joined forces against them, urged on by their mutual fear of the specter of biological determinism—for the former our biological nature robs God of his power; for the latter it robs us of our freedom (McElvaine 18). Hence both sides have put their belief in the way things ought to be over the ways things in fact are, their politics over the truth.

These fears are, to say the least, exaggerated. While it is true that Americans are generally a highly religious people, one where more than half of those polled are likely to admit that the idea of the creation of the world by God corresponds to their personal belief system,[6] apparently a majority of these same people are willing to support or tolerate the teaching of evolution in school. School boards like the one in Kansas that imposed a creationist curriculum tend to be few and far between, and tend to find their way to power via stealth, not popularity. On the other side, the threat is practically nonexistent. Although it is true that most humanistic intellectuals and social scientists have weighed and continue to weigh cultural factors more heavily than biological ones when thinking about the causes of human behavior, this hardly constitutes a ground-swell of public opinion. First, such intellectuals constitute the tiniest minority of a distinctly anti-intellectual public; second, it is understandable that they might emphasize cultural factors, given that their field of inquiry is, as it turns out, culture;

and finally, they are making and defending these claims in a zeitgeist that is, contrary to the claims of supposedly besieged scientists, overwhelmingly biologistic. From weekly news magazines to PBS documentaries, the organs of popularized scientific information continue to hammer the message home that humans, in their most personal, emotional, and seemingly spiritual worlds, are nothing but the result of genetic hardwiring.[7]

Given this picture of the current debates concerning the proper sphere for inquiries into human nature, I would like to make the following series of points: (1) as many intelligent people have been arguing recently, the question of nature versus nurture is more often than not a pointless one.[8] Whereas both physical traits and social expectations, for instance, enter into the identity one assumes as boy or girl—and furthermore as a racial identity, as being desired sexually and socially or relatively neglected, and so forth—neither explains entirely the emotional, intellectual, and hence subjective experience of *being* a sexuated being. *Of course* physicalist phenomenologies must be expressed in the categories presupposed by culture; *of course* the inhabiting of cultural categories can only be experienced by organic beings with physical attributes—either side of the debate can trump the other with its negative thesis, but no theory or adequate description of sexual difference can result therefrom. (2) Given a situation in which both biological (or in this case evolutionary) and cultural factors can be plausibly argued as playing a causal role in the determination of sex traits, there is no reason to believe that one causal theory must be true at the expense of the other. Nevertheless, since traits determined by evolution are selected for over vast periods of time and tend to result in species-wide characteristics, whereas culturally determined traits can change at lightning speed (think of fashions and their associated desires), traits that manifest a high rate of variability between individuals are probably better, albeit not exclusively, explained with reference to cultural factors.[9] (3) When defenders of biological and cultural deterministic positions face off, the dispute invariably concerns questions of causality; but questions of causality are notoriously indeterminate. For instance, when Nadeau ridicules social theories of sexual difference by presenting physical evidence that the female and male brain have been shown to process information differently under PET and MRI analysis, he assumes that, since biology obviously underlies the superstructure of culture, manifest behavioral differences must be an effect of these physiological differences (Nadeau 12). As any philosopher will tell you, however, the assumption that correlated occurrences must have a causal relation is one of the oldest fallacies in the book. Since we know that the brain and its billions of synaptic connections is a fabulously resilient and flexible organ, it is not out of the realm of possibility that men's and women's brains alter their functioning due to fundamentally different socialization processes (for example, it is well documented that brains that have undergone damage are capable of "rewiring" themselves so that healthy portions can help compensate for the functions of damaged portions).[10] Indeed, if physical brain structures were functionally determinate and entirely innate, how could we explain the fact that there are anatomical males who behave in statistically female ways, and vice versa? (4) Finally, and most pertinently, psychoanalysis is not in the causal determinacy business to begin with. In this sense it shares in the philosophical heredity exemplified by Freud's elder and contemporary, Friedrich Nietzsche, which holds that a fundamental part of human nature is to create illusory environments and believe deeply in them.[11] To analyze human beings outside of or in disregard of the fantasy lives we have created for ourselves is like turning out the light in order to analyze without interference the phenomenon of color. Biological, anthropological, historical, and any other number of discourses across a wide range of disciplines, precisely because they trace the causal links that constitute the human present, may add to the understanding of human beings as objective *presences* in the world; nevertheless, as Martin Heidegger argued, the knowledge they thereby provide will add little to the fundamental existential description of how humans *are* in the world (Heidegger, *Being and Time* 44).

Because of this focus, as Charles Shepherdson has recently argued, one of the often unrecognized virtues of psychoanalysis from it inception has been its ability, indeed its necessity, to think outside of the nature/nurture dichotomy (Shepherdson, *Vital* 3).[12] As concerns the question of sexual difference, Lacan's interpretation of the Freudian canon avoids objectively describing sexed beings via either their physical or cultural attributes, aiming, instead, to explore the disclosure of a world as sexed, how one experiences being in a world where there can be no one to offer that final description, but rather where the attempt to recount experience in the singular always leads to the fact of another. Yes, the Lacanian notion of sexual difference exhibits the character of logic, and would hence seem to involve factors unrelated to the specificity of the human body. Nevertheless, the emphasis of this approach is not on how an objective situation came about, or on what factors contributed to its development, but rather on what is it like to be like that—and hence, perhaps, on how I might be *other* than I am.

SEXUATION

That sexual difference refers in Lacan's work to an orientation toward the signifier should not be taken as a code for "everything, sex included, is language," merely another version of social constructivism. As speaking beings, rather, we come into our sexual identities through a process that hermeneutics refers to as interpretation, in the sense that we assume roles, practice identities, speak sentences, believe truths, and so forth, in ways that necessarily presuppose a meaningful background or foundation to those roles, identities, sentences, and beliefs. Every one of our "active" assumptions, in all senses of the word, takes place in the context of and itself assumes the knowledge of a whole series of "passive" interpretations that take place for us or through us. At no time in this process do we cease to be sentient, embodied beings, just as at no point does our sentient embodiedness occur in a way that falls entirely outside the telescoping frameworks of interpretation that do not determine, but rather contextualize or house, the contours of our being.

The biological normativity of two sexes provides a meaningful backdrop that, in its perpetual regress of interpretation, is not permitted to converge upon a single, solid floor of reality, as Monique Wittig has argued it should,[13] but rather diverges along what Lacan will call the two "slopes" of sexual difference.[14] Everywhere we look, the world is rent by sexual difference, a discovery that, experienced subjectively, resolves itself into an irresolvable question, one parallel to the question of origins and the question of the end: what is the nature of those who are other than I? The fact that there are two sexes in which this question is posed—and hence two answers—but only one matrix determining the nature of the answer (one language, one authorized symbolic order, one system of meaning encompassing the quests of two sexes—patriarchy) produces a fundamental dissymmetry between the subjective structures of the sexes, between the basic modes the sexes have of interacting with others and producing meaning.[15]

The specific nature of sexual dissymmetry has to do with the matrix of meaning into which both positions are "thrown": this matrix is the order of signifiers, the symbolic order, which, for the purposes of the current discussion, we might figure as a universal set. It is a set because it is composed of elements; it is universal because it must account for all meaning. The elements of this set interact within a potentially endless combinatory, through which they can function, for example, as a representational mechanism. Within the representational set, elements stand in for other elements and themselves become sets. Insofar as representation is at issue, the combinatory may assign one element, one signifier, to stand in for—to represent—the entirety of the representational mechanism, or the set of sets. At this point the set of elements becomes an apparently paradoxical *set of all sets that includes itself.*

The fact that natural languages potentially constitute such sets is attested to by the liar's paradox,[16] or the fallacy of self-refutation, which, as Barbara Herrnstein-Smith puts it, is better termed self-exemplification (Herrnstein-Smith 113). The basic form of this paradox, distributed historically into any number of iterations, is that the speaker nullifies his or her ability to distinguish the truth from the falsity of a statement by making the enunciation of that statement part of the statement itself. Its most simple and classical formulation, "I am lying," can be judged neither true or false, because its truth implies its falsity and vice versa. In the version of this paradox presented by Cervantes, for example, Sancho "solves" the riddle by mandating that the enunciator be cut in two, or rather, because that sentence seemed too brutal, that he be released for want of a better solution (Cervantes 410–11). Sancho's judgment in turn prefigures the conclusion that Lacan draws from the very existence of the paradox, namely, that there is no paradox as long as we take into consideration the split at the level of enunciation; the subject of enunciation can only ever speak of the subject of the utterance, not self-identically of itself: "It is quite clear that the *I am lying*, despite its paradox, is perfectly valid. Indeed, the *I* of the enunciation is not the same as the *I* of the statement, that is to say the shifter which, in the statement, designates him" (Lacan, *XI* 139). This distinction is essentially the same as the one drawn by Herrnstein-Smith when she accuses the "objectivist" rejection of "relativism" as resting on a fallacy: it is not his or her own use of "true" the relativist is denying when denying the objective validity of truth claims, but rather the objectivist's use of the word, precisely a use that collapses the difference between enunciation and utterance and implicitly believes it is even possible to fall into such a contradiction. As Lisa Block de Behar has argued, this "paradox of paradoxes" that is the tripping stone of self-reflexive utterances lies at the very heart of language (Block de Behar 108) and can only be explained on the basis of language's structure as a set of all sets including itself.

When a speaker attempts to make a *totalizing* statement (e.g., a statement that not only applies the universal categories of speech like truth and falsity to a delimited set of circumstances, but also attempts to incorporate the position of the enunciation of those universal categories)[17] he or she thereby constitutes the set of all elements as a whole, but only at the implicit price of excluding the point of enunciation (e.g., all truth statements are relative to time and space [except this one]). It is thus that in an objectivist (to use Herrnstein-Smith's vocabulary) or realist (to use a more common philosophical vocabulary) world, the relativist position is hopelessly self-refuting; it must use different standards to judge the truth value of other enunciations than it does to judge its own. What the realist position fails to take into account, however, is that the exclusion of the enunciator is inherent in *any* attempt to make *totalizing* statements. Thus, any attempt to speak of the whole excludes itself from the whole, or, to begin to adopt the idiom of Lacanian sexuation theory, all are subject to the function Φ only insofar as there is one that is excluded from the function Φ.

There is, however, another way of making statements using the set of all sets including itself that is language. In this other way, the enunciator does not exclude herself or anyone else from the purview of the utterance, but rather speaks integrally without totalizing. Hence, all truth statements are relative to space and time, including this one; put another way, no statement can claim to characterize a totality, including this one. To reduce this formulation to an axiomatic form parallel to the one above: to not attempt to speak of the whole does not require an exclusion from the whole; or not all are subject to the function Φ and no one is excluded from the function Φ.

These two statements correspond in turn to two ways of figuring or imagining the set of all sets. In the first case the set is imagined to have a distinct border delineating the all. Implicitly, of course, there is a position outside of that border that allows for its very enunciation—that allows, in fact, for the existence of a border. For what is a border without an outside?[18] In the second case the set must be imagined as not having a border, as being, in the mathematician Riemann's terms, finite but boundless, a space that requires multidimensional, non-Euclidean geometry in order to be described.[19] The former is what we could call a transcendentalist position, in that the coherence of the whole is always necessarily guaranteed by the exclusion of a central term; the latter is the immanentist position, in that, while refusing to speak of totalities, there is no position excluded from it.[20] The former has provided the basic form for philosophy since Plato; the latter has been the purview of a few scattered, relatively marginalized thinkers who have only recently gained in stature under the aegis of philosophers like Heidegger and Deleuze. It is Lacan's startling insight that this difference is itself an ontological one, and one, moreover, that corresponds to sexual difference.

What can it mean, then, for an apparently logical distinction to have an ontological status, and for that status to correspond to sexual difference? The distinction is ontological because, to put it in Heideggerian terms, it functions at the level of the disclosure of being that occurs through interpretation; there is, in other words, no level at which the circuit of references (Heidegger, *Being and Time* 73) in which human subjects find themselves does not ultimately diverge into two modes of orientation vis-à-vis the set of all sets that is language. This ontological distinction corresponds to sexual difference because humans, for reasons we will explore below, "choose"—or find themselves retroactively to have chosen, or are chosen by—one or the other of these orientations toward the signifier as a function of their identification with one or another of the two biologically normative sexes. That there are gender identities that do not fall neatly within the two socially accepted categories is not in dispute (Magnus Hirschfeld claimed to have identified literally millions of different genders)[21]; the fact that there need be intergender advocacy groups for those born with ambiguous genitalia is merely evidence for the pervasiveness of the compulsion to sexual bifurcation.[22] Humans are required by their social habitus to choose between two biologically marked identities, and the choice results in a different ontological ground for each sex. Whereas this ground cannot be said to determine a subject's choices, desires, specific freedoms, or ways of thinking or using language at an individual level, it does manifest itself in larger, socially mappable forms, which have been recorded in statistical studies and are also at work in the banalities of gender stereotyping. Moreover, to say that being male and being female involve different ontological grounds also does not imply that men and women cannot have fundamentally similar experiences in many or most aspects of their daily lives; it means, rather, that they will tend to have a different orientation vis-à-vis the ethical fault-line that undergirds and orients desire. Therefore, although an ontological ground can never determine the outcome of a specific characteristic, personality trait, or even mode of experiencing, what it can and does do is establish the directionality, or the conditions of possibility, of ways of experiencing. As I shall argue in the pages that follow, this is the reason why psychoanalysts, new age therapists, conservative gender relations counselors, and engaged feminists often end up speaking similar languages—if only to advocate radically divergent ends—when they speak about gender difference.

IS NOT-ALL REALLY LESS THAN ALL?

Lacan's thought has come under heavy fire from feminists for its doctrine of woman as not-all, and for the claim, presented by Lacan in his seminar of 1973–74, that ~~Woman~~ does not exist (XX 7). While it is not at all my intention to praise or bury Lacan on the basis of his feminist credentials as exhibited on the level of his enunciation, it is precisely in the not-all of his utterance that we can begin to seek the fundamental difference of his theory of the sexes and its relation to the ethical. When I stated the two modes of logical orientation around the signifier above, I also put them into a quasi-algebraic form. These algebraic formulae are equivalent to the formulae of sexuation from the upper half of the famous graph of sexuation that Lacan presented in his seminar.[23] Let us repeat them here, now in the form that Lacan uttered them:

> We'll start with the four propositional formulas at the top of the table, two of which lie to the left, the other two to the right. Every speaking being situates itself on one side or the other. On the left side, the lower line—$\forall x \Phi x$—indicates that it is through the phallic function that man as a whole acquires his inscription, with the proviso that this function is limited due to the existence of an x by which the function Φx is negated: $\exists x\, \overline{\Phi} x$. That is what is known as the father function—whereby we find, via negation, the proposition $\overline{\Phi} x$, which grounds the operativity of what makes up for the sexual relation with castration, insofar as that relation is in no way inscribable. The whole here is thus based on the exception posited as the end point, that is, on that which altogether negates Φx. (Lacan, XX 79–80)

$\forall x \Phi x$: all x are submitted to the function Φ, provided that $\exists x\, \overline{\Phi} x$: there is at least one x that is not submitted to the function Φ. The latter formula, the formula of exclusion, is referred to by Lacan as the father function, and the function Φ is what he calls castration. Recall that I associated this formula with the logic of totalization, and claimed that it was implicit in any attempt to make such a statement that the position of enunciation be excluded from the circumscribed totality. The circumscription of a totality is another way of stating the Lacanian notion of castration: constraint of any kind on the exercise of power, of knowledge; the limit designating what can be known from what cannot be known, what can be said from what cannot be said. That limit is coterminous with a name, the name of the father—of the ultimate father, for example, the name that in the religion of the Old Testament could not be pronounced. This name refers to another function, namely, that of the one who is excluded and whose exclusion

makes operative the limit, castration, or circumscription of totality. This
limit, circumscribed totality, or castration is what makes up for the sexual
relationship, which is in no way inscribable.[24] The sexual relation is not inscribable because to inscribe it would be to know it, and to know it would
mean to be born outside of sexual difference, to have a direct access to the
kind of Being that Wittig speaks of. It would also mean, of course, to speak
from a position of full knowledge, in which the being of one's enunciation
always coincided with the subject of one's utterances, from which one
would never be excluded from the totalizing statements one makes about
reality. When one speaks as a man, according to Lacan, one speaks from
this position and forgets or represses the act of exclusion that enables one's
speech.

"On the other side," Lacan continues,

> you have the inscription of the woman portion of speaking beings. Any speak-
> ing being whatsoever, as is expressly formulated in Freudian theory, whether
> provided with the attributes of masculinity—attributes that remain to be de-
> termined—or not, is allowed to inscribe itself in this part. If it inscribes itself
> there, it will not allow for any universality—it will be a not-whole [not-all], in-
> sofar as it has the choice of positing itself in Φx or of not being of it. (Lacan,
> XX 80)[25]

$\overline{\forall}x\Phi x$: or not all are submitted to function Φ, provided that $\overline{\exists}x\ \overline{\Phi}x$: there
is no one who is excluded from function Φ. Not all are submitted because,
from this enunciative position, there is no *all* to speak of; a totality cannot
be circumscribed; it will not, as Lacan puts it, allow for universality. The
impossibility of saying it all from this position is not to be grasped as a prohibition, but rather as an ever-receding horizon, the flux and transformations of a world that resists totalization.

To speak from this position is not to deny the possibility of truth. Lacan
himself often tries to speak from this position, such as when he says, at the
outset of *Télévision*, "I always speak the truth. Not all though, one can't say
it all. To say it all is impossible, materially: the words come up short. It is,
in fact, by way of this impossible, that truth touches the real" (9). Utterances from this position, female utterances, deploy pragmatic and localized
truths, truths that do not claim, for they could not, a position outside of
discourse from which to hold judgment over such a thing as "the whole
truth."[26] Female utterances also do not necessarily function in reference to
single, central terms whose own liability is denied, whose essence is somehow reified or naturalized into permanent, stable entities outside of a given
field of relations. Hence "justice" or "liberty" and "truth" are not, in female

utterances, held up as ideal and unchanging forms against which the flux of existence is measured, but are rather used in minor, less dramatic, and more contextually specific ways.

So far in this presentation I have been intentionally vague about whether "female utterances" is to be understood as designating the actual speech of real, existing women, or whether it refers exclusively to a philosophical position. Although my goal is to map out the notion of "female" philosophy with the end of exploring its relation to the notion of the ethical, it is of considerable interest to see the extent to which these philosophical generalizations play out at the level of scholarly, popular, and even stereotypical experience. The Lacanian theoretical model of sexual difference can be generalized as associating "maleness" with transcendent structures of knowledge—fields of experience are determined in relation to excluded principles, central but excepted standards of measurement, and so forth—and "femaleness" with immanent structures of knowledge—fields of experience are determined in relation to local, contiguous elements, standards of measurement would not have exceptional status, and so forth. Although the question of difference versus equality has proved to be the fundamental dilemma for feminism (Rhode 5), where difference has been either grudgingly allowed or actively defended researchers (both scholarly and popular) have pointed to a series of characteristics that are remarkably consistent, and that mirror to a striking degree these two logical positions.

Merrill and Jaakko Hintikka have argued, for example, that language is "sexist" in far more profound ways than have been commonly believed, in that sexual difference is operative not merely at the level of what they call the "structural system," but more profoundly at the level of what they term the "referential system"—the level at which more than one immediate referential context is available to inform the structural system underlying the semantics of a given utterance (140–41). Because of the ultimate dependence of concrete meaning production on these ever-receding referential contexts, the referential systems are what in part "determine the individuation of the particular entities we talk about in our language" (143). The identity of objects and individuals in such a model is thus a function of perceived continuity between variances in the referential system; because different referential systems have also been called "possible worlds," the Hintikkas denominate these continuities "world lines."

If boys and girls started to manifest markedly different ways of drawing world lines at a young age, this would augur for the operativity of sexual difference at an ontological level—at the level, in other words, of the very experience of reality itself. Drawing on research reported by David Lewis and Eleanor Maccoby, the Hintikkas argue for just such a conclusion. Boys, it seems, tend to group objects or representations of objects on the basis of the similarity of characteristics intrinsic to all of these objects; they focus, in others words, on a universal term of which the objects in question become particulars. Girls, by contrast, tend to group objects more on the basis of their "functional and relational characteristics" (Hintikka and Hintikka 145). As the Hintikkas conclude:

> All identification which turns on essential properties, weighted similarities, or suchlike, presupposes a predetermined set of discrete individuals, the bearers of these essential properties as similarity relations, and focuses our attention on them. In contrast, an emphasis on relational characteristics of our individuals encourages comparisons of different worlds in terms of their total structure, which leads to entirely different identification methods, which are much more holistic and relational. (146)

It is necessary to interject here that the term "total" has to be understood as opposed to the totalizing gesture of objectivist truth claims, which depend precisely on the delimitation of a "predetermined set of individuals." In contrast, the "total structures" described by the second position are more holistic and relational because they do not presuppose such a predetermined set, but rather incorporate the subject with and as a function of a potentially unbounded set of relations.

A related piece of evidence can be found in the fact that the greatest differences between boys and girls are found in tests that measure spatial performance (Maccoby 42). Spatiality becomes a factor in testing for "analytic ability," or how one groups together objects—and we should not miss the inherent sexism in the semantics of these testing procedures, which denominate putting "objects together on the basis of some elements they have in common" as exhibiting greater analytic ability (27)—because the "analytic" grouping of objects involves a greater "field independence" (i.e., the ability to bracket the environment in which the objects being grouped are found, and to not be "distracted" by elements extraneous to the grouping at hand). In such testing, girls are found to be "more field-dependent and less analytical because of their greater conformity and dependency [sic]" (43).

Perhaps what is needed when faced with such research is not to resist the data, which may be natural to those progressively inclined, but rather to question the very framework used to evaluate the data.[27] Words like "conformity" and "dependency" are chosen by researchers over other possibilities, such as "heightened ambient awareness" or "relational sensitivity." If indeed girls tend to perform at a lower level on tests designed to rate analytic ability, the flip-side is certainly that they would perform higher in tests designed to rate such factors as "holistic sensitivity," were they ever tested for. The difficulty women stereotypically have with directions, for example, might have statistical support;[28] but we must not forget that an aptitude for relating subjective position with cardinal directions on a map requires a kind of persistent abstraction of self from lived reality, which, if highly valued in a patriarchal society, does not for that reason indicate a superior way of being. Indeed, in terms of certain ethico-political considerations, the contrary could turn out to be the case.

These are far from isolated findings and conclusions. Carol Gilligan's influential book *In a Different Voice* has popularized the notion that women are more concerned with personal relationships than with abstract concepts like rights and justice.[29] From an anthropological perspective, Sherry B. Ortner has argued that the universally encountered phenomenon of women's subjugation to men can be in large part explained by an also universal tendency to relate women to nature and men to culture (Ortner 73). Although Ortner has been accused of being a ringleader in a tendency in feminism and recent scholarship to rid social-scientific thought of references to biology and the body,[30] her own anthropological explanation for this equation begins, as she says, with the body, and specifically with the procreative functions of the female body, which have been interpreted in both social and psychical ways as aligning woman with nature. This association is so pervasive that it is found, as Ortner points out, in one of the foundational texts of modern feminism, Simone de Beauvoir's *The Second Sex*, in which de Beauvoir argues that man's lack of direct connection to the reproduction of the species leads him to create in a way that transcends the eternal repetition of animal procreation. Hence man attains more directly to a transcendence definitive of human kind, whereas woman remains behind, somewhere between the two (Ortner 75; de Beauvoir 58–59).

These arguments are echoed in Robert McElvaine *Eve's Seed*, which argues for reinterpreting sexual difference as the motor of history. The cultural denigration of women begins, according to McElvaine, about ten thousand years ago, when human social organization develops from primarily hunter-gatherer societies to agricultural societies. Because, as the inventors of agriculture, women now control the means of both production and *re*production, men develop what amounts to a terrible case of womb-envy and begin to produce a mythic discourse that repositions them on top of the social order, as transcendent creators and sowers of seeds. If women give birth to and hence perpetuate human kind, from now on men will take credit for this accomplishment with the metaphor of the seed, all the while relegating woman, literally, to the ground (McElvaine 14–15).[31]

Ortner herself draws largely from a now famous essay by Nancy Chodorow that appeared in the same 1974 volume, *Woman, Culture and Society*. Chodorow's essay attempts to account for what she also calls "general and nearly universal differences" between the personalities and roles of men and women (Chodorow, "Family Structure" 43). "In any given society," writes Chodorow, "feminine personality comes to define itself in relation and connection to other people more than masculine personality does. (In psychoanalytic terms, women are less individuated than men, they have more flexible ego boundaries)" (44).[32] The reason for this contrast, according to Chodorow's largely object relations-inflected theory, is that in contrast to boys, who are socialized via identification with more distant, largely absent father figures, girls learn their gender roles by identifying with the member of the family who, as the traditional care-giver is by and large more nurturing and tends toward close, physical contact. Whereas boys' experience of identification involves a fundamental negation, a "you shall not be like that," girls are socialized for the most part without recourse to negation (50). A further, and perhaps more Lacanian, extrapolation to this theory[33] would be to note the different nature of the father's intrusion into the child/mother duo in the case of boys and girls: fathers' own sense of rivalry mixed with a desire for their sons to develop a fully masculine personality might prod them to intervene more in the separation of sons from mothers than in the case of daughters.

Philosophical, anthropological, and psychoanalytical generalizations about the differences between the sexes have been corroborated by more quantitative work in the social sciences and confirmed by the conferral of best-seller status on more than one author of popular guides to gender relations. Probably the most influential of all social scientists that have looked at the question of gender difference is the linguist Deborah Tannen, who has repeatedly published tenaciously researched, if heavily anecdotal, accounts of how the ordinary language of men and women varies. Explaining the distinction she makes in her 1990 book, *You Just Don't Understand*, between what she calls report-talk and rapport-talk, Tannen concludes that "[f]or most men, talk is primarily a means to preserve independence and negotiate and maintain status in a hierarchical social order," whereas for women "the language of conversation is primarily a language of rapport: a way of establishing connections and negotiating relationships" (77).[34] For Tannen, men and women speak toward such divergent ends because, as she puts it, "it is as if their life blood ran in different directions"—that of men toward independence, that of women toward intimacy (26).

If there is a gender and relationships guru who is painting a picture of sexual difference that Americans most recognize and identify with, it is John Gray, author of *Men Are from Mars, Women Are from Venus*. Gray's signature tactic in describing gendered behavior is to draw analogies between the sexes and common complementary oppositions. As he puts it in another book, men contract, whereas women expand: "Like the expansive (centrifugal) force, a woman's awareness moves out from her center. Her fundamental nature is to move out from her self and connect with others" (Gray, *Men, Women and Relationships* 57). Similarly, men's perspective on the world is a "focused" one, whereas women see the world from a more "expanded perspective":

> Masculine awareness tends to relate one thing to another in a sequential way, gradually building a complete picture. It is a perspective that relates one part to another part, in terms of producing a whole.
>
> Feminine awareness is expanded; it intuitively takes in the whole picture and gradually discovers the parts within, and it explores how the parts are all related to the whole. It places more emphasis on context rather than on content. (83)

Philosophically speaking, the language in this description is a bit ambiguous, but from the many examples in Gray's work it becomes clear that what one should focus on in the description of men is how they "focus" on building a "complete picture," on "producing a whole." In the case of women, by contrast, we should pay attention to their "intuitively" taking in the "whole picture," discovering the "parts within." The female perspective, in other words, does not approach "the picture" from an external position, but rather discovers itself already "within" the "context" of the whole, where it "explores how the parts are all related to the whole" instead of focusing on them as discrete particulars. This difference is supposed to account for a variety of situations, from familial strife—as with Tannen, the origins of tensions lie in men's tendency to talk to a specific point, in contrast with women's tendency to talk in an expansive, more generally communicative and intimate way—to shopping strategies—women ostensibly enjoy "aimless" shopping and are "energized" by it, whereas it "exhausts" men (hence, according to Gray, the proliferation of comfortable chairs for husbands and boyfriends in department stores) (*Men, Women and Relationships* 89).

What I am interested in gleaning from these popular, "how-to" approaches to difference, as well as from the more scholarly approaches outlined above, is the profoundly consistent contour of a theory of difference that maps almost seamlessly onto the Lacanian logical dyad: men are seen as focused, rational, detached, goal oriented, motivated by universals, oriented spatially via abstract coordinates, valuing independence over intimacy, and speaking primarily in order to communicate information; women, in contrast, are described as expansive, intuitive, connected, relationship oriented, motivated by interpersonal emotions, oriented spatially via landmarks, valuing intimacy over independence, and speaking primarily in order to establish and negotiate relations. There is no doubt that we must take such statistical and anecdotal evidence with a great deal of skepticism; there is no doubt that these patterns are stereotypes that are to some extent reproduced by the very scholarship that seeks neutrally to report them (and that for representing them I must be seen as guilty of the same complicity). There can also be no doubt, however, that these results point to a divergence in behavior and experience that many experience as real, a divergence that can be condensed into a single proposition whose expression we have already derived: what we call being "man" is predicated on a relation to meaning that is transcendental; what we call being woman is predicated on a relation to meaning that is immanent. For all the physiological and evolutionary factors that have played and continue to play a role in the determination of this experience, there is an aspect of the cultural positioning of woman that is of utmost importance, both for understanding why this is the case and for trying to conceptualize this difference in all its richness. This aspect, which we shall call "othering," is at the core of any possible understanding of the ethical.

OTHERING

Lacan presented the formulae of sexuation we have already visited in conjunction with a schema meant to represent the relation of these subject positions to the "Other" (see overleaf). The left or male side of the graph contains the symbols $ and Φ; the right or female side contains three symbols: an S followed by an A with a slash through it in parentheses; a small *a*, and the French feminine indefinite article *La*, also with a slash running through it. The $ on the male side has an arrow pointing to the small *a* on

$$\exists x\ \overline{\Phi}x \qquad \overline{\exists} x\ \overline{\Phi}x$$
$$\forall x\ \Phi x \qquad \overline{\forall} x\ \Phi$$

$$\$ \qquad S(\cancel{A})$$
$$a \quad L\cancel{a}$$
$$\Phi$$

the female side; the slashed *La* on the female side, meanwhile, has two ar-
rows leading out from it, one pointing toward the Φ on the male side, and
the other toward the S with the slashed A on its own side. As arcane as
these drawings appear, their message can be stated quite simply: male desire is characterized by the relation of a lacking or split subject to a fantasy
object; female desire, in contrast, is characterized by the bifurcation of two
vectors. The first leads to Φ, the phallus, the patriarchal symbol of sexual
difference—but also the master signifier, the signifier of exclusion, "for
which there is no signified" (Lacan, *XX* 80). We can conceive of this first
choice as being the correlate of male desire's relation to the fantasy object
a, a belief in an ultimate fulfillment beyond the next barrier. The second
vector, however, does not cross the dividing line—"the division of what is
improperly called humanity insofar as humanity is divided up into sexual
identifications" (80)—but rather points to the third symbol on the female
side, that of the S and the slashed A, what Lacan refers to as the sign of the
lack in the Other (*Autre*).

   This other option for female desire is what constitutes, for Lacan, the
core of sexual difference. Whereas male desire always depends on an object
fantasized to fill in a perceived lack in the subject's constitution, and to that
extent is essentially self-oriented—even if the vector appears to be crossing
the divide into otherness—female desire has the option of being oriented
toward otherness in a radical way, although (and precisely because) it
remains on woman's side of the divide. Female desire exhibits this characteristic because, whereas male desire is other-*regarding*, female desire is
always, to a certain extent, other-*inhabiting*. This difference between other-
regarding and other-inhabiting is an exact correlate of the logical distinction mapped out above between a male position that tends to externalize
and exclude its place of enunciation from the context and objects of
knowledge, and a female position that tends to internalize and include its

place of enunciation, and hence not totalize the object as a bounded, knowable set. This refusal to totalize the object of knowledge is due, in logical terms, to the fact that female subjectivity is constituted not through the exclusion of otherness but rather *as otherness itself*. As a position that is itself already in and of otherness, woman's relation to an Other at the phenomenological level is not predicated on packaging the Other into a comfortable form, one already traced against the specific desires of the self held at a transcendental distance from the object, but involves rather an openness to the Other as radically other:

> Woman has a relation to the signifier of that Other, insofar as, qua Other, it can but remain forever Other. I can only assume here that you will recall my statement that there is no Other of the Other. The Other, that is, the locus in which everything that can be articulated on the basis of the signifier comes to be inscribed, is, in its foundations, the Other in the most radical sense. (Lacan, *XX* 81)

Men, in other words, tend only to relate to otherness insofar as it is an inscribed and inscribable otherness, one that fits, corresponds to, has its place in his images of self and world. The realm of meaning is ultimately foundational for man because he implicitly believes in the existence of an Other—God, Reality, Truth, and so forth—upon which the other of knowledge—the other he describes and articulates in his language—is supported and in which it has its Being. Woman, in contrast, implicitly grasps the radical otherness of the other of knowledge that has no extraworldly guarantee; a world without bounds that must be encountered on its own terms and negotiated encounter by encounter—encounters that never leave the self unchanged, but form an endless series of mutations and revision that we can call, in contrast to the static Being of male desire, becoming.

This insistence on the otherness of women is one factor that makes psychoanalysis potentially interesting for feminist thinkers. As Elizabeth Grosz writes, "[s]uch a notion of desire [one not based on lack] cannot but be of interest to feminist theory, insofar as women have been the traditional depositories and guardians of the lack constitutive of (Platonic) desire, and insofar as the opposition between presence and lack has traditionally defined women and constrained them to inhabit the place of man's other" ("A Thousand" 196). Such an injunction to explore alternative notions of desire does, nevertheless, put the critic working with the language and presumptions of psychoanalysis ill at ease, for it opens up the paradox of critique that abounds in the area of feminist studies: how to describe without one's descriptions taking on a performative efficacity. If patriarchy exhibits patterns, is there a way of describing these patterns without thereby reiterating, reciting, and ultimately reproducing them? The question is even more pertinent, of course, if the author is not a woman, as in the case of Howard Bloch, who in his monumental history of misogyny declares that the only option when reporting on misogynist discourse is simultaneously to deconstruct that discourse and demonstrate where the misogynist writer contradicts himself—where he depends on, for his accusations against women, exactly the same tactics he accuses women of relying on in their dealings with men (*Medieval* 3).

There is, however, one problem with such a strategy: it implicitly assumes that generations and millennia of people can produce, believe in, and inhabit certain categories—can depend on them to structure their most profound experience of the world—without this exerting a powerful, and perhaps even in some ways indelible, effect on the present. Whether the arguments and tirades of countless misogynists of old hold up under current deconstructive scrutiny is, in the end, irrelevant to the question of what it is to, as Grosz puts it, "inhabit the place of man's other." Woman, in other words, not just the way the word is used in sentences but the way it is lived by innumerable beings, is the product of othering; just as to the very same extent man, not only the word but the ways of being it encompasses, is a product of having "othered" woman. If Ortner and others are right in claiming a universal status for the oppression of women, this does not obviate the fact that different cultural histories may account for different processes and experiences of becoming woman and becoming man. In the pages that follow, I will focus on the sexual configuration particular to the Judeo-Christian West, a configuration that has placed the figure of woman in a specific position relative to knowledge, to divinity, and ultimately to the ethical.

THE BURDEN OF REDEMPTION

"The man knew Eve, his wife," says Genesis 4:1, and the note in Édouarde Dhorme's French translation clarifies that "[t]he verb *yâdá*, 'to know,' is regularly used to signify sexual relations, speaking as much of man as of woman. . . . The same expression as in other Semitic languages, with the verbs meaning 'to know.' The initiation to an act covered in mystery seems to us the origin of this use of the verb 'to know' " (*La Bible*, qtd. in Block de Behar chapter 8, note 34). From the beginning, then, knowledge and sexual difference have been conjoined. The tree that was so tempting to Eve was, as we have pointed out, the very tree in whose fruit could be found the knowledge of good and evil—the very knowledge Eve would need in order to know that what she was doing was wrong, that she was being, in fact, tempted. The Old Testament is itself famously uncertain, itself in a position of lacking knowledge or at least of sharing in an overabundance of conflicting knowledge as to the genealogy of Eve: was Eve born with Adam, simultaneously in God's image, as in Genesis 1:27, or did she postdate the naming of animals and Adam's discovery of his loneliness, as reported in Genesis 2:7? The Bible runs through the story of Eve's creation twice—and here we are not even counting the story of Lilith in the apocrypha—its repetition lending Eve a kind of palimpsest, virtual status; was she there already or not? If *she* was already here, then who is *this*?

The dual origin of Eve gave the Church fathers both endless trouble and endless flexibility in defining and redefining woman's role in creation (Bloch, *Medieval* 25–27; Ruether 63): it allowed them to focus on the unity of humanity in Christ, the secondary and belated nature of woman, or both seemingly contradictory options at once. And yet, in a certain sense, it was not a contradiction that woman be seen both as contemporaneous and equal to man and as secondary and belated. The reason for this was that the division of man into two was seen as connected not to his spiritual nature, but to his bodily existence. Insofar as humans were created in God's image, they were created as spiritual beings; but embodiment, the real cause of the fall, was already a manifestation of distance from the deity, a distance quite literally embodied in Eve as the agent of sexual difference (Ruether 64). Woman, in other words, embodies the difference between man and God, but she is also—insofar as she is human, a kind of man—that being who is distanced from God by sexual difference. She is simultaneously the universal humanity of the soul and the embodiment of the fall.[35]

It is, of course, woman's embodiment of the fall from grace that make her the target of misogynist rhetoric, theological and secular alike. It is also in this role that the figure of woman will acquire certain adornments—will be likened, in fact, to adornment per se, or, equally paradoxically, will become the essence of *accident*. As Bloch points out, a consistent tenet of medieval misogyny is the association of women with adornment, disguise, rhetoric (as opposed to truth), and ultimately with the letter itself, as opposed to the meaning the letter so unreliably conveys (Bloch, *Medieval* 23, 32, 58). This, then, is the essence of the misogynist discourse on women:

woman as the embodiment of falsity, deception, temptation and perdition, embodiment and corruption. In the Middle Ages, this discourse came to be accompanied by another, apparently contrary one, in which women were figured as redeemer. This was the period in Church history during which the cult of the Virgin Mary emerged, which historians such as Bullough have claimed was part and parcel of the Church hierarchy's increasingly institutionalized disapproval of sexual activity, both heterosexual and homosexual, but especially the latter, among the cloistered (Bullough 43; Bloch, *Medieval* 67). What is doubtless the case, though, is that the celebration of virginity in general is and was indissociable from the association of the flesh with sin; and if woman was the vehicle for that association, she also became the bearer of ultimate redemption through chastity. How much more virtuous is it for one to resist temptation when one is woman, sign of the flesh and weakness, and not already man, emblem of spirit and moral strength? How much more fortitude must it take for one so far from God to attain perfection (McLaughlin 82)?

Woman, in addition to having been made the sign of man's fall from grace, was now asked to carry the burden of his redemption; and it is this duality that accounts for the troubling bifurcation, in the Western cultural imaginary and in the fantasy space of men, of the image of woman into saint and sinner, virgin and whore.[36] The bifurcation, however, is not merely accidental; it is not merely a case of male culture having haphazardly alighted upon the figure of woman to fulfill two contradictory roles. As Bloch has suggested, the two positions are literally one and the same; they are different twists on the same misogynist myth. If woman is simultaneously the symbol of bodily corruption, deception, and sin on the one hand, and the purity of soul and its ultimate redemption on the other, this is because a border has been made out of her being, a border marking the minimum distance, the last difference separating man from God.[37] If woman is a border, then she is equally and at the same time that which separates man from God and the only thing connecting him to God; she is and must be both devil's gateway and bride of Christ (Bloch, *Medieval* 65–92).

Howard Bloch has argued that there is continuity between the early medieval misogynistic tradition and the tradition of courtly love poetry that sprang up in the twelfth century, the latter a tradition that succeeded in determining Western ideas of love and the relation between the sexes until the present (*Medieval* 196).[38] The continuity of this apparent duality is matched by another, as argued by María Rosa Menocal: namely, the duality between the apparently contradictory interpretations contemporary critics and historians attempt to read into the poetry of adoration of the late Middle Ages. When the poet speaks in divine terms of the beloved, or in profane terms in order to describe the passion of the divine, the modern critic has insisted on understanding this chiasmus as a daring, perhaps even blasphemous transgression. But the poetry, Menocal argues, offers an entirely different story: the love bespoken by the poet's words is not one or the other, not sacred or profane, but both, for there is no difference.

Menocal discusses the Arabic Spanish poet Ibn 'Arabi, pointing out about his poem—so often cited by critics for its possible pantheistic interpretations—that

> the verse that closes that meditation, and closes the poem itself, is almost never cited. The powerful connotation—the essentially inescapable reading imposed—is that the spiritual or mystical dimension is the climax of both the mystical experience and the poem. What we read, in other words is:

> My heart can take on
> any form:
> a meadow for gazelles
> a cloister for monks,
>
> For the idols, sacred ground
> Ka'ba for the circling pilgrim,
> the tables of a Torah,
> the scrolls of the Qur'ān.
>
> I profess the religion of love;
> wherever its caravan turns along the way,
> that is the belief,
> the faith I keep. (Menocal 82)

What is not quoted is this final stanza:

> Like Bish,
> Hind and her sister,
> Love-mad Qays and the lost Láyla,
> Máyya and her lover Ghaylán. (qtd. in Menocal 83)

This suppression of the examples of passionate, profane lovers explains not only the mystical dimension of the Western ideal of love, but also the specific unity between the body of woman and the being of god that underlies the Western ideal of femininity. Their unity is simultaneously proliferated and shunned, written into our acts of devotion and words of love, while at the same time censored in shame. Woman is god, woman is sin, woman is death, woman is redemption.

A literary/devotional form that spread across Europe in the twelfth and thirteenth centuries, lyrical songs praising the Virgin Mary, contains the seeds of this paradoxical association. On the Iberian peninsula collections of such *cantigas* were compiled by the thirteenth-century king Alphonse the Wise, under whose rule in Toledo during the cohabitation of the peninsula by Christians, Moors, and Jews much of the wisdom and folklore of the various peoples of Spain was translated and collected. A typical *cantiga* tells the story of a French knight who wishes to become the lover of a lady who has rebuked his advances. Asking a priest for his advice, he is told that his desires will be fulfilled if he prays before the altar of the Virgin Mary for a year. At the end of the year, the Virgin Mary appears before the knight, who is so taken by her beauty that he renounces his earlier love and dedicates himself to her. To which the Virgin says

> Take your hands away from your face [*dante ta faz*]
> And look and see that I am wearing no mask [*eu non tenno anfaz*];
> Either me or the other woman,
> Take the one you think pleases you more. (Alfonso xvi)

Whereupon the knight chooses the Virgin and is told that he may have her as his lover, *amiga* in the language of courtly love, if he prays for her for another year as much as he already prayed for the other.

Love for the Virgin in this and many other cases is presented in exactly the forms and formulae of courtly, profane love—evidence, in fact, that the distinction between sacred and profane love, as Menocal suggests, is the wrong one to make. If the Virgin differs at all from the beloved of profane love, it is not in the passion that she is owed, but in the manner of presentation—one that itself transcends the paradox inherent to virginity, according to which knowledge of a virgin, indeed any kind of perception of her, is tantamount to the destruction of her virginity, virginity thus being the very instantiation of the impossibility of redemption (Bloch, *Medieval* 93–112). Whereas woman always presents herself in a guise, as deception, materiality, or adornment, a virgin, if she exists, appears unadorned. Mary, as the one true virgin, appears as the impossible, a woman without a mask, hence without deception, materiality, or adornment of any kind.

The mask, the cloth, the veil must be seen, then, as the paradoxical essence of woman.[39] Even in her miraculous virginity, the Virgin can only appear through the mention and negation of the mask of woman. For it is the mask, the material of sexual embodiment, the letter, that separates man from salvation and is at the same time the key to his redemption; only the seeing through of the mask, the lifting of the veil, the interpretation of the letter can bring him home. Perhaps this is why, to turn again to what is possibly the most important founding text of the Western literature of love, the vision of Beatrice with which Dante's *Vita Nuova* begins has as its gravitational center the veil of red cloth draped over her naked body. In his vision Dante makes out the figure of a fearsome lord: "in his arms I seemed to see a person sleeping nude, except that she seemed to be lightly wrapped in a sanguine cloth" [Ne le sue braccia mi parea vedere una persona dormir nuda, salvo che involta mi parea in un drappo sanguigno leggeramente] (Dante 15–16). Robert Harrison has written of this image: "[w]ere it not for that one word in the prose, *nuda*, we could never quite be sure of Breatrice's womanhood, her corporeal facticity, as it were. Everywhere else in the *Vita Nuova* she appears only as dressed, that is to say, she appears above all as her dress" (22). Indeed, we could restrict Harrison's observation even further and note that the corporeal facticity of Beatrice's womanhood is condensed not merely into one word, but into one letter, the letter *a*:[40] like the *aleph* the rabbi inscribes on the forehead of the golem to animate it with the breath, the inspiration of creation, the *a*, the first letter marking the distinction between a primordial intention of God that needed no letter and the degeneracy, the fall of a human, discursive knowledge (Block de Behar 148);[41] or like Derrida's *a*, the difference that is almost not a difference, marking the faintest, almost imperceptible border between identity and difference itself—producing, in fact, identity as a shadow presence beyond the primordial degeneracy of writing (Derrida, "Differance"). Woman is that mark, the veil that degenerates man from a spectral plenitude that is generated, in turn, by her.

Dante begins his *libello* with a reference to another book, that of his memory, in which he finds at a certain point inscribed the words INCIPIT VITA NOVA, and under this marker of the beginning of a new life he claims to find the words that make up the text of his *Vita Nuova*, the text that begins with his encounter with Beatrice and ends with her death. In a world of words, in which the text of the present is recalled from and refers to the text of the past, the body of Beatrice becomes, as Harrison puts it, the "undisclosed substance of revelation" (28).[42] For the theological tradition in which Dante is writing, there can be no doubt that the path to God is a path back through history (Bloch, *Etymologies* chapter 1) and a path built of words, although in the neo-Platonic philosophy to which he was no stranger (Gilson 168; Gorton *passim*) there is something ultimately ir-revocable about the fall, a minimal space between the world of meaning and the being of God that can never be closed.[43] The body of Beatrice, the sublime nudity behind the red veil, is for Dante the embodiment of that irreducible space, just as woman has become, for Western man, the nega-tion and means of an impossible redemption. Which is why Paul, the ori-gin of Church misogyny, can say that man is the image of God, and woman is the *glory* of man (1 Corinthians 11:7).[44]

Given woman's positioning as the veil separating and at the same time leading man to his impossible redemption, it does not seem too far-fetched to argue that an analogous philosophical structure—namely, the episte-mological gap separating the sensible phenomena from the intelligible world of things as they are in themselves—has its origins in a sexual and lyrical ontology.[45] For what, indeed, is the body of Beatrice if not a thing in itself, radiating its noumenal brilliance, albeit not yet stripped of its the-ological aspect.[46] In the closing chapters of *Vita Nuova*, Dante recounts how, after a year's poetic silence following the death of Beatrice, he begins again to write under the influence of another *donna gentile*, one who re-minds him of Beatrice. After an initial flurry of sentiment, however, the poet realizes that what he is falling in love with in the new lady is the self-reflecting gaze of pity in her eyes, and the realization effectively divides him into two parts, one he calls *cuore*, heart, or *appetito*, appetite; and the other he calls *anima*, soul, or *ragione*, reason: "In this sonnet I made of my-self two parts, according to how my thoughts were divided. The one part I call heart, which is the appetite; the other I call soul, which is reason" [In questo sonetto fo due parte di me, second che li miei pensieri erano divisi. L'una parte chiamo cuore, ciò è l'appetito; l'altra chiamo anima, ciò è la ra-gione] (Dante 192). The two sides then enter into battle, his appetite, self-ishly motivated, yearning for the new lady; his soul reminding him that she is nothing but the consolation of a loss. The poet's reason wins over his ap-petite by recalling in his imagination precisely the vision with which the *li-bello* began, of Beatrice in her flaming red drapery (Dante 194).

The poet's return to the intellectual adoration of Beatrice coincides with a group of pilgrims passing through Florence on their way to Rome to view the Veronica, the cloth carrying the imprint of Christ's face, "which Jesus Christ left us as an example of his beautiful face, which my lady is now glo-riously seeing" [la quale Gesú Cristo lasciò a noi per esemplo de la sua bel-lisima figura, la quale vede la mia donna gloriosamente] (Dante 200). Against the backdrop of their journey, the poet writes the last of his sonnets, a spiritual pilgrimage to Beatrice, in which the traveler is not so much the poet himself (who as *pilgrim* will undergo this journey years later in the *Commedia*), but rather the poet's sigh, a breath without words that will travel out beyond the spheres to bring him back a wordless meaning, a new intelligence spoken by the noumenal body of Beatrice.[47] Nevertheless, when the sigh returns to tell of the marvels it has seen, it speaks to the poet in a language he cannot understand: "But it sees her in such a way that when it returns to tell me of it I do not understand, so subtly does it speak to the aching heart that makes it speak" [Vedela tal, che cuando 'l mi ridice, / io non lo 'ntendo, sí parla sottile / al cor dolente, che lo fa parlare] (Dante 208). At the end of the sonnet, the poet tells us that it was accompanied by visions—we can only assume those provoked by the unintelligible speech itself—of such a miraculous nature that he decides to say nothing more of the blessed Beatrice until he can say things worthy of her. His only hope, as he proposes to take on years of study in order to attain to an impossible knowledge, is to be able, sometime before the end of his life and the eventual reunification of his soul with hers, to speak of her, to say of her what has never been said of any one else [io spero di dire di lei quello che mai non fue detto d'alcuna] (Dante 208–9).[48] What Dante concludes, in other words, as Harrison has argued, is that the truth of the poet's speech ultimately remains a veil, the veil of representation, which in its highest, purest, *poetic* manifestation can still carry but an imprint, like the image of Christ on the Veronica, of a body that belongs to another world (Dante 126).

FEMALE PHILOSOPHY

As Dante experiences, the problem of speaking from the place of woman is that your knowledge does not translate into the language of man, those mortal languages spoken here below. When man made woman divine, he also stole her voice or, as thinkers as different from one another as Gilligan, Irigaray, Kristeva, and Cixous have stressed, made her speak in a different voice.[49] Lacan believed that in exceeding the bounds of male knowledge, woman acceded to a divine *jouissance* (Lacan, *XX* 61–72), a claim that Irigaray interpreted as yet another male fantasy, a reduction of woman's being into yet another mode of male pleasure (Irigaray, *This Sex* 103).[50] There may be something to this criticism, for, as she notes, Lacan does say of Bernini's (a man's) statue that "you'll see right away that St. Theresa is coming, there's no doubt about it" (qtd. in Irigaray, *This Sex* 91).

But whatever Teresa is feeling, both Lacan and Irigaray would agree that she is speaking in a different language, a language that comes, as it were, from a place alien to male knowledge—a place, as we have seen, posited by knowledge as unknowable, and where she and her body have been placed as guardian.

In her autobiography,[51] Teresa describes her raptures (*arrobamientos*) in terms that belie expectations—both ours and those of her immediate historical and theological context—of transcendence, although she stresses repeatedly the inadequacy of language to this task of description. Speaking of God, who comes to her "wrapped in love" and lifts her up, corporeally, not merely spiritually, she says:

> That it seems He is not content with taking so truly the soul to Himself, but also wants the body, even being it so mortal and of such soiled earth for all the offenses it has committed. It also leaves a strange selflessness that I will not be able to say how it is; it seems to me that I can say it is different in some way—I mean more than those other things pertaining only to the spirit—because given that things of the spirit are in all ways a selflessness from things, here it seems the Lord wants the body itself to experience it and there comes about a new strangeness for the things of the earth, such that life becomes most painful.[52]

> [que no parece se contenta con llevar tan de veras el alma a Sí, sino que quiere el cuerpo, aun siendo tan mortal y de tierra tan sucia como por tantas ofensas se ha hecho. También deja un desasimiento extraño que yo no podré decir como es; peréceme que puedo decir es diferente en alguna manera—digo más que estotras cosas de solo espíritu—porque ya que estén cuanto a el espíritu con todo desasimiento de las cosas, aquí parece quiere el Señor el mesmo cuerpo lo ponga por obra y hácese una extrañeza nueva para con las cosas de la tierra, que es muy penosa la vida.] (Teresa 91)

The selflessness of which she speaks is literally an out-of-oneself-ness, a turning away from oneself that is produced by a taking up of the soul that is at one and the same time a taking up of the body. Speaking of it, she can only emphasize its ineffability and its difference. It seems, she says, that the Lord wants the body to undergo the turning-away-from-itself of things that the soul might normally undergo, the result being a new strangeness with the things of the world, an abiding pain endured by a corporeal soul. Speaking later of this pain of existence she says, "although the soul feels it, it is in the company of the body, both seem to participate in it" [aunque la siente el alma, es en compañía del cuerpo, entrambos parecen participan de ella] (Teresa 91). A corporeal pain provoked by the sudden absence of

God, in which the soul is as if crucified between heaven and earth:

> But it seems to me that the soul is thus, that neither does it receive consolation from heaven, nor is it there, nor does it want it from the earth, nor it is there, but rather it remains as if crucified between heaven and earth, suffering, without rescue coming to it from either side. Because that which comes from heaven (which is, as has been said, such a marvelous notice from God, well beyond what we can desire), just leads to more torment, because desire grows in such a way that—to my way of seeing—the great pain at times causes one to lose one's sense, if not that it lasts only briefly without it. . . . Understand that the soul wants nothing but its God; but it does not want anything particular of Him, but rather everything together it wants and it does not know what it wants. I say "it does not know" because the imagination does not represent anything; no, to my way of seeing, much of the time that one is thus the faculties do not work; as with pleasure in the union and rapture, here the pain suspends them.

> [mas paréceme que está ansí el alma, que ni del cielo le viene consuelo ni está en él, ni de la tierra le quiere ni está en ella, sino como crucificada entre el cielo y la tierra, padeciendo sin venirle socorro de ningún cabo. Porque el que le viene del cielo (que es, como he dicho, una noticia de Dios tan admirable, muy sobre todo lo que podemos desear), es para más tormento, porque acrecienta el deseo de manera que—a mi parecer—la gran pena algunas veces quita el sentido, sino que dura poco sin él. . . . Bien entiende que no quiere [el alma] sino a su Dios; mas no ama cosa particular de El, sino todo junto lo quiere y no sabe lo que quiere. Digo <<no sabe>> porque no representa nada la imaginación; no, a mi pareceer, mucho tiempo de lo que está ansí, no obran las potencias; como en la unión y arrobamiento el gozo, aquí la pena las suspende."] (Teresa 111)

The state of this great pain robs the faculties of their ability to function, specifically the imagination's ability to represent, such that precisely in the moment of encounter with God the imagination ceases to be able to represent as quality or even as a totality.[53] God, in other words, cannot be faced as an object, even if a deific one; she cannot stand over against Him as separate autonomous being. Desire for God, in Teresa's world, cannot be localized to a single objective absence, but is rather the bereavement of her very being. Even in its utter renunciation of the corporeal, the earthly, the soul remains entirely embodied, the embodiment of raw hunger. Even the rescue God brings is nothing but an advent of further torment, because His occupation of her soul/body can only add force to her desire. If in this state the soul is crucified between heaven and earth, this is because it is experiencing a crucifixion peculiar to the othering of woman, one in which the groundlessness of existence—the perception of which Heidegger called Angst and opposed it to fear, which always has an object (Heidegger, *Being and Time* 174)—is not resolved by a facile prohibition, the name/no of the Father that places the palliative for all earthly ills just out of reach. Crucified between heaven and earth, with one foot in subjectivity and the other in the other that has no other, woman would feel the pain and pleasures of existence in a way that man, insulated from the world by the myth of subjectivity, cannot.[54]

CAN ONLY A GODDESS SAVE US NOW?

It is a trick of perspective. The *I* speaks always from *this* place, in here, about that which is out there. When the other speaks, it also speaks, curiously, from this place, about something else that is out there. This means that when the other speaks, it is not speaking as the Other, but as the original *I*. There is no new voice on the face of the earth except for that of the Other, but when the Other speaks, it speaks the language of the *I*, of the one. "The (male) ideal other has been imposed upon women by men," Irigaray writes, and therefore "[w]oman scatters and becomes an agent of destruction and annihilation because she has no other of her own that she can become" (Irigaray, *Sexes and Genealogies* 64). Irigaray calls for women to create their own God; but listen to the place of that call: *she has no other of her own that she can become.* A call issued from any other place would be an imitation of the one, a repetition of the reification of one subjectivity that speaks as if it were speaking for several, or for all. So the call must issue forth from the very place it must eventually destroy, from the prison it must condemn for the centuries of torture, humiliation, and voicelessness to which is has been subjected. And yet that place is its strength, its difference.

The obvious problem with reading Irigaray the way I am is that she clearly rejects the notion of a female identity that emerges from a phallocentric history: "How can I say it? That we are women from the start. That we don't have to be turned into women by them, labeled by them, made holy and profane by them" (Irigaray, *This Sex* 212). My apparently paradoxical point, however, is simply this: Irigaray's very enunciation of this freedom from history, a freedom put in the terms of an essentialism that, in Diana Fuss's words, does not aim to "imprison women within their bodies but to rescue them from enculturating definitions by men" (67–68), *emerges precisely from such a history.* As Irigaray says in the very lines that follow the above quotation: "That that has always already happened, without their efforts. And that their history, their stories, constitute the locus of our displacement" (Irigaray, *This Sex* 212). Irigaray's essentialism is thus, as Fuss argues, strategic (Fuss 66), but it is strategy that corresponds to an embodiedness linked not exclusively to the anatomical traits of biological women, but also and inextricably to the mode of being that being woman has become.

Is this not, then, the essence of the political paradox endemic to feminism? If women are different then they are different *from* men and disempowered with respect to them; if women are equal then they are *like* them (or at least are judged according to standards that are implicitly male) and disenfranchised of their particularity. Irigaray—and in this sense she is the model of what we are calling "female" philosophy—solves the paradox by affirming it: equality can only come from difference; power comes from activating the potential of powerlessness, from forging a new subjectivity out of the place of otherness in a move that redefines subjectivity and otherness altogether.[55]

Irigaray says at the outset of her Rotterdam lectures that if every epoch is defined by a question, then ours is defined by the question of sexual difference (Irigaray, *Éthique* 13). What is a stake is a changing of the current epoch, the bringing about of a new one, with its incumbent subjectivities. Such a change requires a mutation in the perception and conception of space-time, the inhabiting of places, and the envelopes of identity, and it presupposes a transformation of the relations between form, matter, and what she calls the interval: "Every epoch inscribes a limit in this trinitary configuration: *matter, form, interval*" (Irigaray, *Éthique* 15, my trans.). Our epoch has figured desire in the interval between matter and form, a plus or minus, attraction or tension between poles oriented according to an economy of the interval in which woman has continued to represent, as we have seen, the place of man, a thing or other for his actions. In this way, she becomes an envelope in and against which man delimits himself and the things of his world (17).

The theological discourse of patriarchy made woman's body a veil that both separated man from his redemption and held it up as a promise; hence woman was associated on the one hand with the promise of paradise, and on the other with deceit, with empty adornment. For Irigaray, however, woman's need to veil herself with artificial adornment stems from her lacking adornment proper to herself; insofar as she is the place that envelops man, she lacks her own place, her own envelope, and wants to hide her nudity with clothing, makeup, jewels (Irigaray, *Éthique* 18). It is a trick of perspective. Once we have grasped the fundamental illusion at work in the first formulation, when we can finally understand that the Woman, as Lacan said, like all those other forms of otherness guaranteeing the coherence of man's world, does not exist, only then can we go on to say with Irigaray that the reason for this is that women have been made into the place of man. Only such a realization can avoid repeating the exclusive tropes of subjectivity and make way for a new mode of relating: "That which has never existed between the sexes. Admiration keeping the two sexes insubstitutably in the statute of their difference. Maintaining between them a space, free and attracting, a possibility of separation and alliance" (20).

Perhaps because Irigaray speaks from this place, really speaks from it, she is able to enunciate in a way that Lacan himself might not have. Lacan maps out a notion of sexual difference throughout the seminar called *Encore*, and from time to time, as we mentioned, he seems to speak from a female position. What his discourse does not manage to do, though, is to *speak out* from the veil. Because woman remains veiled, the way to another kind of subjectivity is not fully explored; because of this, psychoanalytic discourse remains descriptive and can be accused, debatably, of retrenching patriarchy.[56] Nevertheless, Lacan goes further than he is given credit for: "I think of you (*Je pense à vous*). That does not mean that I conceptualize you (*je vous pense*). Perhaps someone here remembers that I once spoke of a language in which one would say, 'I love to you' (*j'aime à vous*), that language modeling itself better than others on the indirect character of that attack called love" (Lacan, *XX* 104). The comparison in syntax is intended to reveal the possibility of another kind of relation to the other, one that does not wrap the other into the self-serving shape of an object of knowledge—that which is conceptualized—but rather leaves open a space, leaves the other open to approach the knowing subject on its own terms—clearly a reference to an ethical model most associated with the thought of Lévinas. This way of relating is in turn attached to a notion of ethics. Speaking of behaviorism (and here he could be speaking of any number of disciplines in the human sciences), Lacan says that it has not "distinguished itself by any radical change in ethics, in other words in mental habits, in the *fundamental* habit. Man, being but an object, serves an end. He is founded on the basis of his final cause. . . . What is at stake is the final equation of thought and that which is thought of" (105). Although Lacan is speaking of knowledge, the template for his analysis is the sexual relation. This relation does not exist, because man knows in woman a fantasy object. In the same way, in the human sciences, man has known in man a kind of fantasy object, the object of man as determined by a certain instrumentality or teleology.

The critique of this instrumentalization of man, the equation, as Lacan says, of thought with what is thought of—with, in other words, a shadow reality to which it corresponds—is already well known as Heidegger's great contribution to philosophy. What is different about Lacan's approach is that the question is broached from the inextricable knot of knowledge and sexual difference. As I have shown, for man knowledge and the question of woman have always been intertwined. Because Heidegger neglected this connection, he too would be destined to repeat certain metaphysical gestures, to fall back into a certain nostalgia for a forgotten being (Derrida, "Differance" 30). When asked how an epochal change might come about, Heidegger was stumped by the paradox of instrumentality: if we men try to bring about epochal change, we are treating being as an end and an object of our manipulation, and hence reiterating the very structure we are trying to depose. The answer: a posture of almost total passivity: "Only a god can save us now" (Heidegger, "Only" 57).

Irigaray's philosophy, by contrast, refuses the desperation of Heidegger's last days, because she recognizes that the impasse of metaphysics is primarily the result of a blindness to sexual difference. Irigaray's argument can instead be seen as a reframing of Heidegger's critique of metaphysics in which ontological difference—the difference between beings and Being that is covered over by the metaphysical world-picture—is refigured as sexual difference. In the lecture "Éthique de la différence sexuelle," Irigaray begins her attack on the ostensible neutrality of modern systems of knowledge with a reference to Hegel's reading of *Antigone* in the *Phenomenology of Spirit*. Simply put, Hegel reads Antigone as an allegory of the epochal conflict between two systems of social organization: the traditional system of family, ancestor worship and household gods versus the modern, abstract power structure of the state. But if Antigone represents the ethical demand of the family law, this is because she, as woman, has been delegated this role by default, through the partitioning of spirit between the sexes. Hegel states:

> The brother is the member of the family in whom its spirit becomes individualized, and enabled thereby to turn towards another sphere, towards what is other than and external to itself, and pass over into the consciousness of uni-

> versality. The brother leaves this immediate, rudimentary, and, therefore, strict-
> ly speaking, negative ethical life of the family, in order to acquire and produce
> the concrete ethical order which is conscious of itself. (Hegel, *Mind* 477)

Nevertheless, if Antigone's position as woman and sister deprives her of
spirit, it also locates in her a facet of the divine; it is this spark of the divine
other that Irigaray wishes to salvage by way of an ethics sensitive not
merely to the ways of women—for men and women are assigned their
roles and tasks in Creon's state—but to the difference banished by self-
consciousness, by subjectivity, in its ascent to its current place as arbiter of
all that is.[57] The ethics of sexual difference is an ethics that asks modern
knowledge to consider, for a moment, its own nonneutrality (Irigaray,
Éthique 117).

The emergence of spirit into self-consciousness in Hegel's history, then,
is strictly correlative to the pretensions of modern science to universality,
neutrality, and objectivity—pretensions that Irigaray criticizes in a terminology borrowed explicitly from Heidegger. What is of interest here, however, is the way Irigaray's critique blends Heidegger's conception of metaphysics with a Lacanian understanding of sexual difference. For Heidegger,
modern "man" has achieved his objective knowledge and scientific worldview at the expense of being itself; science, in other words, has only been
able to look at and into the multiplicity of beings by allowing being itself,
and the ontological difference between being and beings, to slip out of
sight (Heidegger, "Question"). For Irigaray this forgetting that founds
physical ontology is a forgetting akin to the moment of individuation in
the psychoanalytic story—the moment, that is, when the child loses and
subsequently forgets the enveloping, nourishing, life-giving presence of the
mother:

> And I will finish with an example of that which a still unpaid debt vis-à-vis the
> maternal, the natural, the matricial, the nourishing can result in or entail.
>   It could only be at the cost of alienating us from our condition as living be-
> ings that we could forget the element that is most indispensable to life: air. The
> air thanks to which we breathe, we live, we speak, we appear, in which every-
> thing "comes into presence," and can come to being. (Irigaray, *Éthique* 122)

Air is Irigaray's metaphor for Heidegger's being, that which we overlook in
order for beings to come into being or to come into presence.[58] The clearing, the open space in which beings are revealed, is created by the with-
drawal of being, and the walls of our enclosure are the very horizon of disclosure whose movement constitutes the experience of truth. But is it not

a reductionism of the most naïve and biologistic kind to identify the enveloping being whose forgetting gives rise to metaphysics with the mother? And yet our very language bears this out: mother, matrix, matter—an etymological family designating the container that is itself not contained.[59]

No, reading the forgetting of being and the forgetting of the mother in the same light is emphatically not a question of simple biologism, for that would assume that our embodied, factical experience as described by Heidegger has its real, objective roots in the loss of the mother's body. What I am arguing is precisely the opposite: that the loss of being and the loss of the mother are structurally identical because the woman in general, and her eternally appointed role as mother in specific, has been called on, from the dawn of metaphysics, to stand in for the being that steadily recedes beyond the horizon of disclosure. The Other is not the Mother, as so often has been claimed, but it is rather the mother, and after her woman per se, who is recruited, positioned by the discourse of metaphysics, in the place of the other: the other of knowledge, the other of desire, and the other of the divine.

Man in his technical house has lost sight of his embodiment; he has forgotten, in effect, the very air he breathes. What could save man from the potential catastrophe—environmental, political, bellicose—of his forgetting? A god perhaps, one brought by "the breath of the cosmos, the song of the poets, the respiration of lovers?" (Irigaray, *Éthique* 124). For Irigaray, however, it must not merely be a question of waiting, but of creation:

> This creation would be our chance, from the humblest of quotidian life to the "greatest," through the opening to a *sensuous transcendental* coming toward us, of which *we* would be the mediators and the bridges. Not only in mourning for Nietzsche's dead God, nor in passive wait of god, but raising him through us, among us, as a resurrection or transfiguration of the blood, of the flesh by way of their language and their ethics. (124)

Such a new ethics, then, entails a resurrection or transfiguration of the blood and the flesh, a recalling of the embodiment of being; it entails an opening up to a transcendental, but a sensuous transcendental—one, I would argue, that is only disclosed to a being who understands itself as immanent to its sensuous horizons.[60]

In her lecture on Merleau Ponty, "L'invisible de la chair," Irigaray urges a reconsideration of the haptic dimension that has been lost to "the privilege of the seeing gaze" (Irigaray, *Éthique* 145), a privilege, it has been argued, that achieved its dominance in modern times (Jay chapter 1; Heidegger, "World Picture").[61] What the phenomenological seer forgets in

giving birth to the things of the visible world is that the invisible world
gave birth to him—that his apparently transcendental distance from objects is the result of the reduction and overcoming of the invisible that allows him to organize his field of vision (Irigaray, *Éthique* 145). For phenomenology, the entire task is to bring what is dark into the light, what is
silent into speech; but in so doing, a presupposition of reversibility, and
hence reducibility, is imposed on these relations. Different terms are reduced to the same. What Irigaray demands is a space or interval that would
confound the expectation of reversibility (Irigaray, *Éthique* 170)—an interval marked by the "to" in the phrase "I love to you," which would indicate the refusal to encapsulate the other in an image or expectation: "I love
to you means I maintain a relation of indirection to you. I do not subju-
gate you or consume you. I respect you (as irreducible). . . . The 'to' is the
site of non-reduction of the person to the object" (Irigaray, *I Love to You*
109). This "to," furthermore, "safeguards a place of transcendence between
us, a place of respect which is both obligated and desired, a place of possible alliance" (Irigaray, *To Be Two* 19).

What is crucial to understand in Irigaray's apparent call for a transcendent place is that such transcendence is radically different from the one we
have been associating with male philosophy. Male philosophy posits the
exceptional status of its place of enunciation so that it can make totalizing
statements about a transcendent reality. The movement toward self-defin-
ition involves a rejection of a feminine background, and this movement is
coupled with a desire for redemption that is encapsulated in the other as a
transcendent object, as a veil. The sensual transcendence of which Irigaray
speaks is only possible from within a sphere of immanence, from a place
that is not initially posited as standing against an excluded background,
from a place that has not wrenched itself free from its sensuous embodiment and environment through the workings of an illusion of autonomy.
The place of woman is this place insofar as woman has been made the
limit of man's knowledge and the safeguard of his desire. From this place,
out of which man was made but into which he has never ventured, another
way takes shape, for it is from this place that a subject can emerge who will
approach another not as the promised answer to the absence around which
he has built his self, the promise of Being, but as one who opens, infinitely
exposed, onto a space of becoming irreducible to fantasies of belonging:
"And the passage from the inside out, from the outside in, the passage between us, is limitless" (Irigaray, *This Sex* 210). The subjects who enter into
such a relation will be able to do so because they will also be changed; no

longer conceived of as transcendent knowers, such subjects will themselves open out onto infinite horizons and conceive of themselves as modes of relation and becoming, as opposed to abstract individuals differentiated from one another by a complex of characteristics.

BECOMING-WOMAN

I implied before that female philosophy was to be equated with antirepresentationalism or noncorrespondence theories of truth, a correlation that would make not only Irigaray and Heidegger female philosophers, but could not fail to include thinkers and movements as varied as neopragmatism; deconstruction; the rhizomatics of Deleuze and Guattari, as well as Deleuze's own rereadings of past philosophers such as Nietzsche, Hume, and Spinoza; and ultimately even Hegel himself, who in certain pragmatic interpretations is not the author of an idealism without bounds but the forerunner of all attempts to think outside the subject-object divide of modern epistemology.[62] Needless to say, such a classification understands the notion of female philosophy in the broadest possible way. Perhaps it is preferable to claim merely that the antirepresentationalism expressed most profoundly by Heidegger but present in all these other thinkers and movements is an important, but only partial instantiation of female philosophy, produced by philosophers whose main limitation was that they did not realize that they were in fact women; that is, that they were speaking from an ontological position made possible by the othering of woman.

In a certain sense, if the central claims of antirepresentationalism are correct and the metaphysical world picture of male philosophy was an epochal error, then it cannot be said that we are becoming women, but rather that we have always been women and have simply forgotten the fact for a long, long time. The problem with this position is that just as male philosophy could not have come into existence without the creation and exclusion of woman, so female philosophy, with its alternate ethical vision, emerges perforce out of this history, much as for Heidegger—and perhaps this is the meaning of his famously obscure suggestion—the danger of technology gives birth to the saving power (Heidegger, "Question" 28). So with female philosophy there can be no Heideggerian nostalgia for the way the Greeks were, no reduction, in fact, of the female to any kind of being whatsoever. The ethical vision of female philosophy lies in its futurity, in its allergy to stability, in its emphasis on becoming.

Despite misgivings by feminist philosophers, including Irigaray, of their work as a possible male appropriation of feminist themes and concerns (Grosz, *Volatile* 164), the thought of Gilles Deleuze and Félix Guattari presents one of the most striking examples of this aspect of female philosophy.[63] In several books and articles, Elizabeth Grosz has detailed the potential use for feminism of Deleuze and Guattari's thought.[64] Rather than examining all of her suggestions, I will focus on a few aspects of their work that strike me as the most emblematic of an ethical female philosophy. To begin with, Deleuze and Guattari have famously rejected the psychoanalytic notion that desire is founded on lack. As Grosz writes, "[l]ack only makes sense insofar as some other, woman, personifies and embodies it for man. Any model of desire that dispenses with the primacy of lack in conceiving desire seems to be a positive step forward and, for that reason alone, worthy of investigation" (165). Before agreeing profoundly with this statement and with much of the philosophical drive of Deleuze and Guattari's work, I will pause to emphasize that, as argued throughout this chapter, desire as lack makes perfect sense *precisely because* woman has always embodied it for man. When this caveat is taken into account, much of the difference that seems to polarize Lacanians and Deleuzians into virulently opposed camps fades away: not just *models* of desire, but also desires (or more precisely, drives) themselves that function in disregard to lack are essential to a female philosophy: "every time the emphasis is put on a lack that desire supposedly suffers from as a way of defining its object, 'the world acquires as its double some other sort of world'" (Deleuze and Guattari, *A-O* 26, quoting Rosset 37), a shadow world, a mirror world decried by Rorty in *Philosophy and the Mirror of Nature*—in short, the metaphysical support upon which male philosophy guarantees its truths.

In addition to refusing the centrality of lack to desire, Deleuze and Guattari's philosophy is concerned not with individuals who enter into relations, but with relations that produce (momentary) individuals. This emphasis can be seen in Deleuze and Guattari's emphasis on packs over groups. A pack is a rhizomatic multiplicity. Unlike a group of individuals, members of the pack establish themselves at the borders and intersections of connections with other members. Characteristics are shared in a contagious or communicative way between heterogeneous terms (Deleuze and Guattari, *Thousand* 238). This is not to say that positions are not differentiated within packs. There are masters, leaders, loners, and demons, figures which, within the economy of the pack Deleuze and Guattari call "anomalous figures" (243). The difference between an anomalous figure and, for example, a fascist leader or typically male leader is that the demonic anomaly is a function of the border of the pack, a border that is ever changing and itself dependent on connections and contagions with other packs, other becomings (245). This is why the economy of pack is susceptible to sorcery, to magic. Only the picture of the world as picture, the world as stage,[65] predicates the impossibility, the irrationality of magic; precisely because it suspends the performativity of what occurs on the stage, it demands the cessation of the participatory involvement of the spectator so common to other modalities of spectacle, ritual, and play.

As a result of Deleuze and Guattari's choice of vocabularies, then, identities are not stable entities preexisting their interactions with others, but rather are the ever-changing functions of those interactions. Such a notion of multiplicity is female insofar as it conceives of relations and contexts, environments and connections, as preceding individuals. An individual exists as excluded from a group; a member of a pack is always grasped in relation to that pack, and by extension to the borders with and members of bordering packs. Hence Deleuze's own reinterpretation of the Leibnizian monad, a house without windows or doors, whose world is contained in the folds of its walls. At first glance this would seem to be the most solipsistic of all "possible worlds," but Deleuze's reading claims precisely the opposite: a monad has no windows, in contrast to a Cartesian subject, because it inflects the entire world in the folds of its walls. The "entire world is enclosed in the soul," in the monad, and no change to the whole does not register in the monad's world (Deleuze, *Fold* 24, 143). A world of windows is a world rent in two, a world of different substances whose contrast implies a negativity, a hole out of which a thinking thing, for example, looks out on extended things. In a similar way, Spinoza is invoked because attributes are conceived of as extensions and continuations—expressions—of essence for which there is only one substance (Deleuze, *Expressionism* 42); Hume is invoked because relations are conceived of as constituted through exteriority, not the contrastive communication between exterior world and interior soul (Deleuze, *Empiricism* 37); Bergson is invoked because he held that possibility is creatively produced out of reality, not that reality is one option in a shadow world of infinite options (Deleuze, *Bergsonism* 20); and Leibniz is invoked because the monad is never conceived of as an individual held out against a background of relationships, but rather as a point of inflection, the only apparently solid and momentary epiphenomenon of an infinitesimal calculus of intensities (Deleuze, *Fold* 23, 47).[66]

Deleuzian philosophy and that of Deleuze and Guattari is concerned, in short, with becoming rather than being. Desiring machines are always in flux, are always constituted by changing assemblages of other machines. Desire is the flow along "a line of flight from identity" (Grosz, *Volatile* 174), always a flowing out into dynamic, "molecular" forms rather than a concentration or grouping into static, "molar" forms. Deleuze and Guattari urge a schizoid mode of production because it is one that follows these lines of flight, as opposed to blocking them:

> It might be said that, of the two directions in *physics*—the molar direction that goes toward the large numbers and the mass phenomena, and the molecular direction that on the contrary penetrates into singularities, their interactions and connections at a distance or between different orders—the paranoiac has chosen the first: he practices macrophysics . . . by contrast the schizo goes in the opposite direction, that of microphysics. (Deleuze and Guattari, *A-O* 280)

When we see a being or a "subject," it is merely a freezing or coagulation of flux and movement, which "is tantamount to saying that the subject is produced as a mere residuum alongside the desiring machines, or that he confuses himself with this third productive machine ["celibate machines"] and with the residual reconciliation that it brings about" (17). Interestingly enough, of all becomings, Deleuze and Guattari privilege becoming-woman. "Although all becomings are already molecular, including becoming woman, it must be said that all becomings begin with and pass through becoming-woman. It is the law to all other becomings" (Deleuze and Guattari, *Thousand* 277). The reason why becoming-woman is central to all becoming is that woman, or girl, is the first object against which men, or boys, are defined as being something—namely, being not *that*. Sexual difference, the difference of woman against which man is defined, in other words, is the first institution or, to use their terms, the first level of stratification or organization that the body undergoes. This means that all becoming, all "reconstruction of the body as a Body without Organs, the anorganism of the body, is inseparable from a becoming-woman, or the production of a molecular woman" (276).[67]

This final point is critically important understanding the connection I am trying to establish between Deleuze and Guattari and the female thought I believe is best exemplified in the work of Irigaray. Deleuze and Guattari, more than any of their male predecessors in female philosophy, express the potential difference of that thought; unlike their predecessors, however, they recognize their own femaleness, and the centrality of femaleness in general, in the genesis of this thought. The primary operative concept, I would argue, in the philosophy of Deleuze and Guattari, is that of the Body without Organs, the BwO. When you theorize the process of desiring from a schizanalytic perspective, one that repudiates notions of lack, desire is seen not as the search for a lost object, but as the project of reconstructing a body without organs, a full body, one converged upon from the position of subjection, subjection to organization, stratification, or territorialization. Deleuze and Guattari are very clear that this concept, and it is a concept in their sense of the word,[68] refers not merely to biological bodies, but to all relations of organization—for example, capital itself is the body without organs of the capitalist (Deleuze and Guattari, *A-O* 10). Bodies of all kinds, biological and social, for example, undergo organization to the point of eventually being conceived in terms of or as a function of their organs—in Spinozian terms, this would be akin to the error of seeing attributes as having some kind of existence independent of substance. In this way it makes sense to see the primary organization as the assignment of gender roles on the basis of the having or not having of a specific organ, although Deleuze and Guattari want to keep this as merely exemplary of a general process of territorialization that occurs constantly and in myriad ways.

Given the opposition between organisms—made by organization, by desiring machines (Deleuze and Guattari, *A-O* 8)—and the BwO, Deleuze and Guattari develop a new vocabulary to speak of desire in terms of flows and production. All organized and territorialized bodies contain within them lines of flight, or better yet are composed and determined by lines of flight, toward their own state of dissolution into a body without organs. The opposition between desiring machines and bodies without organs rewrites a defunct, for Deleuze and Guattari, vocabulary: "The death instinct: that is its name, and death is not without a model. For desire desires death also, because the full body of death is its motor, just as it desires life, because the organs of life are the working machine" (8). Indeed, when we remove the specter of lack, which I will address in a moment, the similarities and potential alliances between schizanalysis and psychoanalysis are striking—and clearly attributed. Recall that Lacan defines the real as that which in the subject suffers from the signifier. Now compare with Deleuze and Guattari: "Desiring machines make us an organism; but at the very heart of this production, within the very production of this production, the body suffers from being organized in this way, from not having some other sort of organization, or no organization at all" (8). This suffering produces the body without organs, the full, unstratified egg with the taut surface, a site of pure, spatial intensity toward which our lines of flight converge (Deleuze and Guattari, *Thousand* 164). We can thus say, without further hesitation, that *the body without organs is a conceptual analogue of the Lacanian real*, once we have come to view the real not from the transcendence of the male side,[69] from which fulfillment always presents itself as an absent, impossible fulfillment, but from the immanent position of female philosophy, a philosophy whose position of enunciation has inhabited the other and knows that it is lacking—knows, in other words, that there is no shadow world, *that lack itself lacks*, that there is nothing "out there" beyond the infinite wealth of the finite world. From this position, desire is not desire for a lost object; desire, in fact, is not desire but drive, the drift of embodiment toward deterritorialization, toward deinstitutionalization. From this position, moreover, the relation to another is not mediated by the elusive and illusory veil of redemption, which packs the other into the form of a convenient filler of our own perceived lack, but is rather mediated by a third and independent term, the openness that pertains as much to the other as to me, and that guarantees her irreducibility to my fantasies.

I have extrapolated, on the basis of their notion of becoming-woman, the pertinence of Deleuze and Guattari's thought to a generalized female philosophy. Although they themselves did not formulate it as such, we can identify this philosophical structure at work in one of their own concepts, namely, that of "minor literature." Minor literature refers to a usage of language that disavows or destabilizes its ordinary or normative form. Ordinary language is the usage that reterritorializes the articulations of sound that had been deterritorialized out of noise (Deleuze and Guattari, *Kafka* 21); this reterritorialization is the function of sense. Language makes sense insofar as it is used according to a set of received designations, which can be referential, when it "presides over the designation of sounds" as things or states of affairs, but also poetic, if that designation turns out to be imagistic or metaphoric (20). Ordinary language is, therefore, representational or extensive, assuming the complementary relation between the subject of enunciation and that of the utterance; what is reterritorialized is what Derrida would call the structurality of language (Derrida, "Structure Sign and Play"), and what De Man would call its literariness (De man, "Resistance"); or, to put it in the language of Lacanian semiotics, its reterritorialization amounts to the production of dead metaphors, the packaging of previously or potentially innovative usage into the staid framework of mundane expectations.

Minor literature is writing that deterritorizalizes this ordinary language use; it leaves behind the protective envelopes of sense by following the lines of flight or escape that such language inevitably carries with it: "a language of sense is traversed by a line of escape—in order to liberate a living and expressive material that speaks for itself and has no need of being put into a form" (Deleuze and Guattari, *Kafka* 21). The minority of a language for Deleuze and Guattari, as exemplified by Kafka's situation as a German-speaking Czech, may stem from its location inside the cultural borders of a major language (20), but we should take this as an instantiation rather than as a definitive determination. For, as they are quick to add, the French of Godard's films also constitutes a minor language within French (23), leading us to speculate that it is not only its cultural situation that determines the minority of a language, but rather the way a particular usage interacts with its surrounding or backdrop language that makes it minor: "We might as well say that minor no longer designates specific literatures but the revolutionary conditions for every literature within the heart of what is called great (or established) literature" (18), a stipulation suggesting that the minority—and hence true greatness, or *authentic* literariness—of a literature is a fully historical phenomenon, in that it is always in reference to an established literature. Minor literature, then, is the name for writing that inhabits the limits of language: "Language stops being representative in order now to move toward its extremities or limits" (23), which need not be seen exclusively as an apology for the avant-garde: a theory such as that of Harold Bloom regarding the battle a poet wages against the influence of his progenitors can also be translated into Deleuze and Guattari's idiom as a minor literature following the lines of flight left to it in the fissures of a great or established literature.

None of this is to say that the social and political conditions of writers are not at stake in a notion of literary minority: "the connection of an individual to a political immediacy" is one of the three characteristics Deleuze and Guattari assign to a minor literature, from which we might venture the following thesis: a literature is minor in precisely the same way as a philosophy is female, namely, the historical circumstances of othering have pushed the enunciator out of the position of absolute subject and into a kind of political immediacy that undermines as much the philosophical claims central to male philosophy as it does the representational territorializations of ordinary language use. Just as thought can wall itself off from the world on the basis of a sovereign confidence in the stability of being, the relation of concepts to a grounding reality, and the subordination of thought itself to preexisting, waiting-to-be-discovered certainties—so does ordinary language subordinate signification, or structurality, to a function of complementarity with a posited world of reference. Such edifices are supported by layers of stratification that leave open lines of escape between them, lines that female philosophy or minor literature follow to their extremities: "To make use of the polylingualism of one's own language, to make a minor or intensive use of it, to oppose the oppressed quality of this language to its oppressive quality, to find points of nonculture or underdevelopment, linguistic Third World zones by which a language can escape, an animal enters into things, an assemblage comes into play" (Deleuze and Guattari, *Kafka* 26–27).

The assemblage is in this case a work of minor literature, for instance a novel by Kafka, such as *The Trial*. Within the very structure of *The Trial* we can discern a variance of perspectives that is operative for the assemblage: "from the point of view of a supposed transcendence of the law, there must be a certain necessary connection of the law with guilt, with the unknowable, with the sentence or the utterance" (44). As the priest in the cathedral explains, "it is not necessary to accept everything as true, one must only accept it as necessary" (276), and this necessity corresponds precisely to the notion of correspondence, of the existence of concepts such as guilt and innocence independent of the enunciation of the law. Kafka's assemblage consists of the very connections that make up the world of the court, it is an assemblage of interlacing hallways and rooms, and by following these lines of escape the assemblage attests to the fact that the unknowability of the law is not due to its transcendence; rather "it is always in the office next door, or behind the door, on to infinity":

> Finally, it is not the law that is stated because of the demands of a hidden transcendence; it is almost the exact opposite: it is the statement, the enunciation, that constructs the law in the name of an immanent power of the one who enounces it—the law is confused with that which the guardian utters, and the writings precede the law, rather than being the necessary and derived expression of it. (Deleuze and Guattari, *Kafka* 45)

The law, then, must be understood as the outcome of performative utterances that purport to describe the law; it is a barrier produced within the confines of language that stakes claim to an extralinguistic existence. This would be the meaning of the doorkeeper's final revelation: the reason the man has gone a lifetime without encountering a single other person seeking access to the law is that this entrance was meant for him alone (Kafka, *Trial* 269).[70]

The revelation that writing precedes the law, consonant with the whole of deconstruction's attitude toward language, relies on a shift of perspective; the reality of the law is not denied, rather its claims to representational justification are undermined. The law is revealed as an effect of enunciation, it is revealed as connected to and in constant movement with desire: according to the shifted perspective, "*where one believed there was the law, there is in fact desire and desire alone.* Justice is desire and not law" (Deleuze and Guattari, *Kafka* 49).[71] Kafka's novel produces this shift in perspective, embodies it, insofar as its assemblage follows the lines of escape of the law's representation in ordinary language, as an autonomous machine dedicated to the pursuit of justice, and finds in the organs of the law, in its offices and corridors, an erotics of justice in which "the authorities of justice are not those who look for offenses but those who are 'attracted, propelled by offense'" (49). In this assemblage, the law as infinitely transcendent is replaced by an "unlimited field of immanence," itself constituted by the "continuum of desire" that is justice, "with shifting limits that are always displaced" (51).[72]

This shift of perspective is immanent to the very architecture of the novel as an assemblage; not in the figurative sense of its architectonics, but in the concrete sense of spatial organization and orientation. The law as transcendental place of enunciation organizes the space of the world around it in discrete blocks, themselves separated by clear and distinct limits (Deleuze and Guattari, *Kafka* 72). Kafka does not renounce this principle of organization, and why would he, "since it is a state of things . . . and since this state functions well in his work" (73)? How could he, we might further ask, because his very perspective functions not as a facile renunciation or opposition (whose political function, we might venture, it serves merely to reinforce, as in "desire against the law"), but rather as parasitic, internally destabilizing, deconstructive? The denial or renunciation of physicalist ontology—the thesis that being is best defined in terms of an accumulation of discrete beings—leads only to the ghetto of antirealist idealism. But if the law in a physicalist ontology is the paranoid despot, the schizoid subject produced by this spatial organization inhabits its lines of flight, experiences the world not as a discontinuous composition of blocks but as a continuity that resolves itself at times and moments into doorways and openings, the way Spinozian substance resolves itself into attributes:

This situation shows up constantly in *The Trial*, where K, opening the door of a tiny room close to his office at the bank, finds himself in the judicial site where the two inspectors are being punished; going to see Titorelli "in a suburb which was almost at the diametrically opposite end of the town from the offices of the court," he notices that the door at the back of the painter's room leads into precisely the same judicial site. (73)

It is perhaps no coincidence that Deleuze and Guattari cite Einstein as an example of someone writing a minor language, speaking of "Einstein and his deterritorialization of the representation of the universe (Einstein teaches in Prague, and the physicist Philipp Frank gives conferences there with Kafka in attendance)" (Deleuze and Guattari, *Kafka* 24). The universe deterritorizalized by relativity was in no uncertain terms a universe of representation, a universalization of a physicalist ontology, with discrete objects relating across empty space; the Einsteinian revolution was to see space as the relations of objects and their relations, forces, as the bending of space; space-time is a result of the very existence of matter, its geometrical properties "are not independent, but they are determined by matter" (Einstein 113). Similarly, in the Riemannian architecture of Kafka's world, that world, the assemblage, "extends over or penetrates an unlimited field of immanence that makes the segments melt and that liberates desire from all its concretizations and abstractions or, at the very least, fights actively against them in order to dissolve them" (Deleuze and Guattari, *Kafka* 86). This last caveat is important, for if we have seen that the law is not a transcendent exception but rather the performative effect of a particular perspective taken on the moving limit of desire, we must also see that this moving limit ceases to move and hence ceases to exist without its concretizations and abstractions, its institutionalizations; desire is nothing other than these and the lines of flight they produce.

ETHICS AND DRIVE

It might appear that Irigaray and Deleuze and Guattari represent an ethics that we could call, in line with the conclusions of Chapter 2, an ethics of drive.[73] In their insistence on the irreducibility of otherness, the immanence of self, the productivity of desire, it could be argued that they are not so much marking their distance from psychoanalysis as fulfilling its promise. In the passage from the classical Freudian and post-Freudian practice to the Lacanian version, "analysis interminable" was also transformed into an analysis with a definite if only possible end, that of becoming an analyst. If the moment marking this transition, called by Lacan "the pass," has the trappings of a religious conversion, it is often described as a transition to a new and radically other ethical field. Miller describes two different ways that a patient can be "cured" of his or her "lack of being" in Lacanian practice: in the first way, which we could compare with a Kojevian ethics of finitude, the analysands stop seeking to rid themselves of their symptoms and come rather to identify with them. The second way involves the so-called "passage through the fantasy." If, Miller writes, "for the first, a feeling of need connotes access to the impossible, for the second, it has an effect of liberty, in other words, of possibility, which gives access to contingency" ("On Semblances" 26). These two ways accord to a certain degree with the very sexual difference that runs throughout psychoanalytic theory, for it is as if, even in the effectuation of a cure to their suffering, men held on to the unity of the phallic function to the very last, as a final barrier protecting them from the nonexistence of the Other. This is their ultimate symptom, and if the fantasy structuring will not give way, then a makeshift, alternate cure is that they come to identify with it, and thus reveal the *jouissance* that sustains it (26).

The other, "most typical, ideal pass is sought on the level of the A [Other], but it must be said that it belongs to women. Lacan privileged the end of analysis on the feminine side, in the same way that he identified the position of the analyst with the feminine position" (Miller, "On Semblances" 27). It is only from this side, according to Miller, that the subject may accede to the kind of radical acceptance of contingency that sloughs off the desperate protection of the substantial veil, of the promise of redemption, and permits entry into relations not founded on the reductive positioning of the Other into particular fantasy schemas. Psychoanalysis, it is true, does not say that the "cure" or "saving power" lies in becoming woman, but neither do Irigaray or Deleuze and Guattari. What they have all said is that the way to an alternate ethical vision cannot stem exclusively from male philosophy, from a metaphysical worldview that instrumentalizes reason in the service of a subject convinced that its salvation lies beyond a veil of representation.[74] Rather, the becoming of the future can only spring from what woman has become, and from what her becoming has made possible. Psychoanalytic thinkers claim that the ideal end of their practice at the clinical level requires pushing through the world of fantasy to the dimension of drive (Žižek, *Tarrying* 60), an experience of the world no longer mediated by the lack of the thing but now open to the presence and wonder of the other, and they have associated this experience with the orientation toward the signifier that Lacan identified with woman. But is it enough to say that with this move we have emerged into a new ethical paradigm? Has the conundrum of the perversity of ethics thereby been resolved?

Ewa Ziarek incorporates this "traversal of fantasy" into her "ethics of dissensus":

> [b]y considering both sides of the ethical relation—the traversal of fantasy and the sublimation of the death drive—this model ceaselessly confronts the subject with the unassimilable otherness within herself and the exorbitant alterity of the Other while deflecting the violence of the death drive toward the transformation of the imaginary and symbolic structures. Consequently, it enables not only a nonviolent response to the Other but also a reconstruction of sociosymbolic relations. (Ziarek 222)

While I am generally sympathetic to Ziarek's position, some differences are important to note. For one, from the perspective of the perversity of ethics, traversing fantasy and sublimating the death drive amount to more or less the same thing. As I have argued, drive or driveness *is* the death drive—the general orientation of drive against the barriers of institutionalization. Both traversing fantasy and sublimation correspond to a way of dealing with the internal disruption of drive's antagonistic relation to the law that alleviates or mitigates problems caused by the idealization typical of "male" or metaphysical desire; both designate an attitude of openness to alterity or even resignation to contingency that in turn corresponds to the ascension of production over reproduction, of creation over representation. Nevertheless, it is misleading to couple this attitude too closely with a notion of nonviolence, if only because what is ultimately attested to by this attitude is the irreducible violence of drive itself: namely, that it is the death drive, internal antagonism, perversity. A certain kind of violence is indeed mitigated—the narcissistic violence of idealization; but another kind of violence—the violence of self-dissolution, of community in Nancy's sense, of contestation—can never be extinguished.

The time has come to address a tension present from the outset of this discussion, but one that now resounds with an insistence impossible to ignore: is the notion of the ethical outlined in this book to be understood as a repudiation of ethics or as a new ethical proposal? If, as I have reiterated on several occasions, attempts to elude the perversity of ethics, the paradox of mediation, or any of its other formulations are doomed to fail because their very impulse is nothing other than a further manifestation of the impossible desire they seek to repudiate, it would seem, then, that this theoretical consideration can have no other conclusion than to declare, in a monotonous rehearsal of so many other ends, the end of ethics. Nevertheless, as each chapter has been concerned to demonstrate in its own way, there is a difference, at least in theoretical terms, between possible attitudes toward the deadlock or limit experience we have called the ethical fault-line.

This difference, which I have stressed can be understood within the framework of Heidegger's much-maligned distinction between authentic and inauthentic modes, is certainly vulnerable to the pragmatist test—namely, whether as a difference it makes any difference at all. What could it possibly mean, in other words, to be resolute, in Heidegger's jargon, or to pierce though the fantasy screen and enter the dimension of drive? What could it mean to accept the Other in its otherness; to relate according to a logic of sublimation rather than of idealization; to slough off the veil of redemption and accept contingency? All of these formulation sound like ethical formulations, because their utterance naturally takes the form of an injunction; they adapt quite well to the structure of the "ought." But it is precisely insofar as they are understood to offer a kind of release from the perversity of ethics that they fail as ethical utterances. There is no beyond to the fantasy screen; there is no real acceptance of the otherness of the Other; there is no way, really, to remove the veil of redemption from our eyes. Our acceptance of contingency will always be saddled by a secret hope for immediacy; our belief in finitude will always give way to dreams of eternity.

Insofar, then, as a theoretical description of ethics contains within itself a kind of ethics of its own, it can only be understood as a manifesto for duplicity. Dreams of radical immanence suffer the same potential consequence as dreams of transcendence: they both have a way of claiming to exceed the law, and hence the paradox of mediation, creating what Agamben calls a "state of exception" in which the law is in force without significance—a state Agamben and many others have accused of being operational for the crimes of totalitarianism (Agamben 52). Nevertheless, any claim whatsoever to outstrip this situation will run the same risk, because—and this is the lesson of Lacan's reading of Kant and Sade—trying to enjoy without the law or have the law without enjoyment necessarily stems from exactly the same urge and leads toward exactly the same potentiality of excess. To embrace duplicity, however, would be one way of taking seriously the curious "ethical" injunction from the end of Lacan's seminar on ethics, not to give way as to one's desire. The phrase "not to give way as to," or *ne pas céder sur*, is not ambivalent by accident; its essence lies in its very ambivalence: it means simultaneously "do not give in to it" and "do not give up on it." In the context of the competing temptations of immanence and transcendence discussed above, this means: do not give in to them, but also do not fall into the trap of thinking you can get away from them.

If this is an ethics, it is a strange one indeed. While on the one hand it constitutes a repudiation of the hope of modern and perhaps of "postmodern" ethics, on the other it seems to hold out its own promise of some kind of effective change that "behaving" in this way, or even that just believing this, can bring about. Of what could such change consist? Perhaps the best way of approaching the problem is to return to the comparatively tangible problems discussed in the first chapter on perversity. There we saw the emergence of an irreducible conundrum for ethical thought: namely, that the constitution of drive through institutionalization predicts the existence of a powerful urge in human desire to transgress whatever social laws are erected, no matter for what purpose. As we further saw in Chapter 2, attempting to deal with such a transgressive urge by totalizing or absolutizing the law in order to eradicate all contrary (pathological) urges in the name of universal morality runs the risk of releasing a pure or totalitarian pathology, whose danger in the political arena is more than evident. Nevertheless, the anarchical attempt to obliterate the law leads to precisely the same state of exception. The lesson of a manifesto for duplicity, then, is that the law will be respected and transgressed continually and in constant measure. At the social level there is nothing ethically new in this formulation, because despite various theoretical attempts to think otherwise, this is what occurs always and everywhere. Our various attempts to uphold the law against its transgression coincide in large measure with other resistances we are engaged in against laws upheld by others. Moreover, the enjoyment we harvest from our transgressive urges are utterly dependent on the laws we oppose, just as the law needs for its very existence the proliferation of urges that forge our resistances to it.

Where this ethical formulation might have a more practical effect is at the level of personal interactions, and clearly this is where psychoanalysis would find reason to deploy it. A constant source of discontent—and here I mean among the middle class of the developed world, where the kind of vital urgency felt by the truly impoverished is not an issue—is the feeling that things would really be better if only. . . . To quote Laurie Anderson's song *Language Is a Virus,* "paradise is exactly like where you are right now, only much, much better." It is the most commonplace example of what

Lacan called the metonymy of desire that this malaise is almost never cured by improving one's lot. One still remains focused on the world of possibilities, and in some way inured to the present world. Given this situation, a natural move is to opt for some "non-Western" set of beliefs that repudiates the very idea of desire itself, such as the Buddhist doctrine of the cessation of desire. The sort of ethics of drive we have been outlining here could not be further from this option. To learn how not to give way as to your desire is to learn to embrace your desire *as* desire, in its essence as nonfulfillment. Here I must immediately take issue with the objection that this is somehow an apology for quietism. To embrace desire as nonfulfillment in no way means that I should—if my desire is socially unacceptable—not act on it, a position that would condemn gays and lesbians, for example, to the darkness of the closet. On the contrary, to not give way as to one's desire would be to act on one's desires in the full knowledge that desire itself will not be thereby fulfilled, that despite and in the face of the most extraordinary experience of rapture, desire, as it always does, will go on.

As discussed in Chapter 3, this is an interpretation on which thinkers influenced by psychoanalysis and deconstruction should converge. That the paradox of mediation cannot be mediated means that we will always be driven by the specter of the immediate, and that at the same time we will always be incapable of fulfilling that drive. As a result, any philosophy that nevertheless strives to banish the lure of immediacy entirely falls into its own world of illusions, meaning that the question of God, like the hope for full presence, cannot be banished, even by a thought as materialistic as that founded by Freud or as rigorous in its attention to the traps of metaphysics as that advanced by Derrida and Nancy.

There can be no doubt, given our discussion of the relation of ethics to sexual difference in this final chapter, that a psychoanalytic perspective privileges the position of woman both clinically, as regards the cure, and philosophically, in its admiration for the developments of what we have called female philosophy. Nevertheless, it would be a mistake to assume that the paradox of ethics has been solved with female philosophy. While a profound suspicion of the redemptive paradigm that dominates metaphysics is salutary for thinking about ethics, to embrace female philosophy as a redemption from that paradigm can obviously do no more than repeat the errors of the past. But perhaps there is something more to the female side than the already formidable sign of the lack in the other. That refusal to buy into the transcendence of the Other as reality, right, or truth is matched, in Lacan's little diagram, by a duplicitous arrow, a vector leading to the sign that stands for the phallus, but also for the authority of another world, transcendence, the state of exception, whatever aspect of otherness that grounds a world or way of life by the mere fact of its absence or the promise of its revelation. While the revolutionary potential of female philosophy is clearly the suspicion it has shown for all these illusions, it may be that its contribution to thinking through the problems of ethics lies not in the sign of pure suspicion, but in its refusal to follow either vector to its logical outcome. In this refusal we find the bifurcation of vectors that seems to condemn desire to a duplicity that will not, for all our efforts, be erased.

Notes

Notes

PREFACE

1. See for example Zupancic; Copjec, *Radical Evil*; and Žižek, *Tarrying*.
2. See, for example, Žižek, *Ticklish* 247–57.
3. In a sense, as I explain below, precisely opposed to how Nancy uses the word.

CHAPTER I

1. Ethical in a thoroughly modern, i.e., Kantian sense, as discussed below.
2. See Gadamer's discussion of prejudices, *Truth and Method* 277–85.
3. See, for example, Augustine Book XI, chapters 17 and 18.
4. See Copjec's discussion, *Radical Evil*, especially x–xi.
5. See Chapter 3 below, and Kant, *Foundations* 23.
6. This is precisely the aspect of Freud's thought that makes him popular among such current schools of thought as neopragmatism. For Rorty, for example, Freud joins the fight against the Kantian/Aristotelian tradition of locating the essence of human being in freedom or in a Sartrean "hole of Being"; in this way Freud becomes a protopragmatist of sorts by avoiding the question of human essence altogether and "making conscience just one more, not particularly central, part of a larger, homogenous machine" (Rorty, "Freud" 157).
7. E.g., Bettelheim 103–12.
8. A choice Lacan termed "bastard," claiming to prefer the English "drive" for its resonances with *dérive*, a notion denoting the drifting/deriving nature of the chain of signifiers (Lacan, "Subversion" 301).
9. It is important to note that Foucault himself largely exonerates Freud in this respect, saying that of all the technologies and institutions of sex it is only psychoanalysis, at least up until the decade of the 1940s, that "rigorously opposed the political and institutional effects of the perversion-heredity-degenerescence system" (Foucault, *History* 119).

10. As Lacan wrote, "every drive is, virtually, a death drive." See "Position de l'inconscient" 848, and Brousse's commentary (Brousse 107). Copjec's elaboration is decisive, and corroborates my reading later in this chapter of the drive as *essentially* equivocal: "The full paradox of the death drive, then, is this: while the *aim* (*Ziel*) of the drive is death, the *proper and positive activity* of the drive is to inhibit the attainment of its aim" (Copjec, *Imagine* 30).

11. See also Freud, *Abriss* 44.

12. "We came to know what the 'sexual instincts' were from their relation to the sexes and to the reproductive function. We retained this name after we had been obliged by the findings of psycho-analysis to connect them less closely with reproduction" (Freud, "Instincts" 265).

13. See Laplanche's analysis of Freud's theory of sadomasochism, in which he writes, "[s]exuality appears as a drive that can be isolated and observed only at the moment at which the nonsexual activity, the vital function, becomes detached from its natural object or loses it. For sexuality it is the reflective (*selbst* or *auto-*) moment that has become constitutive, the moment of a turning back towards self, an 'autoerotism' in which the object has been replaced by a fantasy, by an object reflected within the subject" (88). It is crucial to note that, in Laplanche's view, sexuality is associated with the perversion (turning) of the drives, which is simultaneously related to autonomy and fantasy. It is as if our very potential for autonomy (ethics) required the primordial distance from self (fault-line) produced by the drive's fundamental perversity and recorded in fantasy both as fundamental fiction and as the minimal detachment from lived reality needed to stage a desire in the first place.

14. In this light, then, in the section that follows we will consider masochism as the paradigmatic perversion, for it is in masochism that the negative terms of the polarities are most clearly manifest.

15. This is perhaps the moment to express what should be obvious: namely, that Freud's neurological speculations correspond to the infancy of a scientific discipline that has changed a great deal in the interceding years. Nevertheless, Freud recognized that his descriptive language functioned essentially by analogy, and did not intend it as a literal representation of the brain's mechanical functioning (Wallwork 35). It is in this spirit that I am reading his metapsychological theses as contributions to a theory of the ethical.

16. Let me note here the parallels between this reading of Freud and Derrida's deconstruction of primary and secondary processes in "Freud and the Scene of Writing." For Derrida, Freud's metapsychological apparatus reveals the effects of writing in the place of what one would suppose to be original, virginal being. Speaking of the "breaching" of the *Bahnungen* that structure the unconscious, he notes that "there is no pure breaching without difference," because a choice of neural itinerary always requires a preference (Derrida, "Freud" 201). Sin requires choice; choice requires knowledge; the first choice is never pure.

17. This formulation resonates with Heidegger's assertion that Dasein *is* temporality, insofar as its fundamental existential mode, care (*Sorge*), entails the projection of its possibilities into the future (Heidegger, *Being and Time* 179). This and other parallels will receive further elaboration below.

18. "presses, untamed, ever onward."

19. See also Freud, "A Child" 193–94.

20. Sadism "proper" here refers to a sadism as perversion, rather than the merely aggressive sadism that is concerned with domination. Deleuze, who wishes to distinguish rigorously between sadism and masochism, and to deny their supposed complementarity, nonetheless allows for the complexity of their relationship when this distinction is taken into account: "Thus Freud's first model is more complex than its seems, and suggests the following sequence: aggressive sadism— turning around of sadism upon the self masochistic experience—hedonistic sadism (by projection and regression)" ("Coldness" 43–44). As it is my claim that the "aggressive sadism" is not a perversion of drive but merely a description of its active tendency to overcome a stimulus, the only sadism to speak of would be that resulting from the internalization of the masochistic experience, what Deleuze calls hedonistic sadism. The result, of course, is that the two are very complementary indeed.

21. This corresponds as well to Freud's argument in "A Child" 199. The fact that sexual possession at the hands of some substitute for the father constitutes a "normal" drive for women explains why "feminine" masochism is a perversion primarily reserved for men. In other words, its manifestations must be far more extreme to be even noticed in women (Silverman 189).

22. See Airaksinen 27–35.

23. As Silverman notes, perversions perform the transgression of boundaries, separating such basic categories as food and excrement, human and animal, life and death, pleasure and pain, adult and child, and so forth (Silverman 187).

24. This position was also held by proponents of what could be called the anthropological approach to the perversions. See Medard Boss's discussion (33–34).

25. See, for example, Freud, *Interpretation* 276.

26. See Žižek: "Following Freud, Lacan repeatedly insisted that perversion is always a socially constructive attitude, while hysteria is much more subversive and threatening to the predominant hegemony. . . . The pervert is thus the 'inherent transgressor' *par excellence*: he brings to light, stages, practices the secret fantasies that sustain the predominant public discourse, while the hysterical position precisely displays doubt about whether those secret perverse fantasies are 'really *it*'" (*Ticklish* 247–48). As Copjec says, "[t]he conflation of Kant with Sade, or of ethical action with perversion, is no doubt due, in large part, to a theoretical laxity on the question of transgression." But as she goes on to argue, "[t]here has to be some *fissure* in the law itself in order for transgression to get a foothold" (*Imagine* 208). The notion of the perversity of ethics points precisely to such a primordial, mutual

imbrication of law and transgression; indeed, the law is always divided between the rule presented to us and that prior manifestation whose institutionalization structures our desire vis-à-vis the rule.

27. See Butler's development of these notions in *Gender Trouble* and *Bodies that Matter*; in *The Psychic Life of Power* she focuses on the "passionate attachments" that enable or drive the "subjectivation" (*assujetissment*) that accounts for both the formation of a subject and its simultaneous conformity to often oppressive social models of behavior and identification (*Psychic Life* 7).

28. I see parallels between this argument and Ewa Ziarek's, who writes: "I rethink antagonisms and the instability of social relations in democracy [her referent here is Laclau, along with Butler and Chantal Mouffe] in the context of the subject's conflicting relation to 'the Other within' and ask under what conditions it can function either as a condition of responsibility or as an exacerbation of social conflict" (Ziarek 10). To reiterate, that social antagonism should be understood in a psychical context does not mean that resistance ceases to be problematic; what it does mean is that the conditions for perverse or ethical desire underlie individuals' interactions in the social sphere, even as these conditions are themselves the very mark of the individual's primordial sociality (i.e., institutionalization).

29. A sense precisely opposite to the notion of immanence defined in conjunction with Deleuze's thought in Chapter 4 below.

CHAPTER 2

1. By calling this a turning point and putting emphasis on the *Ethics* seminar, I am not thereby claiming that the seminar need be seen as instituting a "radical break" in the development of Lacan's thought. Indeed I agree with Tim Dean that the tendency to locate such breaks can lead to the creation of "early" and "late" intellectual personalities such that one period or another of the thinker's work may be more easily repudiated (Dean 37). The turning point in question has more to do with the kinds of questions to which Lacan turns his attention during this period, and can in no way be understood as a "turning away" from, for instance, his ideas concerning language and the unconscious.

2. This claim of influence is contested by some followers of Lacan, who base their arguments on Lacan's own insistence that his interest in Heidegger had been largely "propaedeutic" (*XI* 18). Lee accepts this argument (136), as does Zupancic (259), but one must keep in mind that it was not good form among French intellectuals to openly espouse the thought of such a politically notorious thinker. For a (somewhat biased) history and overview of the relation between Heidegger and French thought, see Rockmore, esp. 153–62. If one pays attention to the content of Lacan's thought in the 1960s and after, one can certainly conclude, as Recalcati does, that Heidegger remained among Lacan's most important influences, although he also maintains that Lacan incorporated and then transcended Heidegger's thought. See, for example, Recalcati 181–206.

3. Another important example of those who looked to Freud is Erich Fromm.

4. This analogy concerns the *akrates*, or morally weak man, who is led like a slave by his passions, and it is inherited almost unaltered from Plato. Nevertheless, Aristotle is concerned in Book Seven of the *Nicomachean Ethics* to distinguish *akrasia* from mere ignorance of the good, as it is explained in Plato. For Aristotle, the *akrates* acts against the good out of weakness of will, without being ignorant of the good. See Amélie Rorty's comments (268, 275).

5. This joke comes from an anthology of Jewish witticisms, *Warum hat Kain Abel erschlagen? Weil Abel ihm alte jüdische Witze erzählt hat.*

6. This explanation owes a great deal to Freud's own theory of jokes. See, for example, *Der Witz* 166–67.

7. In all cases where Lacan quotes in ancient Greek, I will write the term in Latin letters.

8. An essential element of Nussbaum's argument in *Upheavals of Thought.*

9. "After all, what can I presume Aristotle knew? Perhaps the less I assume he has knowledge, the better I read him" (Lacan, *XX* 67).

10. See Lacan, *XX* 48, where Lacan clarifies that the unconscious is not structured *by* language but *like* a language.

11. See Wittgenstein, *Philosophical Investigations* paragraph 256. See also Stern 103.

12. This insight puts psychoanalysis in league with pragmatism and other contemporary anti-representationalist discourses. See my "Keeping Pragmatism Pure: Rorty with Lacan."

13. See, for example, Deleuze and Guattari, *A Thousand Plateaus* 154.

14. See Žižek, *The Ticklish Subject,* perhaps the most detailed installment of this argument. See Chapter 4 below for discussion of a possible rapprochement with Deleuze and Guattari's position.

15. As expressed in the proposition: "you cannot learn a language whose terms express semantic properties not expressed by the terms of some language you are already able to use" (Fodor 59).

16. "We could not have acquired any language unless its fundamental properties were already in place, in advance of experience, as argued in the epistemic rationalism of early rationalist psychology" (Chomsky, *Language and Thought* 48).

17. Technically we should speak of the preconscious, as consciousness would then refer to active awareness: "It is from that moment when we speak of our will and our understanding as distinct faculties that we have a preconscious, and that we are able, in effect, to articulate in a discourse something of that chattering by means of which we articulate ourselves inside ourselves, we justify ourselves, or we rationalize for ourselves, with reference to this or that, the progress of our desire" (Lacan, *VII* 61–62). Implicitly, *will* must correspond to the unconscious organization of *Sachvorstellungen* and *understanding* to the discourse of *Wortvorstellungen*; like the straw and the grain, their very existence is a function of their distinction.

18. The persistent Derridean critique of Lacan finds its target here, in the idea

of some center, be it substantial or absent, toward which desire somehow always returns. See especially Derrida, *Post Card* 437. Nevertheless, it should be clear from the above formulation that the place of *das Ding* and the absent center of desire are all formulations for what is fundamentally an effect of the insitutionalizations of the reality principle. The "return" only retroactively produces the phantasmatic presence of an object to be refound and always misses it at that. "A letter always arrives at its destination" implies a difference between the destination it has become as an effect of the arrival, and the destination that is claimed for it prior to its arrival. Nevertheless, that phantasmatic, absent presence is crucial for understanding what can only be called the metaphysics of desire. Derrida, for his part, often comes across as supporting such a formulation: "The prime mover, as 'pure act' (*energéia he kath' hautén*), is pure presence. As such, it animates all movement by means of the desire it inspires. Desire is the desire of presence" (Derrida, "Ousia" 52). It is also not an objection to claim that Derrida is here critiquing the deployment of presence in Aristotle and Hegel, since the point of the argument is to claim, *pace* Heidegger, that time or temporality cannot be thought *without* reference to presence. I am grateful to Martin Hägglund for his insights into this debate.

19. See Lacan, "Agency of the Letter."

20. A point hammered home most insistently by Wittgenstein, who never tired of repeating that although we *can* think of meanings as images accompanying our words, we do not *have* to. See, for example, his *Blue Book* 3.

21. For example: "[I]t is a duty to preserve one's life, and moreover everyone has a direct inclination to do so. But for that reason, the often anxious care which most men take of it has no intrinsic worth, and the maxim of doing so has no moral import" (Kant, *Foundations* 13).

22. See discussion in Chapter 3 below.

23. A position that resonates with the Buddhist doctrine of cessation of desire. This connection has been explored with some frequency. See, for example, John Suler.

24. That the "evential" represents just such a dimension can be seen in Badiou's rendering of Paul's revelation into ontological terms: "The ontological substructure of this conviction (but ontology is of no interest to Paul) is that there is no evential [*événementiel*] One that can be the One of a particularity. The only possible correlate to the One is the universal" (Badiou, *Saint Paul* 80, my translation).

25. It is also crucial to point out, as I will spell out in the next chapter, that to deny the positivity of transcendence is not to cling to a strictly immanentist position; rather, while refusing to posit a positive content to transcedence, the psychoanalytic position also insists on the inevitability of a transcendent production of some kind. Copjec, for example, writes approvingly of both Badiou and Agamben for refusing to embrace the body as "the limit, par excellence, that which puts an

end to any claim to transcendence. What Badiou is here proposing, however, is that our idea of bodily finitude assumes a point of transcendence. Like Agamben, Badiou argues that death becomes immanentized in the body only on condition that we presuppose a beyond" (Copjec, *Imagine* 29). Although I share Copjec's view, as I argue here and in later notes, at times Badiou and Agamben have recourse to a transcendence that clearly exceeds the status of necessary presupposition.

26. See Zupancic 53–58.

27. "The fact is that idealization involves an identification of the subject with the object, whereas sublimation is something quite different" (Lacan, *VII* 111).

28. Ziarek writes of an "undoing of the idealization of the Other" as essential to a nonnarcissistic love (135). I agree with her, but take partial issue with her notion of sublimating the death drive, as I explain in Chapter 4 below.

29. Here, again, we see parallels with Badiou's notion of the event, although Lacan's association of the moment of *creatio* with sublimation makes it clear that the context is aesthetic, passionate, and not one that we can evaluate ethically by virtue of its relation to truth. As we will see below, Lacan's engagement with Heidegger led him to conceive of *creatio* and truth as, indeed, vitally linked, but neither of their positions allows for the kind of evaluative distinctions that Badiou's political interests require him to make.

30. See Christopher Fynsk's discussion of Lacan and Heidegger, and specifically of their conceptions of "the thing," in section two of his *Infant Figures*. Specifically, for Fynsk, Lacan's reading of the Freudian unconscious engages "something on the order of what Heidegger tried to think as the 'ontico-ontological difference' " (Fynsk, *Infant Figures* 99), an argument with which I am in complete agreement. Žižek's analysis is simultaneously astute and amusing, as he brackets the history of civilization between the enclosing of the void of the Thing by the Greek vase and its correlate enclosure in today's chocolate *Kinder Eggs*: "the two moments of the Thing in the history of the West: the sacred Thing at its dawn, and the ridiculous merchandise at its end" (*Puppet* 147). The trick, he points out, is to realize that the vase was also, of course, a commodity.

31. See Lacan, "Subversion" 303, and Žižek's discussion of "quilting points" in *Sublime Object*, chapter 3.

32. See Roudinesco 219–31.

33. Cf. Heidegger's transformation of the "old proposition" *ex nihilo nihil fit* (nothing comes from nothing) into "*ex nihil omne ens qua ens fit* (from the nothing all beings as beings come to be)" (Heidegger, "What Is" 95).

34. See Capobianco for a preliminary discussion of convergences in the ethical thought of Heidegger and Lacan. See also Richardson and Recalcati. Krzysztof Ziarek's discussion of these two thinkers and their revision by Irigaray is of great interest as well.

35. Albeit as only one aspect of that concept.

36. Conscience as awareness leads into the highly problematic distinction between the authentic and the inauthentic, which I address at the end of this chapter in relation to the ethics of psychoanalysis.

37. Derrida takes up Heidegger's failure to think through the human-animal distinction in *Of Spirit* (11, passim).

38. As several commentators have pointed out, this substitution amounts not only to an impoverishment, but also to a corruption or perversion of the very intent of Kant's ethics. Zupancic invokes the Lacanian definition of a pervert as one who enjoys for the other, who makes himself an instrument of God and hence bucks his ultimate responsibility to choose as a case utterly opposed to that of an ethical act (60, 97), while Juliet Flower MacCannell claims even more directly that Eichmann occupies the position of the pervert (145).

39. See Lacan, "Kant with Sade" 55: "we will say that it [*Philosophy in the Bedroom*] gives the truth of the *Critique*." My arguments here echo those of Zupancic. See especially pages 85 and 90–92.

40. Here my reading agrees with that of Joan Copjec, who argues, "Lacan's attack on 'Poland' is a radical one, it is an attack on the transcendental categories and the assurances they provide us" (*Imagine* 5). The existence of such "transcendental categories" depends on erasure of the difference at the heart of the self from which the moral law emerges; in other words, the ethical attests not to the existence of transcendental categories, but to their impossibility. In a similar vein, she says of perversion: "On the contrary, perversion is the attempt to avoid the very status of subject, precisely by avoiding the split embodied in a whole series of antinomies that characterize and unsettle the (neurotic) subject" (223). This is, of course, exactly what, for Lacan, Kant's ethics amount to.

41. To the outburst of one of the fellow participants in his orgy, that he may be going too far, Dolmancé responds, "Get it into your head once and for all, my simple and very fainthearted fellow, that what fools call *humaneness* is nothing but a weakness born of fear and egoism; that this chimerical virtue, enslaving only weak men, is unknown to those whose character is formed by stoicism, courage, and philosophy" (Sade 360). How can we fail but note that the language with which Dolmancé urges on his cohorts is that of duty, pressing them on against their natural inclination, born of fear and egoism, to stop.

42. For a far more detailed comparative analysis of Kant's and Sade's ethical systems, see Martyn, who argues that both thinkers fail in their projects in similar, and similarly productive ways.

43. See Barbara Johnson's discussion of this trope in "Is Female to Male as Ground Is to Figure?" I choose the term "imbrication" because of its evocation of overlapping tiles, in which the shape of each tile is in part a function of the absence or obscuring of another.

44. Lewis and Short's Latin dictionary defines *vel*, the word Lacan uses for this algebraic conjunction, as a "disjunctive conjunction, to introduce an alternative as

a matter of choice or preference, or as not affecting the principal assertion" in other words, precisely the sort of radically ambiguous negation implied by the phrase "identity founded on radical nonreciprocity."

45. For further commentary see Lee 143 and Clément 179.

46. See, for example: Dunand 247, 253–54; Lacan, *VII* 282, 304, 319.

47. See Lee 148–49.

48. And purification of desire is still seen as a necessary aspect of becoming an analyst. See Brousse 101.

49. But Poe would also call this *perverse*, which raises the question of the relation between *perversity*, as the universal effect of the ethical fault-line on desire, and *perversion* as the symptomatic manifestation of the pervert, who, as Lacan writes, "makes himself the instrument of the Other's jouissance" (*Écrits* trans. 320). This is the principal grounds for why the various transgressions the pervert imagines or puts into practice cannot amount to a subversive act on the political or social level. The pervert passes the buck, as it were, as to his or her own *jouissance* by believing, in spite of the evidence against it, that the Other is not lacking. This is obviously one of a number of possible defense strategies against the uncanny effects of the lack of the Other on the subject, of which psychosis, as the absolute refusal of this lack, is the most radical. If the fault-line is the most intimate marker of the Other's nonexistence, then the perversity of Antigone's desire is in fact opposed to the structure of the perversions, precisely because in her refusal to pass the buck she chooses to be "the guardian of the being of the criminal as such." For an excellent discussion of the structure of the perversions see Dor's *Structure and Perversions*. While Dor repudiates the theoretical separation of perversity from the perversions, he does so only insofar as the former term calls upon us "to make moral judgments on behavior" (64), and he does not focus on the philosophical sense I have developed here. Likewise, in Bruce Fink's definition "perversion involves the attempt to prop up the law so that limits may be set to jouissance" ("Perversion" 38), the symptom in question is secondary and reactive, not primordial. James Penney has also developed a similar distinction between primary and secondary perversions in his *The World of Perversion*.

50. The lines are: "My husband could die and I could marry, / My child could die, my womb could bear another / But Oedipus and Jocasta cannot / Make another brother for Antigone. / That is why I did you special honour." (Sophocles 50).

51. Here Judith Butler emphasizes a reading that I do not share. After quoting several times the phrase "the ineffaceable character of what is," she next quotes as Lacan's "controversial conclusion": "that separation of being from the characteristics of the historical drama he has lived through, is precisely the limit or the *ex nihilo* to which Antigone is attached" (Lacan, *VII* 279). Butler's critique runs as follows: "Here, again, one might well ask how the historical drama she has lived through returns her not only to this persistent ineffaceability of what is but the certain prospect of effaceability. By separating the historical drama she lives

through from the metaphysical truth she exemplifies for us, Lacan fails to ask how certain kinds of lives, precisely by virtue of the historical drama that is theirs, are relegated to the limits of the ineffaceable" (*Antigone's Claim* 50). Lacan, however, is not talking about Antigone in the quoted passage; he is talking about her attachment to Polynices, and why this attachment is radically affective in utter disregard to the specificities of Polynices' crime, the details of his life history, or even his kinship to Antigone: "Antigone's position represents the radical limit that affirms the unique value of his being without reference to any content, to whatever good or evil Polynices may have done, or to whatever he may be subjected to" (*VII* 279).

52. See Zupancic's discussion, 7–19.

53. Here I am indebted to Charles Shepherdson's brilliant discussion in "Of Love and Beauty in Lacan's Antigone." See also Christopher Fynsk's excellent essay, "Between Ethics and Aesthetics," in which he argues that "[t]he aesthetic funtion, as Lacan refers to it, *indicates* the originary relationality that I have termed the an-archic ground of praxis, and does so in a manner (in a 'usage') that constitutes a kind of essential exigency for any political or ethical thought" (85). Fynsk's "an-archic ground of praxis" is, in my reading, equivalent to the point of absolute affect I am theorizing here.

54. I discuss this passage in relation to the notion of theatricality in *How the World Became a Stage*.

55. There is a profound connection between this psychoanalytic notion of aesthetics, as involving the emergence of presence within representational frameworks, and the aesthetic theory developed Hans Ulrich Gumbrecht, whose book *The Production of Presence* is offered as an attempt to rescue aesthetics from the persistent obligation to interpret (in a non-Lacanian way) by focusing on what he calls the silent side of meaning, in which objects, events, and literature make themselves felt in our lives precisely by not meaning something.

56. See Nussbaum, *Upheavals of Thought* (22): "all of these features not only are compatible with, but actually are best explained by, a modified version of the ancient Greek Stoic view, according to which emotions are forms of judgment that ascribe to certain things and persons outside a person's own control great importance for the person's own flourishing." Needless to say, I am not espousing what Nussbaum calls the adversorial position either: "the view that emotions are 'non-reasoning movements,' unthinking energies that simply push the person around, without being hooked up to the ways in which she perceives or thinks about the world" (24–25).

57. "Instead, he staged the singular desire of the philosopher and thereby contributed considerably to opening the space for a sort of new philosophical culture. In which we are situated, despite efforts to make us forget it so as to turn back the clock" (Derrida, *Resistances* 46).

58. Charles Shepherdson, "Of Love and Beauty," discusses these lines from

Antigone and Heidegger's reading of them as well as that of Lacan in a longer version of the above-cited essay. Heidegger's reading is from *Introduction to Metaphysics* 151–52.

59. I am in agreement here with Copjec's reading in *Imagine There's No Woman*: "She gives herself her own law and does not seek validation from any other authority." In other words, it is not the otherness but the nonexistence of the Other on which Lacan's interpretation turns.

60. Thanks to David E. Johnson for bringing this reading to my attention.

61. Rorty's understanding of "authenticity" is characteristically straightforward: "What the younger Heidegger tells us about the sociohistorical situation of Dasein is just what the older Wittgenstein tells us about our situation in regard to language that when we try to transcend it by turning metaphysical we become self-deceptive, inauthentic" ("Wittgenstein" 51).

62. Adorno's *Jargon of Authenticity* is the classic critique in this respect, although to my mind it depends on a profound misreading of the text. For Adorno, Heidegger's obsession with a totalizing philosophy ("In Heidegger, as in idealism, that which tolerates nothing beyond itself is understood to be the whole. The least trace which went beyond such identity would be as unbearable as anyone who insisted on his own individuality is to the fascist" [Adorno 140]) is what accounts for the idealization of death in his notion of authenticity (Adorno 137). Where Adorno reads the notion of totality at work in Heidegger's thought as a kind of radical idealist negation of anything exceeding my horizon, it is more consistent with Heidegger's argument in *Being and Time* and elsewhere to read precisely the opposite movement in his affirmation of the whole: namely, that I cannot expect any more of myself than my horizon in its essential limitedness, or finitude, and yet philosophy in both its materialistic and idealistic manifestations do precisely that: point to my outermost limits and then point to that something other that exceeds those limits, not recognizing that pointing to it effectively incorporates it into my horizon. Death is the name for that essential finitude that cannot be tamed in this way. I make this argument in much greater detail in chapter 4 of my *The Philosopher's Desire*. Lévinas's distancing from Heidegger, which I discuss in Chapter 3 below, is also largely based on a misunderstanding of what Heidegger means by totality.

63. Derrida's argument against Lacan in "The Purveyor of Truth" ["Le facteur de la verité"]: "a letter does *not always* arrive at its destination, and from the moment that this possibility belongs to its structure one can say that it never truly arrives…" (Derrida, *The Post Card* 489).

64. Here I would like to propose a parallel between this "authentic" knowledge and Judith Butler's notion of a nonviolent ethical stance, which she elaborated in her 2002 Adorno Lectures, *Kritik der ethischen Gewalt*: "I would say that this new ethical meaning springs from a certain preparedness to recognize the very limits of recognition, and to admit that, there where we claim to know and represent ourselves, we fail in certain ways, in ways, however, that are essential to what we are;

and this new ethical meaning also springs from a certain preparedness to admit that we can also not expect anything else from others" (Butler, *Kritik* 55, my translation). This recognition is, rather than a certainty, as she asks, "Can we know in an unlimited way that our recognition is always limited?" very much what I argue authentic knowledge is for Heidegger: knowledge as unavoidable uncertainty, disorientation, anxiety: "I come from something that precedes me and that oversteps my borders, and that in no way frees me from the duty to give an account of myself. If, despite this, I act as though I could reconstruct the norms responsible for my status as subject, then I deny that very disorientation and interruption of my narrative implied in the social dimension of these norms" (*Kritik* 93). Authentic knowledge, ethical meaning in Butler's terms, is the recognition that the self is always-already conditioned, undermined, and divided by the social world it springs from. This constitutive division is what I am calling the fault-line, but its function as precisely something *real* in the Lacanian economy, a term that Butler has otherwise been firm in rejecting from her thought. See her critique of Žižek and the concept of the real in *Bodies that Matter*. My thanks to Christopher Fynsk for reminding me of this important connection.

65. Again, the full argument is made in my *The Philosopher's Desire*.

66. As Derrida writes of deconstruction's own analytic desire, "[b]ut here, without delay, comes the double bind: to analyse such a desire does not mean to renounce its law and to suspend the order of reason, of meaning, of the question of the origin, of the social bond" (*Resistances* 36). Indeed, it cannot. In order for the analytic drive at work in deconstruction to be at all possible, it must simultaneously rely on (a hope for) the very simplicity of meaning its own analytic movement dissolves.

67. I see this reading as highly amenable to the best interpretations of deconstruction. As Martin Hägglund writes in his excellent analysis of Derrida and Lévinas "The Necessity of Discrimination," "In effect, every attempt to organize life in accordance with ethical or political prescriptions will have been marked by a fundamental duplicity. On the one hand, it is necessary to draw boundaries, to demarcate, in order to form any community whatsoever. On the other hand, it is precisely because of these excluding borders that every kind of community is characterized by a more or less palpable instability."

CHAPTER 3

1. See, for example, Rorty, *Consequences* 28. Actually, Rorty himself quotes this passage disapprovingly as evidence of the young Wittgenstein's belief in a possibility of "getting beyond language altogether" ("Wittgenstein" 63). His reading is indebted to James C. Edwards, who, while recognizing indications in the "Lecture" of the sort of dismissal of philosophical chimeras typical of the *Investigations*, nevertheless insists that the work remains well within the realm of concerns of the younger Wittgenstein: "But should one not be hard-nosed and just call such 'judg-

ments' nonsense rather than supernatural? Yes, but at the same time one should not forget that there undoubtedly are situations in which we would use value expressions in an absolute sense" (Edwards 86). Nevertheless, it seems to me that while "respecting deeply" these "tendencies" ("Lecture" 14), Wittgenstein's decision that "[t]his running against the walls of our cage is perfectly, absolutely hopeless" ("Lecture" 13) is a resounding condemnation of treating the ethical as an appropriate topic for philosophical consideration.

2. See Wittgenstein, *Philosophical Investigations* paragraph 256.

3. As we will see in greater detail throughout this chapter, this moment of being-outside-itself is the reason that one can speak at all of an ethical concern in deconstruction. That said, it is crucial to distinguish a concern with ethics with an ethics per se, or with somehow being ethical. For instance, Simon Critchley identifies an ethical concern in the former sense when he claims that "for Derrida, the ethical moment is the interruption of the general context of conditioned hypothetical imperatives by an unconditional categorical imperative. Ethics arises in and as the undecidable yet determinate articulation of these two orders" (Critchely 40). He slips, however, into an ethical position of the latter kind when he writes,"[t]he ethical moment that motivates deconstruction is this Yes—saying to the unnameable, a moment of unconditional affirmation that is addressed to an alterity that can neither be excluded from nor included within logocentric conceptuality" (41). There is nothing, in my view, inherently more or less ethical about affirming the appearance of unconditionality than there would be of denying it. In another, more Lévinasian formation, Critchley writes, "[f]or me, by contrast, the paradigmatic ethical moment is that of being pre-reflectively addressed by the other person in a way that calls me into question and obliges me to be responsible" (48). What, I am forced to ask, would constitute a prereflective form of address? Moreover, from the perspective of being-outside-itself, "I" am already called into question from the outset. Finally, the obligation I feel to respond could take myriad forms, including all sorts of colorfully violent variations that would probably not pass popular muster as "responsible" forms of behavior.

4. The present participle "gaping" translates "béance" (Lacan, *Écrits* 524), a nominal form that is rare in French, but whose dissemination in intellectual circles seems at least in part due to Lacan's frequent usage. See Peggy Kamuf's contribution to the *CR* volume on Nancy, which explores this term in the context of Nancy's *L'intrus*.

5. And here, I think, deconstruction can be heard to assent to the attestation Heidegger locates in the call of conscience: not a call of the same, but the calling of irreducible difference at the heart of identity.

6. See the discussion of *an* below.

7. In Kant's case, this is true because the existence of practical reason depends on practical laws that determine the will (and hence are of the subject) (Kant, *Critique* 32); and in Heidegger's case, he explicitly states that "Dasein calls itself in

conscience" (Heidegger, *Being and Time* 254), which, as we have seen above, is the equivalent of a trembling in identity of nonidentity to self. In Derrida's words, identity "can only affirm itself as identity by opening itself to the hospitality of a difference from itself or of a difference with itself" (Derrida, *Aporias* 10; qtd. in Winkler 85).

8. A point already argued persuasively by Heidegger in his reading of Kant, in *Kant and the Problem of Metaphysics* (136).

9. We should also note that this point of "absolute affect" is precisely the place where, like Antigone, one is affected to act regardless of any reason, and hence the place that represents the vanishing point of ethics and aesthetics.

10. See, for example, Chanter and Critchley. See also Hägglund's critique of this appropriation.

11. See my *The Philosopher's Desire*.

12. See Chapter 4.

13. A critique that echoes that of Derrida's "Purveyor of Truth": "The proper place, first of all. The letter has a place of emission and of destination. This is not a subject, but a hole, the lack on the basis of which the subject is constituted" (Derrida, *Post Card* 437).

14. I do not think we can count Nancy among those whom, with Lacan, Deleuze and Guattari reject offhand as "priests of lack" (Deleuze and Guattari, *Thousand* 154). For even if "Man," as he says, "bears witness foremost to a lack in being" [manque à être], this is only the case so long as one does not conceive of this lack as implying a backdrop of normative plenitude from which it withdraws. See Nancy, "Is Everything Political?" 18.

15. Several years later Nancy returned to this question in the opening section of his *Ego sum*, in which he categorizes Lacan's treatment of subjectivity as the vanguard of a persistent, modern anthropologization of the subject, one that replaces the utter undecidability that characterizes the place of the subject of enunciation with a certainty, an identity of some kind. That this attitude toward psychoanalysis might be related to a mistrust of its institutional power is suggested by his comparison of psychoanalysis to an empire, and of Lacan to Caesar, to whom one might as well render the coin (of the subject), a coin to which true philosophy has no claim. See *Ego sum* 17–18.

16. See Miguel de Beistegui, who draws analogies between Nancy's thoughts on sacrifice and Lacan's notion of a "pure signifier behind which no signified could be hidden" (163).

17. That Lacan insists on being as always formulating a question would seem to argue against the reading in *Ego sum* that psychoanalysis repeats the anthropological gesture of replacing undecidability with certainty. See note 15 above.

18. See Nancy's *The Sense of the World*, in which he relates sense to openness and spacing, the space opened by one's orientation toward world (7, passim).

19. The resonance with Heidegger is again striking. "What has been circumspectly interpreted with regard to its in-order-to as such, what has been *explicitly*

understood, has the structure of *something as something.* . . . [However] [t]he fact
that the explicitness of a statement can be lacking in simple looking, does not
justify us in denying every articulate interpretation, and thus the as-structure, to
this simple seeing. The simple seeing of things nearest to us in our having to do
with . . . contains the structure of interpretation so primordially that a grasping of
something which is, so to speak, *free of the as* requires a kind of reorientation"
(Heidegger, *Being and Time* 140). Logic as an analysis of predication, as Heidegger
then goes on to argue, will always fail as long as it does not realize the derivative
relation of predicative statements to the as-structure already operative at an existential level (150). This "equivalence of non-equivalence itself" is exactly what I am
identifying with "the void at the heart of being." Moreover, although this is not
the place for an extended discussion of Derrida's engagements with theology, this
void corresponds as well to the point in Derrida's thought at which he, in
Rodolphe Gasché's words, "like Heidegger . . . makes room for God, so to speak":
"God, or what Derrida calls in *Dissemination* the 'theological trap,' is the dream of
an absolute erasure of the trace, that is, of the inevitable negativity and endless referral to Other that all attempts to think a positive infinity and full presence must
meet, and of making the trace subservient to full presence. But this exemplary
function of the name of God also demonstrates, in an exemplary fashion, that the
dream of full presence is not possible without the trace. For what is the trace but
the minimal reference to an Other without which no God can come into His own,
and which, on this account, always makes God differ from himself? In this sense
God is necessarily the effect of the trace, of a structure that retains the Other as
Other in the full plenitude of a self-present entity. Yet since a trace is only a trace
if it is erasable . . . it harbors in a structural fashion the possibility and site of its
occultation and oblivion by the idea of God. As a necessary possibility, necessary
because structurally always possible, 'the theological trap' is thus an inevitable, if
not a necessary trap. It is not an illusion that could simply be disposed of"
(Gasché, *Inventions* 161). I quote at such length because I find this to be a lucid
and compelling overview of Derrida's theological position, neither, as Gasché argues, a negative theology nor a disavowal of the theological question, but rather a
profound recognition of its inevitability as, in Derrida's words, "a determined moment in the total movement of the trace" (Derrida, *Grammatology* 47, qtd. in
Gasché, *Inventions* 161). I need only add, then, that the trace, as "the inevitable
negativity and endless referral to Other that all attempts to think a positive infinity and full presence," another name for what we will call with Kierkegaard the
paradox of mediation, is also analogous to "the void at the heart of being," to that,
in other words, which makes even God differ from Himself. See also, Caputo,
Prayers and Tears 20: "Everything in deconstruction, we are contending, turns on a
passion for the impossible, on setting a place at the table for the tout autre, which
is the impossible." Caputo also goes on to discuss the relation between Derrida's
and Lévinas's thought in some detail on this point.

    20. Charles Shepherdson has also emphasized the idea that the Lacanian real,

of which *das Ding* was an earlier theoretical manifestation, cannot be grasped as being that which lies outside of signification, but rather as that which exceeds symbolization within the symbolic, is "excluded from within." See his discussion in "The Intimate Alterity of the Real."

21. A brief and clear explanation of the torus motif, which Lacan elaborated in his unpublished seminar on *Identification*, can be found in Joël Dor's "Epistemological Status."

22. Georg Friedrich Bernhard Riemann was the nineteenth-century German mathematician whose non-Euclidean geometry provided Einstein with the mathematics needed to work out General Relativity. (Riemann lived after Hegel, so any retroactive influence must be chalked up to the Cunning of Reason.)

23. *Relèver*, French for *Aufheben*, often translated in English as "to sublate."

24. At least in its "male" version. See Chapter 4.

25. Nancy's reading of Hegel can be found in *La remarque speculative*. See, for example, page 112, where Nancy argues that the speculative work, the *Aufhebung* of propositions, occurs precisely *at* the preposition *an*: " 'this *is* that' is transformed into 'this passes to/occurs at that' " ["ceci *est* cela" se transforme en "ceci (se) passe à cela"]. Although Nancy's ultimate point is to critique Hegel's implicit exclusion of grammar from speculative transformations, what seems most pertinent to this discussion is how the speculative moment, while transforming fixed being into movement, seems necessarily to turn around a fixed position, in this case a pre-position that is itself not subject to speculative transformation. Nancy refers to such a point of nondialecticity as "that point where the negative itself, in order to be the negative (in order to be the *nihil negativum* and not just the *nihil privatum*) must avoid its own operation and be affirmed as the absolute remainder that cannot be captured in a concatenation of procedure or operation. (It is the critical, suspended, inoperative point at the heart of the dialectic)" (Nancy, *Being Singular* 91).

26. The infinite judgment is the judgment that no longer takes the object that is judged as a mere immediacy, but rather grasps it as category, that is, as the immediate unity of being and self (*Sein und Seinen*, which we may better translate as "being and belonging to one"). Consciousness as an observer arrives at a point at which it declares itself to be a thing, and in so doing enunciates an infinite judgment, one that "suspends itself," because to be true it would also have to be false—the immediacy of the object is thus transformed into negativity, its category becoming this very "self-superseding antithesis" embodied in the judgment (Hegel, *Spirit* 209). Negativity, or the limit determining the object, is now revealed to be internal to the observing self.

27. See Lisa Block de Behar's discussion (44).

28. It seems to me that this is exactly the sense in which we need to understand Heidegger's invocation of the apparently messianic "Moment" as the authentic alternative to the "now" of inauthentic temporality: "Resolute, Da-sein has brought itself back out of falling prey in order to be all the more authentically

'there' for the disclosed situation in the 'Moment' [Augen*blick*]" (Heidegger, *Being and Time* 301–2).

29. See Robert P. Harrison's beautiful reading of the poem in *The Body of Beatrice*.

30. The reference is to *De Dieu qui vient à l'idée* (250), where, it seems to me, Lévinas is making a similar point.

31. A great deal has appeared recently on the subject of deconstruction and theology in particular, and the so-called religious turn in continental philosophy in general. See especially Hent de Vries, *Philosophy and the Turn to Religion*; Gil Anidjar's introduction to his edited volume of Derrida's religious writings, *Acts of Religion*; and John D. Caputo's collection of essays and readings in religious thought, *The Religious*.

32. Žižek makes a similar point at the outset of his *The Puppet and the Dwarf: The Perverse Core of Christianity*. Criticizing the reduction of religious experience to a kind of generalized ethicality or openness to radical otherness, he writes that "[w]hat we are getting today is a kind of 'suspended' belief, a belief that can thrive only as not fully (publically) admitted, as a private, obscene secret" (6). The point, of course, with which I am in full agreement, is that the urge to believe has exactly the same force as does the private, obscene secret, namely, the perverse force of the ethical.

33. And which, as we saw above, has a political dimension through its appropriation by Badiou.

34. In some ways this is an elaboration of a more familiar argument, traceable to Hegel, that connects Christianity historically with the modern world. According to Vattimo, reading Dilthey, "Christianity is the condition that paved the way for the dissolution of metaphysics and its replacement by gnoseology" (107).

35. Although in my reading the two positions are hard to distinguish.

36. The formulation *à même soi* translates *an sich* for Nancy, and thus connotes both the beyond of the noumenal thingness and the at-itselfness of pure identity. See Gasché's discussion in "Alongside" 144.

37. Descartes held that the fact of thought (as opposed to its content) was incorrigible; that ideas, or mental images (whether accompanying sensory perception or not), were forms of thought; and that therefore the fact of mental images (as opposed to their content) was also incorrigible. Here is the relevant passage: "Now, with respect to ideas, if these are considered only in themselves, and are not referred to any object beyond them, they cannot, properly speaking, be false; for, whether I imagine a goat or chimera, it is not less true that I imagine the one than the other. Nor need we fear that falsity may exist in the will or affections; for, although I may desire objects that are wrong, and even that never existed, it is still true that I desire them. There thus only remain our judgments, in which we must take diligent heed that we be not deceived. But the chief and most ordinary error that arises in them consists in judging that the ideas which are in us are like or

conformed to the things that are external to us; for assuredly, if we but considered
the ideas themselves as certain modes of our thought (consciousness), without referring them to anything beyond, they would hardly afford any occasion of error."
Meditations III, 6.

38. Indeed, in opting to translate the Danish *Tro* as *belief*, Swenson would
seem to precipitate us toward the deconstructive reading at the cost of betraying
the continuity of the word *Tro* throughout the passage upon which the passage's
deconstructive force depends. That is to say, the one word *Tro* in Kierkegaard's
passage serves to bridge precisely the unbridgeable chasm between the historical
and the eternal, but only insofar as it maintains its undecidability with regard to
whether it signifies *faith* or *belief*, the certainty of the eternal or the uncertainty of
the temporal. Derrida comments on the same issue in Heidegger's use of *Glaube*,
which can also be translated as *faith* or *belief*, asking how he can "at the same time
affirm one of the possibilities of the 'religious,' " while "rejecting so energetically"
Glaube as having no place in thought. The answer can only be that Glaube "remains therefore metaphysical in some way" for Heidegger, insofar as it signifies
"taking for true something represented." This latter usage would seem to correspond to *belief* rather than *faith* in English (as in having one's belief or opinion
confronted with hard fact); the crucial point here, however, is to recognize that the
power of the concept of *faith* relies at least in part on a mutual haunting with *belief* and ultimately *knowledge* that the precipitation of translation can smooth over
but not exorcise. See Derrida, "Faith and Knowledge" 97.

39. Hence the subtitle of Derrida's confrontation with Kierkegaard's *Fear and
Trembling*, "Whom to Give to (Knowing Not to Know)."

40. See David Wood, "Thinking God in the Wake of Kierkegaard" 62; and
Jean-Paul Sartre, "Kierkegaard: The Singular Universal" 168.

41. See also Wood 70, for a commentary of the same passage as translated by
Howard V. and Edna H. Hong.

42. On the relation of deconstruction to negative theology, see Coward and
Foshay, *Derrida and Negative Theology*.

43. Cf. Safranski 23. Kant also noticed this apparent contradiction, although
he named it in a different way: "reason can find no further ground for the human
propensity to hypocrisy (esprit fourbe), although this propensity must have been
present before the lie; for, an act of freedom cannot (like a natural effect) be de-
duced and explained in accordance with the natural law of the connection of effects with their causes, all of which are appearances" (*Metaphysics of Morals*
183–84). What Kant's remark points to is the paradox of institutionalization, or
mediation, evident in the tale of Eve's transgression: namely, that the very idea of
temptation indicates a transgressive urge prior to the first rule that would give one
the knowledge necessary to transgression. Kant moreover ties this into freedom as
that cause which is not traceable to the connection of causes to effects that characterizes the world of appearances. Freedom, in other words, is the source of all

ethical actions, and at the same time is always, ineluctably rent by the decisions of transgression and conformity whose enactment signals that one has already entered the realm of institutions. My thanks to David E. Johnson for bring this passage to my attention.

44. Thanks to Anita Traninger for bringing this objection to my attention.

45. See Heidegger, *Being and Time* 176.

46. A compatible interpretation comes to us from Spinoza, who distinguishes between law and eternal truth, arguing that, unlike an eternal truth, a law depends "solely on the will and absolute power of some potentate, so that the revelation in question was solely in relation to Adam, and solely through his lack of knowledge a law." What is at stake here is precisely that Adam's innocence is nothing other than a necessary ignorance of a knowledge that, like the language he learns to speak, preexists his entry into it, and is thus revealed to him in such a way that deprivation, and hence evil, is integral to that very revelation. God is not caught up in contradiction because contradiction emerges necessarily, as is implied by Spinoza's emphasis on the word "solely," the moment the universality of God's eternal truth is particularized in the understanding of an individual (Spinoza 63).

47. See Taylor's commentary on Kierkegaard's Abraham-critique and its relation to Derrida's thought in *Nots* 78–84.

48. For Kierkegaard's original *Snak*, "chatter" is preferred over "nonsense" in the 1980 translation of *The Concept of Anxiety* by Reidar Thomte and Albert B. Anderson; although "nonsense" is always listed, most entries engage with the semantic field of speech, and hence support the notion that what faith as a resting place [*Hvilepunkt*] offers is something that precisely resists transmission through mere talk. The original passage can be found in Kierkegaard, *Begrebet Angest* 143.

49. See Peter Fenves's book on Kierkegaard, *Chatter*, where he discusses the intricate play of communication and the incommunicable: "It is impossible to avoid communication, even if, and especially when, one attempts to void communication of its necessity by communicating mere possibilities, sheer fictions. For the communication of a void does not avoid communication; avoiding communication communicates a void" (Fenves 145).

50. Fenves makes a similar point concerning the proximity of Kant and Kierkegaard: "nowhere is the grasp of 'Kant's skepticism' stronger than in *The Concept of Anxiety*. For this skepticism, like all skepticism, denies the ability of concepts to grasp everything; the limits of the grasp of the concept is as much a problem for Kant as it is for Kierkegaard" (Fenves 69).

51. "It is, in fact, absolutely impossible by experience to discern with complete certainty a single case in which the maxim of an action, however much it might conform to duty, rested solely on moral grounds and on the conception of one's duty" (Kant, *Foundations* 23).

52. A notion also at the heart of the Christian concept of charity, that it should be practiced in secret.

53. That is, as "respect," a "singular feeling which cannot be compared to any pathological feeling," and hence a paradoxical feeling that is at the same time not a feeling (Kant, *Practical* 97).

54. Talk given at Stanford University on February 5, 1997, as part of the speaker series discourse@networks.2000, on the epistemology of information technology.

55. Here I quote a particularly pertinent description of the ethical by William Haver: "The question of the ethical comes to us, first and last, from beyond any possible epistemological horizon as a scream of abject, sovereign terror; it is indeed the call of a sovereign curse, which calls us and condemns us to a certain attention to an inassimilable singularity. The call of the ethical, the thought of the ethical, the thought that there is, or at least might be, an ethicality, is in its essence cruel, the very cruelty of thought itself" (181). When Derrida speaks of justice it is very much in the same terms we are using to theorize the ethical: "Abandoned to itself, the incalculable and giving [*donatrice*] idea of justice is always very close to the bad, even to the worse for it can always be reappropriated by the most perverse calculation" ("Force" 257).

56. This corresponds exactly to what Derrida says regarding the decision of justice, which unlike that of legality must always remain undecidable: "At no moment, it seems, can a decision be said to be presently and fully just. Either it has not yet been made according to a rule, and nothing allows one to call it just, or it has already followed a rule . . . which, in its turn, nothing guarantees absolutely; and moreover, if it were guaranteed, the decision would have turn [*sic*] back into calculation and one could not call it just" ("Force" 253).

57. The call of conscience, which calls, as Heidegger says, in silence ("The call speaks in the uncanny mode of silence" [Heidegger, *Being and Time* 255]) is also beyond good and evil in precisely the same way: as the absolutely incommunicable impetus of action that is necessarily prior to the justificatory practices that are capable of categorizing according to standards of morality.

58. This, it seems to me, is parallel to Badiou's movement, in which he steps beyond a recognition of the excessive and ultimately transcendental moment of the event to the assumption, ungrounded and ultimately still a symptom of the "situation," that the ethics of the event has to do with the "capacity to enter into the composition and becoming of some eternal truths" (Badiou, *Ethics* 90). This overstepping, clearly reminiscent of the hubris Kant criticized as the transcendental illusions of pure reason (Kant, *Pure* 387–93), is also present in Lévinas's ethics, in such formulations as, "[e]thics is not a moment of being, it is otherwise and better than being; the very possibility of beyond. In this reference [*renvoi*] from the Desirable to the Undesirable, in this strange mission commanding the approach to the other, God is pulled out of objectivity, out of presence, and out of being. He is neither object nor interlocutor. His absolute remoteness, his transcendence, turns into my responsibility—the non-erotic par excellence—for the other" (Lévinas, *Of God* 69). Yes, ethics is otherwise than being, but from there to add, cru-

cially, that it is *better*, is to ground one's very utterance in the knowledge of a being whose certainty the utterance has tried to undermine. In my view, Lévinas's consistent error is to suppose that such moments of absolute affect as infinite responsibility are really "non-erotic par excellence." On the contrary, as I have tried to show, the moment of the *undesirable* in desire is as profoundly erotic as it is inevitable.

59. Kierkegaard's insistence on attributing his writings to pseudonyms attests to a suspicion toward the capacity of speech to universalize without a destructive remainder, to be, in other words, the revelatory instrument of perfect subjective truth and hence close the gap between the universal and the particular. Nevertheless, it is precisely when he ceases to write within the confines of this self-imposed distance to self, when he writes toward the end of his life on the topic of *My Work as an Author*, that he succumbs to what might be called ethical temptation, and writes as if his own words sprang from the authority of the divine. See 321–22 especially.

60. See the texts collected in *The Purloined Poe* as well as Jean-Luc Nancy and Philippe Lacoue-Labarthe's critique in *The Title of the Letter*, discussed above.

61. See Lacan, *VII* 75; for Žižek's earliest critiques of deconstruction see, for example, *The Sublime Object of Ideology* 153–55. Some of Derrida's readings of psychoanalytic texts are collected in *Resistances of Psychoanalysis*. Among new critical voices suggesting affinities and convergences between the two discourses, a recent and forceful example is that of Wolfram Bergande.

62. Derrida affirms as much himself with some consistency in his work. In the essay on justice, for example, he ends by locating beyond and prior to the institution of the law what he calls a pure violence: "God is the name of this pure violence, and just in essence: there is no other, there is none prior to it and before that it has to justify itself. Authority, justice, power, and violence all are one in him. . . . God is the name of the absolute metonymy, what it names by displacing the names, the substitution and what substitutes itself in the name of this substitution" ("Force" 293). Since violence is per force impure, the "pure" violence prior to the institution of the law is nothing other than the unsurpassable displacement of names underlying all institutions, which, precisely insofar as it is unsurpassable, provides a force and an attraction that provoke the name of God.

63. The critical voices need not be limited to the strict deconstructivists; as Deleuze and Guattari say, for psychoanalysis it always comes back to "playing mommy and daddy" (*Anti-Oedipus* 7).

64. See Žižek's definition of the Holy Spirit: "the community deprived of its support in the big Other" (*Puppet* 171); faith is what remains.

CHAPTER 4

1. See Dor, *Structure and Perversions*: "because of the relation that the woman necessarily maintains with the real of phallic absence, her perverse manifestations are difficult to ascribe to sexual perversion in the strict sense" (200).

2. For studies focused more specifically on Freud's theories of sexual difference, see Teresa Brennan, *The Interpretation of the Flesh*, the chapters on Freud in Paul Verhaeghe's *Does the Woman Exist?*, and Samuel Slipp's *The Freudian Mystique*.

3. I must pause here to state the obvious and yet important caveat, that as I write in this chapter about men and women, or man and woman, these words should always be read with implicit quotation marks around them. Howard Bloch writes that any predicate to the sentence beginning "Woman is . . ." must necessarily be misogynist (5); and yet, from the psychoanalytic perspective I am defining in these pages, it is impossible to achieve the kind of unity between utterance and enunciation that would allow me to objectively define either woman or man.

4. By virtue of the close relation between "female" philosophy and deconstructive or "postmodern," which I outline in greater detail below, ethics may certainly be connected to earlier questions of "écriture féminine." For a now-classic overview, see Toril Moi 106–26.

5. Beyond Sokal and Bricmont's popular attack on poststructuralism, *Fashionable Nonsense*, Nadeau and McElvaine are examples of the pervasiveness of this thesis.

6. Fox News/Opinions Dynamic Poll, August 25–26, cited in McElvaine 17.

7. The PBS eight part series *Evolution*, which aired in September 2001, is just one recent example. Darwin has, moreover, been undergoing a resurrection of sorts in the least expected places. Feminist philosopher Elizabeth Grosz, for instance, devoted a course in part to Darwin at the University at Buffalo; philosopher Daniel Dennett produced a provocative rereading of him in *Darwin's Dangerous Idea*; and George Levine has written on his influence on literature in *Darwin and the Novelists*.

8. As William Allman puts it, "genes and environment are not separate, conflicting influences on the development of the human mind. Rather, they work in concert, and are designed to be that way" (176–77). His view is cited approvingly by McElvaine (26).

9. Hence the, to my mind, utter absurdity of the thesis of Randy Thornhill and Craig Palmer's book, *A Natural History of Rape*, which, by claiming that the impulse to rape is a result of natural selection, manages to naturalize a brutal crime without thereby adding one whit to the understanding of why some men are rapists and some not.

10. As the biologists Huberto Maturana and Francisco Varela describe it, this is a generalizable truth concerning nervous systems: "the neurons, the organism they integrate, and the environment in which they interact operate reciprocally as selectors of their corresponding structural changes and are coupled with each other structurally" (170). Moreover, as they argue, "innate and learned behavior are, as behaviors, indistinguishable in their nature and in their embodiment" (171–72). Perhaps even more decisively, in April 2004 Michael Meany of McGill University was widely reported as having established that the treatment rats receive from their mothers affects their genetic structure. See Robinson, "Genomics."

11. "The will to appearance, to illusion, to deception, to becoming and change, is deeper, more 'metaphysical' than the will to truth, to reality, to being" (Nietzsche, *Will* 369). See also Joshua Landy's excellent treatment of the subject of what he calls "lucid self-delusion" in Nietzsche and Proust.

12. See also Copjec, who quotes Freud's refusal to found psychoanalysis on either "anatomy or convention" (*Read My Desire* 204). Freud's original quote is to be found in "Femininity" 114.

13. "Gender is an ontological impossibility because it tries to accomplish the division of Being. But Being as being is not divided" (Wittig 81). Compare this ontological assumption with that of one we would assume to be an archetypically "male" philosopher, Hegel, who says of Being, what he calls the "absolute Notion," "the division into two moments has already taken place, difference is excluded from the self-identical and set apart from it" (Hegel, *Spirit* 100).

14. Lacan will also refer to the different sexes as two countries "towards which each of their souls will strive on divergent wings, and between which a truce will be all the more impossible since they are actually the same country and neither can compromise on its own superiority without detracting from the glory of the other" (Lacan, "Agency" 152). The problem of two countries that are also the same parallels the logical problem, exposed below, of a single symbolic matrix being called upon to account for the existence of two sexes.

15. "This Lacanian solution, different from Freud's, nevertheless suggests an aporia: how do we write two sexes with only one signifier?" (Morel 31).

16. For an exhaustive history of the paradox and its various (attempts at) solutions, see Rüstow.

17. That is, the speaker believes he or she can mediate the paradox of mediation.

18. This is also the nature of the scholastic paradox concerning the edge of the universe: when you come to the edge of the universe, stick your hand out across the edge; if you can, then you are not at the edge; if you cannot, then there is something stopping you, and it must be beyond the edge (Grant 41).

19. See my discussion in "On Dante, Hyperspheres, and the Curvature of the Medieval Cosmos."

20. Cf. Žižek's discussion, in which he compares the female side of the formulae of sexuation to Kant's mathematical antinomies and the male side to the dynamic antinomies (*Tarrying* 56–57), as well as Copjec's more extended explanation (*Read* 201–36). As Copjec puts it in her more recent work, "[s]he [woman] is constituted by the negation of any transcendent beyond and thus lives in a 'soup and dumplings' world of immanence" (*Imagine* 101). The distinction between immanentist and transcendentalist positions can be confusing, especially because we have already seen that Nancy calls "immanentist" precisely what I am calling the "male" or transcendentalist model of identity (see Chapter 1). But in a sense, the female or immanentist position is indeed a kind of transcendentalism, because by refusing to be all it remains open, or "infinitely exposed," to an otherness that

transcends it. The pretension of the "male" or transcendentalist position, even in positing its transcendental other, is that by claiming to speak for the totality it negates the possibility of real otherness.

21. See James Steakley, "*Per scientiam ad justitiam.*"

22. Foucault famously aligns this injunction to be one of two sexes with psychoanalysis's conviction that sex "harbors what is most true in ourselves" (*Herculine* xi); Judith Butler speaks of the "heterosexual imperative" (*Bodies* 15); yet both offer evidence and argument supporting the notion of the pervasiveness of this social pressure. Butler's theory of performativity in *Gender Trouble*, or materialization in *Bodies that Matter*, would seem to be emphatically opposed to any notion of a "fixed" division between the sexes. As she writes, "[t]he presumption that the symbolic law of sex enjoys a separable ontology prior to and autonomous to its assumption is contravened by the notion that the citation of the law is the very mechanism of its production and articulation" (Butler, *Bodies*15). Nevertheless, as she also says, "the matrix of gender relations is prior to the emergence of the 'human' " (7), indicating that there is a matrix, and presumably a heterosexual one, that is responsible for the very materialization of bodies as sexed beings. If, then, the distinction from Lacanian theory that Butler wants to emphasize is that the matrix of gender relations not be thought of as a "separable ontology prior to and autonomous to its assumption," but is nevertheless a matrix prior to the emergence of the human, then we can only agree. For the ontological difference of sex is in no way separable and prior to its assumption by individuals, but is indeed entirely coterminous with its many recitations. It has no content prior to its assumption, but is rather the very form of assumption itself.

23. For a thorough commentary of these formulae, see Fink 108–12.

24. As Copjec says, "When we speak of language's failure with respect to sex, we speak not of its falling short of a prediscursive object, but of its falling into contradiction with itself. Sex coincides with this failure, with this inevitable contradiction" (*Read* 206).

25. Translation modified; see French original on page 74.

26. Lacan also parodizes male language, from which, for example, it would appear that "[r]egarding feminine sexuality, our colleagues, the lady analysts, do not tell us the whole story" (Lacan, *XX* 57). I personally have no doubt that this and other such statements are highly ironic, but that claim is entirely undecidable, since it deals with intentionality, and ultimately irrelevant, since what is at stake is an idea and an argument, not the intention of a master. As for manifesting a "preference" for one or the other mode, he makes it quite clear that analytic discourse is at odds with a metaphysical worldview that makes statements about the "whole" (43). Grosz also notes that Lacan "seems to want to retain some of the allure and the mystery of the Eternal Feminine," although she argues that he is in the service of denying woman any pleasure of their own (Grosz, *Jacques Lacan* 139–40).

27. This is an argument made by Deborah Rhode (5), who also cites supporting claims by Carol Gilligan, Nel Nodding, and Mary O'Brien, among others.

28. Nadeau cites research in which women and men are tested for their ability to navigate mazes both with and without landmarks, the result being that women's performance decreases when the landmarks are removed, whereas men's remains unaffected. When the dimensions of a maze with landmarks are changed, however, men's performance is adversely affected, whereas women's remains unchanged. The apparent conclusion to be drawn is that men are statistically more dependent on an abstraction of distances and directionality, whereas women are more dependent on ambient markers (Nadeau 56).

29. Gilligan's position has naturally stirred dissent. See, for example, Seyla Benhabib and Cynthia Fuchs Epstein.

30. The accusation can be found in Nadeau 101–2. McElvaine concurs with his assessment of twentieth-century anthropology's overall detrimental effect on attempts to think through sexual difference, an effect due to anthropology's assertions of the total determinism of culture on human behavior.

31. Cf. Barbara Johnson's discussion of another, more morbid connotation of this consignment of woman "to the ground" in "Is Female to Male as Ground Is to Figure?" (259).

32. In her later work, Chodorow has cautioned against the sort of generalizations such statements seem to imply, claiming, for example, that "men and women love in as many ways as there are men and women" (Chodorow, *Femininities* 71). Nevertheless, it may be said that one of the purposes of theory is to explain observed trends and differences, and as long as it is understood that generalizations are not to be taken as determinant at the individual level, it seems clear that thought cannot do without them.

33. These connections are worth making despite Chodorow's characterization of Lacanian and object relations theories as largely incompatible with regard to sexual difference (Chodorow, "Psychoanalytic Feminism" 129). Frosh draws a similar connection between Lacanian and object relations theory (81).

34. These and other apparent banalities discussed below are not the exclusive domain of popularizing social scientists. Luce Irigaray, whom we will discuss in more detail further on, would seem to concur: "My experience as a woman demonstrates, as does my analysis of the language of women and men, that women almost always privilege the relationship between subjects, the relationship with the other gender, the relationship between two" (*To Be Two* 17); "The results from the first cue reveal the fact that women seek communication with the other, the other-man in particular, whereas men do not" (Irigaray, *I Love to You* 80).

35. See Kofman 44.

36. For a psychoanalytic study of this phenomenon, see Teresa Brennan, *History After Lacan*; for a more philosophically inflected analysis, see Kofman's *Le respect des femmes*. The classic treatment is, of course, in de Beauvoir's *The Second Sex*.

37. An immediate connection can be established here between cultural history and Freud's clinically derived theories. As Paul Verhaeghe has argued, the trauma

at the basis of hysteria, which he identifies as the utter passivity of being an infant, is "situated *outside* or beyond all forms of psychical working-over" (40). The first representation of this outside in the psyche, then, is a "boundary representation" that substitutes for it: in other words, primary repression. The convergence becomes clear when we realize that the excluded trauma substituted by the boundary signifier is identified with femininity. Moreover, as Toril Moi states, insofar as women is conceived of as a symbolic border, they will "share in the disconcerting properties of *all* borders" (167).

38. For more on the history of courtly love, see Bullough 402–5; Denis de Rougemont's classic study, *Love in the Western World*; C. S. Lewis, *The Allegory of Love*; and more recently and indirectly, María Rosa Menocal's *Shards of Love*.

39. Woman as masquerade is the logical counterpart to the Lacanian dictum that the Woman does not exist (Lacan, *XX* 72). As Jacques-Alain Miller says: "The fact that Woman does not exist does not mean that the place of Woman does not exist, but rather that this place remains essentially empty. The fact that this place remains empty does not mean that we cannot find something there. But in it, we find only masks, masks of nothingness, which are sufficient to justify the connection between women and semblances" ("On Semblance" 14). It only takes a slight turn of perspective to positivize this absence as Irigaray does, and argue that the mask or adornment is the place women make for themselves in lieu of the place not granted them by patriarchy (Irigaray, *Éthique* 18).

40. Although, technically, her gender seems to dissipate asymptotically as we focus our philological lens, for once we take into account that the *a* of *nuda* refers grammatically to *persona*, the sex of Beatrice vanishes entirely from this introductory sentence; her sex, in other words, is both strikingly present and absent.

41. On the golem, see Block de Behar chapter 12; on knowledge as degeneration, see Bloch's *Etymologies and Genealogies* chapter 1; on its relation to the Fall, see Bloch, *Medieval* 99.

42. Ginsberg suggests a further analogy between the relation of Dante's *libello* to the intellectual memory-text it purports to transcribe and that of Beatrice's physical body to her function as embodiment of beatitude (26).

43. Romano Guardini also stresses an implicit Platonism in the hyperrational nature of love, which overcomes reason in its attempts to grasp it conceptually (303), as does Ronald Martinez, in the context of the loss of Beatrice: "one of the principal metaphysical legacies of logical division in Christian culture is reference to separation and loss: division characterizes human existence both absolutely, in that creation itself is in Neoplatonic terms a distancing of the creature from the creator, and historically, in that the Fall of Man brought separation from God and from his best self and consigned him to temporal existence" (14).

44. The literary history of Modernity has been indelibly stamped with this relation, although the sacred nature of its origins is more often than not concealed. Paul-Laurent Assoun, in his *Le pervers et la femme*, sees one of the fundamental

structures of modern literature as being the axis pervert-woman, the basic plots grounded on a transgressive urge to penetrate an ultimately empty mystery. This thesis is tightly related to Lacan's claim that the structure of masculine desire is basically perverse, in that it can only relate obliquely, via dissimulation and substitution, to its objects of desire (Lacan, *XX* 72).

45. Kant, to whom this division is often attributed, is careful to disavow it: "The division of objects into *phaenomena* and *noumena*, and of the world into a world of sense and a world of understanding, can therefore not be permitted at all" (*Pure* 350–51). Nevertheless, an implicit division remains, because the limitation of sensibility so central to the first Critique permits the thought of the noumenal precisely as a way of denying "knowledge in order to make room for faith" (117).

46. Cf. Sarah Kofman's *Le respect des femmes*, in which she argues that repugnance and horror in the face of women is a simple reversal of the natural *inclination* toward a return to the mother's body; respect for women, like respect for the sublimity of the moral law, is a radically ambivalent sentiment (Kant refers to it in the *Critique of Practical Reason* as the only moral sentiment, virtually a contradiction in terms [99–101]), implying, "almost simultaneously, attraction and repulsion" (Kofman 41).

47. For a recent study of the relation of knowledge and erotics to astronomy, see Cornish 12–25. The classic theological interpretation of the *Vita Nuova* is Charles Singleton's *Essay on the "Vita Nuova."*

48. Cf. Miller: "The truth is that because of the nature of speech, women embody that which cannot be said—a secret, veiled knowledge—and that is why they are held to be subjects-supposed-to-know. All the fuss about what they should be taught cannot mask the male fear of the supposed knowledge of women" ("On Semblances" 23).

49. In her *Tales of Love*, Kristeva also refers to a history that could be likened to that of what I am calling "othering," one in which the "sacred invocation" of the troubadour's songs becomes "psychological," and in which the lady becomes actually the object, as the form of courtly love evolves from lyricism to narrative (189).

50. Michelle Montrelay explains the distinction of feminine *jouissance* as a function of othering: "For the woman enjoys her body as she would the body of another" (262; quoted in Copjec, *Imagine* 101).

51. Irigaray continues, "[f]or where the pleasure of the Theresa in question is concerned, her own writings are perhaps more telling" (*This Sex* 91).

52. In this translation I have tried to retain the awkwardness of Teresa's prose, which regularly drives her bibliographers into spasms of editorial creativity. This passage has a different syntactic arrangement in almost every edition.

53. Miller speaks of clinical manifestations of exactly this kind of psychic pain as being largely specific to women: "And so now we must speak of a being of nothingness, and of the pain specific to this being of nothingness. . . . In treating women, we also encounter testimonies to a psychic pain linked to an affect of

non-being, of being nothing, of moments of absence from oneself. There are also testimonies of a strange relation with the infinite, which can present itself on the level of something unfinished—in other words, of a feeling of radical incompleteness" ("On Semblance" 16–17).

54. For a detailed historicization of Teresa's works, Bernini's portrayal of her, and Lacan's interpretation, see Hayes. In the chapter of *La fable mystique* in which he deals with Teresa, Michel de Certeau describes the enunciative function of the mystic's discourse as situating itself in the place of the inaudible speech of God; the "I" of the mystics "takes over for the enunciative function, but in the name of the Other" (de Certeau 257). And mystic, finally, is the name Lacan gives to those who, regardless of biological sex, speak from the position of woman, hence of the Other: "There are men who are just as good as women. It happens. And who also feel just fine about it. Despite—I won't say their phallus—despite what encumbers them that goes by that name, they get the idea or sense that there must be a jouissance that is beyond. Those are the ones we call mystics" (Lacan, *XX* 76). It seems likely that Lacan was influenced in this regard by Bataille. As Amy Hollywood argues, "Bataille . . . suggests that mysticism can be an unassuageable desire for 'what is there' in its historical particularity" (113–14). Later, reading Lacan on mysticism, she writes, "mysticism, as a quest for the absolute . . . encounters instead that which radically destabilizes subjectivity and meaning," two moments that are related in Lacan to phallic and an other jouissance respectively (149).

55. The potential of radical new visions emerging from otherness is discussed with regard to postcolonial subjectivities in Homi K. Bhabha's *The Location of Culture*: "In this salutary sense, a range of contemporary critical theories suggest that it is from those who have suffered the sentence of history—subjugation, domination, diaspora, displacement—that we learn our most enduring lessons for living and thinking" (Bhabha 172). See also Spivak's classic discussion of the question of the voice of such subjectivities in her "Can the Subaltern Speak?" In his recent *Undoing Empire*, José F. Buscaglia-Salgado employs a similar trope: "Accordingly, when I refer to the mulatto subject as the receptacle of the essence of *mulataje* I am thinking of a social and historical agent that, although inevitably inscribed within the world of the coloniality of power in the most infinitely torturous ways, nevertheless represents the very possibility and describes the vectorial intention of the nonracialized" (xviii). The critique that to look for utopian politics in such positions amounts to an affirmation of destitution is a common one, but it strikes me as one that depends on a somewhat outdated (i.e., pre-Foucauldian), theory of power relations. For the implicit assumption in such a critique is that power is unidirectional and oppressive, whereas what Foucault brought to the discussion of power relations was precisely the realization that there is no void of power, no lack of power over which substantive, real power holds sway, but rather that power describes a multivalent, multidirectional field of relations in which a vast variety of subject positions can be identified. See Heller, as well as Deleuze's

theoretical extrapolations of Foucault's method in *Foucault* (especially 34–44). This critique is also one that exactly parallels the most likely objection to this entire chapter: namely, that I am celebrating as well as repeating the gestures that have condemned women to secondary status since the beginning of recorded history. The answer, it seems to me, is to point to the difference between identifying with the gaze of the subjector and identifying (but not claiming to speak from) a position whose normative silence holds utopian potential. This critique is also familiar to psychoanalytic feminists. Juliet Mitchell's response, that it is important to "know the devil" and that this knowledge is not equivalent to doing his work, seems to me to be beyond reproach (364).

56. "Psychoanalytic theory thus utters the truth about the status of female sexuality, and about the sexual relation. But it stops there. Refusing to interpret the historical determinant of its discourse . . . and in particular what is implied by the up to now exclusively masculine sexualization of the application of its laws, it remains caught up in its phallocentrism, which it claims to make into a universal and eternal value" (Irigaray, *This Sex* 102–3).

57. This, it seems to me, is also the fundamental point of Grace M. Jantzen's argument in *Becoming Divine*, which locates a paradigm for feminist ethics in, for example, Lévinas's claim that, in her words, "the ethical takes its rise from relationship to another person. What we may want is to 'know' this other person—but knowledge here cannot mean just contemplating from a distance, nor can it mean devouring, if the relationship is to be ethical" (Jantzen 234). Obviously, the largely Lévinasian-inspired ethics of otherness, of the "saying" (*dire*) over the "said" (*dit*) (Critchley 7) are exemplifications of a version of ethics arising from "female" philosophy.

58. Cf. Irigaray's book on Heidegger, *The Forgetting of Air in Martin Heidegger*.

59. Cf. Irigaray, *Speculum* 18.

60. As Claire Colebrook argues, the notion of the sensuous transcendental also allows Irigaray to refuse the injunction in philosophy to choose between empiricism and transcendentalism, in that it reveals the transcendental to be dependent on the sensuous, and hence empirical, realm, while also insisting on the transcendent (i.e., other-orientedness of ethics) (Colebrook 121–22).

61. Irigaray's work can be characterized by the constant revelation of such other dimensions of conceptualization. Olkowski recognizes, for example, Irigaray's association of women and fluidity (Irigaray, *This Sex* 106–18) as a grounds for subverting what Olkowski calls the logic of "hegemonic and rigid hierarchies" (Olkowski 94), whereas Grosz suggests that it is the multivalent nature of flows that threatens masculine identity with the specter of reversal, of passivity (Grosz, *Volatile* 201).

62. See Gimmler, Margolis, as well as Egginton, "From the End of History to the Death of Man."

63. See the volume *Deleuze and Feminist Theory* for various perspectives on this issue. Alice Jardine and Rosi Braidotti are often evoked as examples of an early feminist mistrust of Deleuzian thought (e.g., Andermat Conley 18; Colebrook 112; Olkowski 86), although Braidotti distances herself in this volume from her earlier, more hesitant stance in *Nomadic Subjects*, by distinguishing between short- and long-run potentials of Deleuzian thought (Braidotti. "Teratologies" 162). Olkowski's contribution to the volume also reads Deleuze and Irigaray together, albeit in a different way than I do, claiming that out of this meeting can emerge a new philosophical framework that "embraces multiplicity without producing binaries" (Olkowski 90).

64. See, for example, Grosz, "A Thousand Tiny Sexes," *Volatile Bodies* 160–83, and "Deleuze's Bergson."

65. See my *How the World Became a Stage*.

66. For the convergence of these and various other Deleuzian "series," see Boundas.

67. This is, I believe, the place in Deleuze and Guattari's text that most clearly responds to the worry of feminists that, in Colebrook's words, "if difference is no longer an originary condition, and if difference is no longer the difference of the genesis of the subject, then sexual difference is no longer foundational, no longer the difference from which all other (given) differences are effected" (Colebrook 118). This is also the place in their text that might serve to differentiate Deleuze and Guattari from Derrida, for whom sexual difference would only be one particular determination of *différance* (Colebrook 120). Finally, there is a definite parallel between this argument and Žižek's attempt to read for points of approximation between Deleuze and Lacan, in his *Organs Without Bodies*. Although in this book Žižek differentiates between the Deleuze of earlier works like *The Logic of Sense* and what he takes to be the weakening of his thought through his collaborations with Guattari, the crucial element that joins Deleuzian and Lacanian thought is, in my reading, strongly present in the collaborative works as well. In Žižek's view, this element is the "symbolic castration," which, although it appears in altered form in Deleuze's vocabulary, is nevertheless operative there in a fundamental way. Far from being exclusively a force for restriction and territorialization, "*Oedipus*," in Žižek's reading, is the very "*operator of deterritorialization. . . .* So, far from tying us down to our bodily reality, 'symbolic castration' sustains our very ability to 'transcend' this reality and enter the space of immaterial becoming" (Žižek, *Organs* 83). Of course, becoming is the farthest thing from "immaterial" in Deleuze's thought, and what Žižek really means here is "virtual," as can be seen from this passage: "the very extraction of the virtual from the real ('symbolic castration') constitutes reality—*actual reality is the real filtered through the virtual*" (Žižek, *Organs* 84). Now, if symbolic castration is also the primordial distinction the body suffers that coincides with sexual difference, it is clear that becoming-woman as the most fundamental becoming is a direct correlate to the separation of virtual multiplici-

ties from the actual world. See Delanda's discussion of the virtual and the actual, 114–16.

68. See Deleuze and Guattari's, *What Is Philosophy?* 5.

69. Indeed, the organization of the body into organs is aligned by Deleuze and Guattari with Artaud's "Judgement of God," the body as viewed, as known, from the ultimate transcendent perspective (*A-O* 150). See Peto's description of a transference phenomenon in which the patient reported fantasies of a total fusion with the analysis to the point of becoming an undifferentiated "mass of flesh" (Peto 228, cited in Verhaeghe 143). Given Deleuze and Guattari's affirmation of schizoid subjectivities, it is suggestive that Peto referred to the episodes discussed as "psychotic" ones.

70. Indeed, this is suggested by one of the many interpretations the priest offers in his subsequent dialogue with K, namely, that the doorkeeper is "really subordinated to the man" (Kafka 274). The "necessity" of the law augurs for the opposite interpretation: that "[w]hatever he may seem to us, he is yet a servant of the Law; that is, he belongs to Law and as such is beyond human judgment. In this case one must not believe that the doorkeeper is subordinate to the man" (Kafka 276).

71. Giorgio Agamben's treatment of Kafka's legend offers an intriguing if ultimately problematic interpretation. According to Agamben, the imposing openness of the door to the law reveals the "zero point" of the law, where the law remains "in force without significance." "What, after all, is the structure of the sovereign ban if not that of a law that *is in force* but does not *signify*? Everywhere on earth men live today in the ban of a law and a tradition that are maintained solely as the 'zero point' of their own content, and that include men within them in the form of a pure relation of abandonment. All societies and all cultures today . . . have entered into a legitimation crisis in which law (we mean by this term the entire text of tradition in its regulative form, whether the Jewish Torah or the Islamic Shariah, Christian dogma or the profane *nomos*) is in force as the pure 'Nothing of Revelation.' But this is precisely the structure of the sovereign relation, and the nihilism in which we are living is, from this perspective, nothing other than the coming to light of this relation as such" (Agamben 51). Nihilism, for Agamben, is this zero point at which the traditional laws structuring a social body no longer signify, but still maintain the mystical "force of law" that Derrida discusses in his essay by the same name. Agamben goes on to identify this force with Kant's "simple form of law," in his ethics, and "to the transcendental object," in his epistemology (Agamben 51–52). The lesson Agamben takes from the legend is that of a "task that our time imposes on thinking," namely, "to think the Being of abandonment beyond every idea of law (even that of the empty form of law's being in force without significance)," to move "out of the paradox of sovereignty toward a politics freed from every ban" (Agamben 59). What Agamben fails to see, and yet what his intervention illustrates in clarion terms, is that, just like Kant's simple form of law,

the urge to escape "the paradox of sovereignty"—another version of Kierkegaard's paradox of mediation—is yet another inevitable iteration of the man's attempt in Kafka's legend to cross the threshold of the door. While it is of the greatest urgency to recognize the effects of what Agamben calls the state of exception, "life under a law that is in force without signifying" (Agamben 52), to wish oneself out of the paradox of sovereignty is one of the surest ways to posit, unaware, yet another state of exception.

72. This reading is highly redolent of Derrida's: "the inaccessible transcendence of the law [*loi*], before which and prior to which 'man' stands fast, only appears infinitely transcendent and thus theological to the extent that, nearest to him, it depends only on him, on the performative act by which he institutes it" ("Force" 270).

73. A connection can be made here between a Lacanian psychoanalytic position and the position of recent feminist contributions toward thinking a new model of ethics. Cf. Grosz: "Rather, Deleuze and Guattari are participants in what might be described as the advent of a 'postmodern ethics,' an ethics posed in the light of the dissolution of both the rational, judging subject and the contract based, liberal accounts of the individual's allegiance to the social community" ("A Thousand" 196).

74. This latter potion corresponds to what Lacan called "bachelor ethics," against which he situated the discourse of psychoanalysis. See Colette Soler's description: "By claming to determine a will by excluding all motivations and so-called pathological objects of the senses, what the categorical imperative of moral law and its extremism ends up proscribing is evidently woman. This ethics is also 'beyond sex' [*hors sexe*]; it short-circuits the Other in favor of the Self" (47). Later, "[t]he conclusion I draw is that psychoanalysis, contrary to the dominant discourse, shuns all complicity with the rising bachelor ethic in its different forms" (51). As Verhaeghe puts it, "[i]n the world of make-believe, 'le monde du semblant,' we are all narcissistically alike, but beyond this world we are all fundamentally different" (113). This is why Lacan speaks of the desire of the analyst as being a "desire to obtain absolute difference" (Lacan, *XI* 276).

Works Cited

Adorno, Theodor W. *The Jargon of Authenticity*. Trans. Knut Tarnowski and Fredric Will. Evanston, Ill.: Northwestern University Press, 1973.

Agamben, Giorgio. *Homo Sacer: Sovereign Power and Bare Life*. Trans. Daniel Heller-Roazen. Stanford, Calif.: Stanford University Press, 1998.

Airaksinen, Timo. *The Philosophy of the Marquis de Sade*. New York: Routledge, 1991.

Alfonso X. *Cantigas de Santa María*. Ed. Walter Mettman. Madrid: Castalia, 1986.

Allman, William F. *The Stone Age Present*. New York: Simon and Schuster, 1994.

Andermat Conley, Verena. "Becoming-Woman Now." In *Deleuze and Feminist Theory*. Eds. Ian Buchanan and Claire Colebrook. Edinburgh: Edinburgh University Press, 2000. 18–37.

Anidjar, Gil. "Introduction: 'Once More, Once More': Derrida, the Arab, the Jew." In *Acts of Religion*. Ed. Gil Anidjar. New York/London: Routledge, 2002. 1–39.

Arendt, Hannah. *Eichmann in Jerusalem: A Report on the Banality of Evil*. New York: Viking Press, 1963.

Aristotle. *Nicomachean Ethics*. Trans. Martin Ostwald. Indianapolis: Bobbs-Merrill Educational Publishing, 1962.

Artaud, Antonin. "To Have Done With the Judgment of God, A Radioplay." 1947. In *Selected Writings*. Ed. Susan Sontag. New York: Farrar, Straus, and Giroux, 1976. 555–574.

Assoun, Paul-Laurent. *Le pervers et la femme*. 2nd ed. Paris: Anthropos, 1996.

Augustine, Saint. *City of God*. Trans. Marcus Dods. New York: Modern Library, 1950.

Badiou, Alain. *Ethics: An Essay on the Understanding of Evil*. Trans. Peter Hallward. London: Verso, 2001.

———. *Saint Paul: La fondation de l'universalisme*. Paris: Presses Universitaires de France, 1997.

Benhabib, Seyla. "The Generalized and the Concrete Other: The Kohlberg-Gilligan Controversy and Feminist Theory." In *Feminism as Critique: Essays on the Politics of Gender in Late Capitalist Society*. London: Polity, 1987. 77–79.

Bergande, Wolfram. *Lacans Psychanalyse und die Dekonstruktion*. Vienna: Passagen Verlag, 2002.

Bersani, Leo. *The Freudian Body: Psychoanalysis and Art*. New York: Columbia University Press, 1986. 38–39.

———. "Is the Rectum a Grave?" *October* 43 (1987) 197–222.

Bettelheim, Bruno. *Freud and Man's Soul*. New York: Alfred A. Knopf, 1983.

Bhabha, Homi K. *The Location of Culture*. London/New York: Routledge, 1994.

Bloch, Howard. *Etymologies and Genealogies: A Literary Anthropology of the French Middle Ages*. Chicago: University of Chicago Press, 1983.

———. *Medieval Misogyny and the Invention of Western Romantic Love*. Chicago: University of Chicago Press, 1991.

Block de Behar, Lisa. *Borges: The Passion of an Endless Quotation*. Trans. William Egginton. Albany: SUNY Press, 2003.

Bloom, Harold. *The Anxiety of Influence: A Theory of Poetry*. Oxford: Oxford University Press, 1973.

Boss, Medard. *Sinn und Gehalt der sexuellen Perversionen*. Frankfurt: Fischer, 1984.

Boundas, Constantin V. "Deleuze: Serialization and Subject-Formation." In *Gilles Deleuze and the Theater of Philosophy*. Eds. Constantin V. Boundas and Dorothea Olkowski. New York: Routledge, 1994. 99–116.

Braidotti, Rosi. *Nomadic Subjects. Embodiment and Sexual Difference in Contemporary Feminist Theory*. New York: Columbia University Press, 1994.

———. "Teratologies." In *Deleuze and Feminist Theory*. Eds. Ian Buchanan and Claire Colebrook. Edinburgh: Edinburgh University Press, 2000. 156–172.

Brennan, Teresa. *History After Lacan*. London/New York: Routledge, 1993.

———. *The Interpretation of the Flesh: Freud and Femininity*. London/New York: Routledge, 1992.

Breuer, Joseph, and Sigmund Freud. *Studies on Hysteria*. Trans. James Strachey. New York: Basic Books, 1957.

Brousse, Marie-Hélène. "The Drive (I)." In *Reading Seminar XI: Lacan's Four Fundamental Concepts of Psychoanalysis*. Eds. Richard Feinstein, Bruce Fink, and Maire Jaanus. Albany: SUNY Press, 1995. 99–107.

Bullough, Vern L. *Sexual Variance in Society and History*. New York: Wiley, 1976.

Buscaglia-Salgado, José F. *Undoing Empire: Race and Nation in the Mulatto Caribbean*. Minneapolis: University of Minnesota Press, 2003.

Butler, Judith. *Antigone's Claim: Kinship between Life and Death*. New York: Columbia University Press, 2000.

———. *Bodies that Matter: On the Discursive Limits of "Sex."* New York: Routledge, 1993.

———. *Gender Trouble: Feminism and the Subversion of Identity*. New York: Routledge, 1990.

————. *Kritik der ethischen Gewalt.* Frankfurt am Main: Suhrkamp, 2002.

————. *The Psychic Life of Power: Theories in Subjection.* Stanford, Calif.: Stanford University Press, 1997.

Capobianco, Richard. "Lacan and Heidegger: The Ethics of Desire and the Ethics of Authenticity." In *From Phenomenology to Thought, Errancy, and Desire: Essays in Honor of William J. Richardson, S. J.* Ed. Babette E. Babich. Dordrecht/Boston/London: Kluwer Academic Publishers, 1995. 201–206.

Caputo, John D. *The Prayers and Tears of Jacques Derrida: Religion without Religion.* Bloomington and Indianapolis: Indiana University Press, 1997.

————, Ed. *The Religious.* Malden, Mass./Oxford: Blackwell Publishers, 2002.

Cervantes, Miguel de. *El ingenioso hidalgo Don Quijote de la Mancha* 2 vols. Madrid: Cátedra, 1996.

Chamberlain, Jane, and Jonathan Rée. *The Kierkegaard Reader.* Oxford/Maldon, Mass.: Blackwell Publishers, 2001.

Chanter, Tina. *Time, Death, and the Feminine: Levinas with Heidegger.* Stanford, Calif.: Stanford University Press, 2001.

Chodorow, Nancy J. "Family Structure and Feminine Personality." In *Woman, Culture and Society.* Eds. Michelle Zimbalist Rosaldo and Louise Lamphere. Stanford, Calif.: Stanford University Press, 1974. 43–66.

————. *Femininities, Masculinities, Sexualities: Freud and Beyond.* Lexington: University Press of Kentucky, 1994.

————. "Psychoanalytic Feminism and the Psychoanalytic Psychology of Women." In *Feminism and Psychoanalytic Theory.* New Haven: Yale University Press, 1989. 178–198.

Chomsky, Noam. *Language and Thought.* Wakefield, RI, and London: Moyer Bell, 1993.

————. *Femininities, Masculinities, Sexualities: Freud and Beyond.* Lexington, KY: University Press of Kentucky, 1994.

————. "What Is the Relation between Psychoanalytic Feminism and the Psychoanalytic Psychology of Women?" In *Theoretical Perspectives on Sexual Difference.* Ed. Deborah Rhode. New Haven/London: Yale University Press, 1990. 114–130.

Clément, Catherine. *The Lives and Legends of Jacques Lacan.* Trans. Arthur Goldhammer. New York: Columbia University Press, 1983.

Colebrook, Claire. "Is Sexual Difference a Problem?" In *Deleuze and Feminist Theory.* Eds. Ian Buchanan and Claire Colebrook. Edinburgh: Edinburgh University Press, 2000. 110–127.

Copjec, Joan. "Introduction: Evil in the Time of the Finite World." In *Radical Evil.* Ed. Joan Copjec. London: Verso, 1996. vii–xxviii.

————. *Imagine There's No Woman: Ethics and Sublimation.* Cambridge, Mass.: MIT Press, 2002.

————. *Read My Desire: Lacan Against the Historicists.* Cambridge, Mass./London: MIT Press, 1994.

Cornish, Alison. *Reading Dante's Stars*. New Haven/London: Yale University Press, 2000.

Coward, Harold, and Toby Foshay, eds. *Derrida and Negative Theology*. Albany: SUNY Press, 1992.

Critchley, Simon. *The Ethics of Deconstruction: Derrida and Levinas*. Oxford/Cambridge, Mass.: Blackwell Publishers, 1992.

Dante Alighieri. *La vita nuova*. Ed. Tommaso Casini. Firenze: Sansoni, 1962.

Davidson, Arnold I. "How to Do a History of Psychoanalysis: A Reading of Freud's Three Essays on the Theory of Sexuality." In *The Trials of Psychoanalysis*. Ed. Françoise Meltzer. Chicago: University of Chicago Press, 1988. 39–64.

Dean, Tim. *Beyond Sexuality*. Chicago/London: University of Chicago Press, 2000.

De Beauvoir, Simone. *The Second Sex*. Trans. H. M. Parshley. New York: Knopf, 1953.

De Beistegui, Miguel. "Sacrifice Revisited." In *On Jean-Luc Nancy: The Sense of Philosophy*. Eds. Darren Sheppard, Simon Sparks, and Colin Thomas. London: Routledge, 1997. 157–173.

De Certeau, Michel. *La fable mystique, 1. XVIe–XVIIe siècle*. Paris: Gallimard, 1982.

Delanda, Manuel. *Intensive Science and Virtual Philosophy*. New York: Continuum, 2002.

Deleuze, Gilles. *Bergsonism*. Trans. Hugh Tomlinson and Barbara Habberjam. New York: Zone, 1991.

———. "Coldness and Cruelty." In *Masochism*. Trans. Jean McNeil. New York: Zone Books, 1989. 9–138

———. *Empiricism and Subjectivity: An Essay on Hume's Theory of Human Nature*. Ed. Constantin V. Boundas. New York: Columbia University Press, 1991.

———. *Expressionism in Philosophy: Spinoza*. Trans. Martin Joughin. New York: Zone, 1990.

———. *The Fold: Leibniz and the Baroque*. Trans. Tom Conley. Minneapolis: University of Minnesota Press, 1993.

———. *Foucault*. Trans. Sean Hand. Minneapolis: University of Minnesota Press, 1988.

———. *The Logic Of Sense*. Trans. Mark Lester. New York: Columbia University Press, 1990.

———. *Pure Immanence: Essays on a Life*. Trans. Anne Boyman. New York: Zone, 2001.

Deleuze, Gilles, and Félix Guattari. *Anti-Oedipus: Capitalism and Schizophrenia*. Trans. Robert Hurley, Helen R. Lane, and Mark Seem. Minneapolis: University of Minnesota Press, 1983.

———. *Kafka: Toward a Minor Literature*. Trans. D. Polan. Minneapolis: University of Minnesota Press, 1986.

———. *A Thousand Plateaus: Capitalism and Schizophrenia*. Trans. Brian Massumi. Minneapolis: University of Minnesota Press, 1987.

————. *What Is Philosophy?* Trans. Hugh Tomlinson and Graham Burchell. New York: Columbia University Press, 1994.

De Man, Paul. "The Resistance to Theory." In *Modern Criticism and Theory*. Ed. David Lodge. 2nd ed. Harlow, England: Longman, 2000. 332–348.

Dennett, Daniel C. *Darwin's Dangerous Idea: Evolution and the Meaning of Life.* New York: Simon and Schuster, 1995.

Derrida, Jacques. *Aporias.* Trans. Thomas Dutoit. Stanford, Calif.: Stanford University Press, 1993.

————. "Differance." In *Margins of Philosophy*. Trans. Alan Bass. Chicago: University of Chicago Press, 1982. 1–31.

————. "Faith and Knowledge: The Two Sources of 'Religion' at the Limits of Reason Alone." Trans. Samuel Weber. In *Acts of Religion*. Ed. Gil Anidjar. New York/London: Routledge, 2002. 40–101.

————. "Force of Law: The 'Mystical Foundation of Authority.' " Trans. Mary Quaintance. In *Acts of Religion*. Ed. Gil Anidjar. New York/London: Routledge, 2002. 228–298.

————. "Freud and the Scene of Writing." In *Writing and Difference*. Trans. Alan Bass. Chicago: University of Chicago Press, 1978. 196–231.

————. Limited Inc. Evanston, Ill.: Northwestern University Press, 1988.

————. *Of Grammatology.* Trans. G. C. Spivak. Baltimore: Johns Hopkins University Press, 1976.

————. *Of Spirit.* Trans. Geoffrey Bennington and Bachel Bowlby. Chicago: University of Chicago Press, 1989.

————. "Ousia and Gramme: Note on a Note from *Being and Time*." In *Margins of Philosophy*. Trans. Alan Bass. Chicago: University of Chicago Press, 1982. 29–68

————. *The Post Card: From Socrates to Freud and Beyond.* Trans. Alan Bass. Chicago/London: University of Chicago Press, 1987.

————. *Resistances of Psychoanalysis.* Trans. Peggy Kamuf, Pascale-Anne Brault, and Michael Naas. Stanford, Calif.: Stanford University Press, 1998.

————. "Structure, Sign, and Play in the Discourse of the Human Sciences." In *Modern Criticism and Theory*. Ed. David Lodge. 2nd ed. Harlow, England: Longman, 2000. 89–103.

————. "Violence and Metaphysics: An Essay on the Thought of Emmanuel Levinas." In *Writing and Difference*. Trans. Alan Bass. Chicago: University of Chicago Press, 1978. 79–153.

————. "Whom to Give to (Knowing Not to Know)." Chapter 3 of *The Gift of Death*. Trans. David Wills. Chicago: University of Chicago Press, 1995. Reprinted in *Kierkegaard: A Critical Reader*. Eds. Jonathan Rée and Jane Chamberlain. Oxford/Maldon, Mass.: Blackwell Publishers, 1998. 151–174.

Descartes, René. *Meditations.* A trilingual HTML edition. Eds. David B. Manley and Charles S. Taylor. http://www.wright.edu/cola/descartes/meditations.html.

Dor, Joël. "The Epistemological Status of Lacan's Mathematical Paradigms."

Trans. Pablo Nigel. In *Disseminating Lacan*. Eds. David Pettigrew and François Raffoul. Albany: SUNY Press, 1996. 109–121.

———. *Structure and Perversions*. Trans. Susan Fairfield. New York: Other Press, 2001.

Dunand, Anne. "The End of Analysis (I)." In *Reading Seminar XI: Lacan's Four Fundamental Concepts of Psychoanalysis*. Eds. Richard Feinstein, Bruce Fink, and Maire Jaanus. Albany: SUNY Press, 1995. 243–250.

Edwards, James C. *Ethics Without Philosophy: Wittgenstein and the Moral Life*. Tampa: University Presses of Florida, 1982.

Egginton, William. "From the End of History to the Death of Man." *Analecta Husserliana* 51 (1996): 33–58.

———. *How the World Became a Stage: Presence, Theatricality, and the Question of Modernity*. Albany: SUNY Press, 2002.

———. "Keeping Pragmatism Pure: Rorty with Lacan. In *The Pragmatic Turn in Philosophy: Contemporary Engagements Between Continental and Analytic Thought*. Eds. William Egginton and Mike Sandbothe. Albany, NY: SUNY Press, 2004.

———. "On Dante, Hyperspheres, and the Curvature of the Medieval Cosmos." *Journal of the History of Ideas* 60.2 (1999): 195–216.

———. "The Philosopher's Desire: Psychoanalysis, Interpretation, and Truth." Unpublished manuscript.

Einstein, Albert. *Relativity: The Special and the General Theory*. Trans. Robert W. Lawson. New York: Crown Trade Paperbacks, 1961.

Epstein, Cynthia Fuchs. *Deceptive Distinctions: Sex, Gender, and the Social Order*. New Haven, Conn.: Yale University Press, 1988.

Fenves, Peter. *Chatter: Language and History in Kierkegaard*. Stanford, Calif.: Stanford University Press, 1993.

Fink, Bruce. *The Lacanian Subject: Between Language and Jouissance*. Princeton, N.J.: Princeton University Press, 1995.

———. "Perversion." In *Perversion and the Social Relation*. Eds. Molly Anne Rothenberg, Dennis A. Foster, and Slavoj Žižek. Durham, N.C. and London: Duke University Press, 2003.

Fodor, Jerry. *The Language of Thought*. Cambridge, Mass.: Harvard University Press, 1975.

Foucault, Michel. *The History of Sexuality.* Vol. 1: *An Introduction*. Trans Robert Hurley. New York: Vintage Books, 1990.

———. *Herculine Barbin. Being the Recently Discovered Memoirs of a Nineteenth-Century French Hermaphrodite*. Trans. Richard McDougall. New York: Pantheon Books, 1980.

Freud, Sigmund. *Abriss der Psychoanalyse*. Frankfurt: Fischer, 1998.

———. "Beyond the Pleasure Principle." In *The Essentials of Psychoanalysis*. Ed. Anna Freud. Trans. James Strachey. London: Hogarth Press, 1986. 218–268.

———. "'A Child Is Being Beaten' A Contribution to the Study of Origin of Sexual Perversions." In *The Standard Edition of the Compete Psychological Works of Sigmund Freud*. Trans. and Ed. James Strachey. Vol. 17. London: Hogarth Press, 1966. 179–204.

———. *Civilization and Its Discontents*. Trans. and Ed. James Strachey, New York and London: W. W. Norton, 1961.

———. *The Complete Letters of Sigmund Freud to Wilhelm Fliess, 1887–1904*. Trans. and Ed. Jeffrey Moussaieff Masson. Cambridge, Mass., and London: Belknap Press of Harvard University Press, 1985.

———. *Der Witz und seine Beziehung zum Unbewußten*. Studienausgabe IV. Frankfurt am Main: Fischer Verlag, 1970.

———. "The Economic Problem of Masochism." In *General Psychological Theory: Papers on Metapsychology*. Ed. Philip Rieff. New York: Collier Books, 1963. 190–201.

———. "The Ego and the Id." In *The Standard Edition of the Complete Psychological Works of Sigmund Freud*. Trans. and Ed. James Strachey. Vol. 19. London: Hogarth Press, 1961. 3–68.

———. "Femininity." In *The Standard Edition of the Complete Psychological Works of Sigmund Freud*. Vol. 22. Trans. James and Alix Strachey. London: Hogarth Press and the Institute for Psycho-Analysis, 1964.

———. "Formulations Regarding Two Principles in Mental Functioning." In *General Psychological Theory: Papers on Metapsychology*. Ed. Philip Rieff. New York: Collier Books, 1963. 21–28.

———. "Instincts and Their Vicissitudes." In *The Essentials of Psychoanalysis*. Ed. Anna Freud. Trans. James Strachey. London: Hogarth Press, 1986. 197–217.

———. *The Interpretation of Dreams*. Trans. James Strachey. New York: Avon Books, 1965.

———. "The Most Prevalent Form of Degradation in Erotic Life." In *Sexuality and the Psychology of Love*. Ed. Philip Rieff. New York: Collier Books, 1963. 48–59.

———. "Project for a Scientific Psychology." In *The Standard Edition of the Complete Psychological Works of Sigmund Freud*. Trans. and Ed. James Strachey. Vol. 1. London: Hogarth Press, 1966. 283–398.

———. *Three Essays on the Theory of Sexuality*. Trans. James Strachey. New York: Basic Books, 1962.

Fromm, Erich. *Anatomy of Human Destructiveness*. New York: Holt, Rinehart and Winston, 1973.

Frosh, Stephen. *Sexual Difference: Masculinity & Psychoanalysis*. London/New York: Routledge, 1994.

Fukuyama, Francis. *The End of History and the Last Man*. New York: Free Press, 1992.

Fuss, Diana J. " 'Essentially Speaking': Luce Irigaray's Language of Essence." *Hypatia* 3 (1989): 62–80.

Fynsk, Christopher. "Between Ethics and Aesthetics." *L'esprit créateur* 35.3 (1995): 80–87.

———. *Infant Figures*. Stanford, Calif.: Stanford University Press, 2000.

Gadamer, Hans-Georg. *Truth and Method*. Second rev. ed. Trans. Joel Weinsheimer and Donald G. Marshall. New York: Continuum, 1998.

Garber, Marjorie, Beatrice Hanssen, and Rebecca L. Walkowitz, eds. *The Turn to Ethics*. New York/London: Routledge, 2000.

García Ponce, Juan. *De anima*. Bogotá: Tercer Mundo Editores, 1989.

Gasché, Rodolphe. "Alongside the Horizon." In *On Jean-Luc Nancy: The Sense of Philosophy*. Eds. Darren Sheppard, Simon Sparks, and Colin Thomas. London: Routledge, 1997. 140–156.

———. *Inventions of Difference: On Jacques Derrida*. Cambridge, Mass./London: Harvard University Press, 1994.

Gilligan, Carol. *In a Different Voice*. Cambridge: Harvard University Press, 1982.

Gilson, Somin A. *Medieval Optics and Theories of Light in the Works of Dante*. Lewsiton/Queenston/Lampeter: Edwin Mellen Press, 2000.

Gimmler, Antje. "Pragmatic Aspects of Hegel's Thought." Trans. Reinhild Steingrover-McRae. In *The Pragmatic Turn in Philosophy: Contemporary Engagements Between Analytic and Continental Thought*. Eds. William Egginton and Mike Sandbothe. Albany: SUNY Press, 2002.

Ginsberg, Warren. *Dante's Aesthetics of Being*. Ann Arbor: University of Michigan Press, 1999.

Goldschneider, Filipp. *Warum hat Kain Abel Erschlagen?* Frankfurt. Eichborn, 1996.

Gorton, Lisa. "The Paradox Topos." *Journal of the History of Ideas* 61.2 (2000): 343–346.

Grant, Edward. "Medieval and Seventeenth-Century Conceptions of an Infinite Void Space Beyond the Cosmos." *ISIS* 60 (1969): 39–60. Rpt. in Grant, Edward. *Studies in Medieval Science and Natural Philosophy*. London: Varorium Reprints, 1981.

Gray, John. *Men Are from Mars, Women Are from Venus*. New York: HarperCollins, 1992.

———. *Men, Women and Relationships*. New York: HarperCollins, 1993.

Grosz, Elizabeth. "Deleuze's Bergson: Duration, the Virtual and a Politics of the Future." In *Deleuze and Feminist Theory*. Eds. Ian Buchanan and Claire Colebrook. Edinburgh: Edinburgh University Press, 2000. 214–234.

———. *Jacques Lacan: A Feminist Introduction*. London: Routledge, 1990.

———. "A Thousand Tiny Sexes." In *Gilles Deleuze and the Theater of Philosophy*. Eds. Constantin V. Boundas and Dorothea Olkowski. New York: Routledge, 1994. 187–210.

———. *Volatile Bodies: Toward a Corporeal Feminism*. Bloomington/Indianapolis: University of Indiana Press, 1994.

Guardini, Romano. *Dantes Götliche Komödie: Ihre philosophischen und religiösen Grundgedanken*. Mainz: Matthias-Grünewald-Verlag, 1998.

Gumbrecht, Hans Ulrich. *The Production of Presence: On the Silent Side of Meaning*. Stanford, Calif.: Stanford University Press, 2004.

Hägglund, Martin. "The Necessity of Discrimination: Disjoining Derrida and Levinas." Forthcoming in *Diacritics* (2005).

Harrison, Robert Pogue. *The Body of Beatrice*. Baltimore/London: Johns Hopkins University Press, 1988.

Haver, William. *The Body of This Death: Historicity and Sociality in the Time of AIDs*. Stanford, Calif.: Stanford University Press, 1996.

Hayes, Tom. "A *Jouissance* Beyond the Phallus: Juno, Saint Teresa, Bernini, Lacan." *American Imago* 56.4 (1999): 331–355.

Hegel, G. W. F. *The Phenomenology of Mind*. Trans. J. B. Baillie. New York/Evanston: Harper Touchstone, 1967.

———. *The Phenomenology of Spirit*. Trans. A. V. Miller. Oxford/New York: Oxford University Press, 1977.

Heidegger, Martin. "The Age of the World Picture." In *The Question Concerning Technology and Other Essays*. Trans. William Lovitt. New York: Harper & Row, 1977. 53–114.

———. *Being and Time*. Trans. Joan Stambaugh. Albany: State University of New York Press, 1996.

———. *Introduction to Metaphysics*. Trans. Ralph Mannheim. New Haven, Conn.: Yale University Press, 1959.

———. "Introduction to 'What Is Metaphysics?' " Trans. Walter Kaufman. In *Pathmarks*. Ed. William McNeill. Cambridge: Cambridge University Press, 1998. 277–290.

———. *Kant and the Problem of Metaphysics*. 5th ed. Trans. Richard Taft. Bloomington: University of Indiana Press, 1997.

———. "Letter on Humanism." Trans. Frank A. Capuzzi. In *Pathmarks*. Ed. William McNeill. Cambridge: Cambridge University Press, 1998. 239–276.

———. "Only a God Can Save Us Now." "The Spiegel Interview, 1966." Trans. William J. Richardson. In *Heidegger: The Man and the Thinker*. Ed. Thomas Sheehan. Chicago: University of Chicago Press, 1981.

———. "The Origin of the Work of Art." In *Poetry, Language, Thought*. Trans. Albert Hofstadter. New York: Harper Colophon Books, 1975. 17–87.

———. "The Question Concerning Technology." In *The Question Concerning Technology and Other Essays*. Trans. William Lovitt. New York: Harper & Row, 1977. 53–114.

———. "The Thing." In *Poetry, Language, Thought*. Trans. Albert Hofstadter. New York: Harper Colophon Books, 1975. 161–184.

———. "Was ist Metaphysik?" *In Gesamtausgabe. Band 9. Wegmarken*. Frankfurt: Vottorio Klosterman, 1996. 103–122.

———. "What Is Metaphysics?" Trans. David Ferrell Krell. In *Pathmarks*. Ed. William McNeill. Cambridge: Cambridge University Press, 1998. 82–96.

———. "The Word of Nietzsche: 'God Is Dead.'" In *The Question Concerning Technology and Other Essays*. Trans. William Lovitt. New York: Harper & Row, 1977. 53–114.

Heller, Kevin Jon. "Power, Subjectification, and Resistance in Foucault." *SubStance* 79 (1996): 78–110.

Herrnstein-Smith, Barbara. *Contingencies of Values: Alternative Perspectives for Critical Theory*. Cambridge, Mass./London: Harvard University Press, 1988.

Hintikka, Merrill B., and Jaakko Hintikka. "How Can Language Be Sexist?" In *Discovering Reality: Feminist Perspectives on Epistemology, Metaphysics, Methodology, and Philosophy of Science*. Eds. Sandra Harding and Merrill B. Hintikka. London/Dordrecht/Boston: D. Reidel Publishing, 1983. 139–148.

Hoem, Sheri. "Community and the 'Absolutely Feminine.'" *Diacritics* 26.2 (1996): 49–58.

Hollywood, Amy. *Sensible Ecstasy: Mysticism, Sexual Difference, and the Demands of History*. Chicago: University of Chicago Press, 2002.

Huntington, Samuel P. *The Clash of Civilizations and the Remaking of World Order*. New York: Simon and Schuster, 1996.

Irigaray, Luce. *Éthique de la différence sexuelle*. Paris: Éditions de Minuit, 1984.

———. *The Forgetting of Air in Martin Heidegger*. Trans. Mary Beth Mader. Austin: University of Texas Press, 1999.

———. *I Love to You*. Trans. Alison Martin. New York/London: Routledge, 1996.

———. *Sexes and Genealogies*. Trans. Gillian C. Gill. New York: Columbia University Press, 1993.

———. *Speculum of the Other Woman*. Trans. Gillian Gill. Ithaca, N.Y.: Cornell University Press, 1985.

———. *This Sex Which Is Not One*. Trans. Catherine Porter. Ithaca, N.Y.: Cornell University Press, 1985.

———. *To Be Two*. Trans. Monique M. Rhodes and Marco F. Cocito-Monoc. New York: Routledge, 2001.

Jantzen, Grace A. *Becoming Divine: Toward a Feminist Philosophy of Religion*. Bloomington/Indianapolis: Indiana University Press, 1999.

Jardine, Alice. *Gynesis: Configurations of Woman and Modernity*. Ithaca, N.Y.: Cornell University Press, 1985.

Jay, Martin. *Downcast Eyes: The Denigration of Vision in Twentieth-Century French Thought*. Berkeley: University of California Press, 1994.

Johnson, Barbara. "Is Female to Male as Ground Is to Figure?" In *Feminism and Psychoanalysis*. Eds. Richard Feldstein and Judith Roof. Ithaca, N.Y./London: Cornell University Press, 1989. 255–268.

Johnson, David E. "Marking (Out) Ethics, In Other Words: On a Single Line in Kant and Juan García Ponce." *Interdisciplinary Literary Studies*, 5.2 (spring, 2004): 50–72.

Kafka, Franz. *The Trial*. Trans. Willa Muir and Edwin Muir. New York: Knopf, 1968.

Kamuf, Peggy. "Béance." *CR: The New Centennial Review* 2.3 (2002): 37–56.

Kant, Immanuel. *The Conflict of the Faculties*. Trans. Mary J. Gregor. Lincoln/London: University of Nebraska Press, 1992.

———. *Critique of Practical Reason*. Trans. T. K. Abbot. Amherst, N.Y.: Prometheus Books, 1996.

———. *Critique of Pure Reason*. Trans. Paul Guyer and Allen W. Wood. Cambridge: Cambridge University Press, 1998.

———. *Foundations of the Metaphysics of Morals*. 2nd ed. Trans. Lewis White Beck. New York: Library of Liberal Arts, 1990.

———. *Kritik der praktischen Vernunft. Grundlegung zur Metaphysik der Sitten*. Ed. Wilhelm Weischedel. Frankfurt: Suhrkamp, 1997.

———. *The Metaphysics of Morals*. Ed. Mary Gregor. Cambridge: Cambridge University Press, 1996.

———. *Religion Within the Limits of Reason Alone*. Trans. Theodore M. Greene and Hoyt H. Hudson. New York: Harper, 1960.

Kierkegaard, Søren. *Begrebet Angest*. Borgen: Danske Klassikere, 1991.

———. *The Concept of Anxiety*. Trans. Reidar Thomte and Albert B. Anderson. Princeton, N.J.: Princeton University Press, 1980.

———. *The Concept of Dread*. Trans. Walter Lowrie. Princeton, N.Y.: Princeton University Press, 1957.

———. *Concluding Unscientific Postscript to Philosophical Fragments*. Eds. and trans. Howard V. Hong and Edna H. Hong. Princeton, N.J.: Princeton University Press, 1992.

———. *Fear and Trembling/Repetition. Kierkegaard's Writings, VI*. Trans. Howard V. Hong and Edna H. Hong. Princeton, N.J.: Princeton University Press, 1983.

———. *The Journals of Søren Kierkegaard*. Trans. Alexander Dru. London/New York/Toronto: Oxford University Press, 1938.

———. *My Work as an Author*. In *The Kierkegaard Reader*. Eds. Jane Chamberlain and Jonathan Rée. Oxford/Maldon, Mass.: Blackwell Publishers, 2001.

———. *Philosophical Fragments, or a Fragment of Philosophy*. Trans. David F. Swenson. Princeton, N.J.: Princeton University Press, 1962.

———. *Philosophical Fragments, or a Fragment of Philosophy*. Trans. Howard V. and Edna H. Hong. Princeton, N.J.: Princeton University Press, 1985.

Kofman, Sarah. *Le respect des femmes*. Paris: Éditions Galilée, 1982.

Kristeva, Julia. *Tales of Love*. Trans. Leon S. Roudiez. New York: Columbia University Press, 1987.

La Bible. Ancient Testament. Trans. Édouard Dhorme. Paris: Gallimard, 1956.

Lacan, Jacques. "The Agency of the Letter in the Unconscious or Reason Since Freud." In *Écrits: A Selection*. Trans. Alan Sheridan. New York/London: W. W. Norton, 1977. 146–178.

———. *The Four Fundamental Concepts of Psycho-Analysis.* Trans. Alan Sheridan. New York/London: W. W. Norton, 1977.

———. "Kant with Sade." Trans. James B. Swenson, Jr. *October* 51 (1989): 55–104.

———. "Of Structure as an Inmixing of an Otherness Prerequisite to Any Subject Whatever." In *The Languages of Criticism and the Sciences of Man: The Structuralist Controversy.* Eds. Richard Macksey and Eugenio Donato. Baltimore/London: Johns Hopkins University Press, 1970.

———. "Position de l'inconscient." In *Écrits.* Paris: Éditions du Seuil, 1966. 829–850. Translation by Bruce Fink appears in *Reading Seminar XI: Lacan's Four Fundamental Concepts of Psychoanalysis.* Eds. Richard Feinstein, Bruce Fink, and Maire Jaanus. Albany: SUNY Press, 1995. 259–282.

———. *Le séminaire, livre VII: L'éthique de la psychanalyse.* Paris: Seuil, 1986.

———. *Le séminaire de Jacques Lacan, Livre XX, Encore, 1973–1974.* Paris: Éditions du Seuil, 1975.

———. *The Seminar of Jacques Lacan, Book 1: Freud's Papers on Technique 1953–1954.* Trans. John Forrester. New York/London: W. W. Norton, 1991.

———. *The Seminar of Jacques Lacan, Book VII: The Ethics of Psychoanalysis 1959–1960.* Trans. Dennis Porter. New York/London, W. W. Norton, 1992.

———. *The Seminar of Jacques Lacan, On Feminine Sexuality, The Limits of Love and Knowledge, Book XX, Encore 1972–1973.* Trans. Bruce Fink. New York/London: W. W. Norton, 1998.

———. "The Subversion of the Subject and the Dialectic of Desire." In *Écrits: A Selection.* Trans. Alan Sheridan. New York/London: W. W. Norton, 1977. 292–324.

———. *Télévision.* Paris: Éditions du Seuil, 1974.

Laclau, Ernesto. "Can Immanence Explain Social Struggles?" *Diacritics* 31.4 (2001): 3–10.

Landy, Joshua. "The Cruel Gift: Lucid Self-Delusion in French Literature and German Philosophy, 1851–1914." Dissertation. Princeton University, 1997.

Laplanche, Jean. *Life and Death in Psychoanalysis.* Trans. Jeffrey Mehlman. Baltimore/London: Johns Hopkins University Press, 1976.

Lee, Jonathan Scott. *Jacques Lacan.* Cambridge: MIT University Press, 1990.

Lévinas, Emmanuel. *De Dieu qui vient à l'idée.* Paris: Vrin, 1982.

———. "Existence and Ethics." In *Kierkegaard: A Critical Reader.* Eds. Jonathan Rée and Jane Chamberlain. Oxford/Maldon, Mass.: Blackwell Publishers, 1998. 26–38.

———. *God, Death, and Time.* Trans. Bettina Bergo. Stanford, Calif.: Stanford University Press, 2000.

———. *Of God Who Comes to Mind.* Trans. Bettina Bergo. Stanford, Calif.: Stanford University Press, 1998.

———. *Totality and Infinity. An Essay on Exteriority.* Trans. Alphonso Lingis. Pittsburgh: Duquesne University Press, 1969.

Levine, George L. *Darwin and the Novelists: Patterns of Science in Victorian Fiction.* Cambridge, Mass.: Harvard University Press, 1988.

Lévi-Strauss, Claude. *The Raw and the Cooked. Introduction to a Science of Mythology: I.* Trans. John and Doreen Weightman. New York: Harper Colophon Books, 1969.

Lewis, C. S. *The Allegory of Love: A Study in Medieval Tradition.* Oxford: Oxford University Press, 1946.

Locke, John. *An Essay Concerning Human Understanding.* London: Dent, 1965.

———. *An Essay Concerning Human Understanding.* Oxford: Clarendon Press, 1975.

MacCannell, Juliet Flower. "Facing Fascism: A Feminine Politics of Jouissance." *Topoi* 12 (1993): 137–151.

Maccoby, Eleanor E. "Sex Differences in Intellectual Functioning." In *The Development of Sex Differences.* Ed. Eleanor E. Maccoby. Stanford, Calif.: Stanford University Press, 1966. 25–55.

MacIntyre, Alasdaire. *A Short History of Ethics.* New York: Simon and Schuster, 1966.

Margolis, Joseph. "Cartesian Realism and the Revival of Pragmatism." In *The Pragmatic Turn in Philosophy: Contemporary Engagements Between Analytic and Continental Thought.* Eds. William Egginton and Mike Sandbothe. Albany: SUNY Press, 2002.

Martinez, Ronald. "Mourning Beatrice: 'The Rhetoric of Threnody in the *Vita nuova.*'" *MLN* 113.1 (1998): 1–29.

Martyn, David. *Sublime Failures: The Ethics of Kant and Sade.* Detroit, Mich.: Wayne State University Press, 2002.

Maturana, Humberto, and Francisco Varela. *The Tree of Knowledge. The Biological Roots of Human Understanding.* rev. ed. Trans. Robert Paolucci. Boston and London: Shambhala, 1998.

McElvaine, Robert S. *Eve's Seed: Biology, the Sexes, and the Course of History.* New York: McGraw-Hill, 2001.

McLaughlin, Eleanor Commo. "Equality of Souls, Inequality of Sexes: Woman in Medieval Theology." In *Woman in Western Thought.* Ed. Martha Lee Osborne. New York: Random House, 1979. 77–88.

Menocal, María Rosa. *Shards of Love: Exile and the Origins of the Lyric.* Durham, N.C.: Duke University Press, 1994.

Menninghaus, Winfried. *Ekel. Theorie und Geschichte einer starken Empfindung.* Frankfurt: Suhrkamp, 1999.

Miller, Jacques-Alain. "Extimacy." In *Lacanian Theory of Discourse.* Eds. Mark Bracher, Marshall W. Alcorn, Jr., Ronald J. Corthell, and Françoise Massardier-Kennedy. New York and London: New York University Press, 1994. 74–87.

———. "On Semblances in the Relation Between the Sexes." Trans. Sina Najafi and Marina Harss. In *Sexuation.* Ed. Renata Salecl. Durham, N.C./London: Duke University Press, 2000. 13–27.

Mitchell, Juliet. *Psychoanalysis and Feminism: Freud, Reich, Laing and Women*. New York: Vintage Books, 1975.

Moi, Toril. *Sexual/Textual Politics*. London: Methuan, 1985.

Montrelay, Michelle. "Inquiry into Femininity." In *The Woman in Question*. Eds. Parveen Adams and Elizabeth Cowie. Cambridge, Mass.: MIT Press, 1990. 253–273.

Morel, Geneviève. "Psychoanalytical Anatomy." Trans. Sina Najafi and Marina Harss. In *Sexuation*. Ed. Renata Salecl. Durham, N.C./London: Duke University Press, 2000. 28–38.

Muller, John, and William J. Richardson, eds. *The Purloined Poe*. Baltimore: Johns Hopkins University Press, 1988.

Nadeau, Robert L. *S/he Brain: Science, Sexual Politics, and the Myths of Feminism*. Westport, Conn./London: Praeger, 1996.

Nancy, Jean-Luc. *Being Singular Plural*. Trans. Robert D. Richardson and Anne E. O'Byrne. Stanford, Calif.: Stanford University Press, 2000.

———. *The Birth to Presence*. Trans. Brian Holmes et al. Stanford, Calif.: Stanford University Press, 1993.

———. "La Déconstruction du Christianisme." *Études philosophiques* 4 (1998): 503–19. Translated as "The Deconstruction of Christianity." Trans. Simon Sparks. In *Media and Religion*. Eds. Hent de Vries and Samuel Weber. Stanford, Calif.: Stanford University Press, 2001. 112–130.

———. *Ego sum*. Paris: Flammarion, 1979.

———. *The Inoperative Community*. Trans. Peter Connor, Lisa Garbus, Michael Holland, and Simona Fynsk. Minneapolis: University of Minnesota Press, 1991.

———. "Is Everything Political? (A Brief Remark)." Trans. Philip M. Adamek. *CR: The New Centennial Review* 2.3 (2002): 15–22.

———. *La remarque speculative*. Paris: Galilée, 1973.

———. *L'intrus*. Paris: Galilée, 2000.

———. *The Sense of the World*. Trans. Jeffrey S. Librett. Minneapolis: University of MinnesotaPress, 1997.

Nancy, Jean-Luc, and Philippe Lacoue-Labarthe. *The Title of the Letter*. Trans. Francois Raffoul and David Pettigrew. Albany: SUNY Press, 1992.

Nasio, Juan-David . *Les yeux de Laure: le concept d'objet a dans la théorie de J. Lacan*. Paris: Aubier, 1987.

New Oxford Annotated Bible with the Apocrypha, The. Eds. Herbert G. May and Bruce M. Metzger. New York: Oxford University Press, 1977.

Nietzsche, Friedrich. *Nachgelassene Werke. Nietzsche's Werke*. Band XIV. Leipzing: Naumann, 1904.

———. *The Will to Power*. Trans. Walter Kaufman and R. J. Hollingdale. New York: Random House, 1967.

Nodding, Nel. *Caring: A Feminine Approach to Ethics and Moral Education*. Berkeley: University of California Press, 1984.

Nussbaum, Martha C. *Upheavals of Thought: The Intelligence of Emotions*. Cambridge/New York: Cambridge University Press, 2001.

O'Brien, Mary. *The Politics of Reproduction*. Boston: Routledge and Kegan Paul, 1981.

Olkowski, Dorothea. "Body, Knowledge and Becoming-Woman: Morpho-logic in Deleuze and Irigaray." In *Deleuze and Feminist Theory*. Eds. Ian Buchanan and Claire Colebrook. Edinburgh: Edinburgh University Press, 2000. 86–109.

Oller, D. Kimbrough. *The Emergence of the Speech Capacity*. Mahwah, N.J./London: Lawrence Erlbaum, 2000.

Ortner, Sherry. "Is Female to Male as Nature Is to Culture?" In *Woman, Culture and Society*. Eds. Michelle Zimbalist Rosaldo and Louise Lamphere. Stanford, Calif.: Stanford University Press, 1974. 67–88.

Penney, James. *The World of Perversion. Psychoanalysis and the Impossible Real of Desire*. Albany: SUNY Press, 2005.

Peto, Andrew. "Body Image and Archaic Thinking." *International Journal of Psycho-Analysis* 40 (1959): 223–231.

Poe, Edgar Allan. *The Complete Works of Edgar Allan Poe*. Ed. James A. Harrison. 17 vols. New York: AMS Press, 1965.

Recalcati, Massimo. *Der Stein des Antosses: Lacan und das Jenseits des Lustprinzips*. Trans. René Scheu. Vienna: Turia and Kant, 2000.

Rée, Jonathan, and Jane Chamberlain. "Introduction." In *Kierkegaard: A Critical Reader*. Oxford/Maldon, Mass.: Blackwell Publishers, 1998.

Rhode, Deborah L. "Theoretical Perspectives on Sexual Difference." In *Theoretical Perspectives on Sexual Difference*. Ed. Deborah Rhode. New Haven/London: Yale University Press, 1990. 1–12.

Richardson, William. "Psychoanalysis and the Being-Question." In *Interpreting Lacan*. Ed. Joseph H. Smith and William Kerrigan. New Haven: Yale University Press, 1983.

Ricoeur, P. "Philosophy after Kierkegaard." In *Kierkegaard: A Critical Reader*. Eds. Jonathan Rée and Jane Chamberlain. Oxford/Maldon, Mass.: Blackwell Publishers, 1998. 9–25.

Robinson, Gene E. "Genomics: Beyond Nature and Nurture." *Science* 304 (2004): 397–399.

Rockmore, Tom. *Heidegger and French Philosophy: Humanism, Antihumanism, and Being*. London/New York: Routledge, 1995.

Rorty, Amélie O. "Akrasia and Pleasure: Nicomachean Ethics Book 7." In *Essays on Aristotle's Ethics*. Ed. A. O. Rorty. Berkeley/Los Angeles/London: University of California Press, 1980. 267–284.

Rorty, Richard. *Consequences of Pragmatism (Essays: 1972–1980)*. Minneapolis: University of Minnesota Press, 1982.

———. "Freud and Moral Reflection." In *Essays on Heidegger and Others. Philosophical Papers* Vol. 2. New York: Cambridge University Press, 1991.

————. "Justice as a Wider Loyalty." In *Justice and Democracy: Cross-Cultural Perspectives*. Eds. R. Bontekoe et al. Honolulu: University of Hawaii Press, 1997.

————. *Philosophy and the Mirror of Nature*. Princeton, N.J.: Princeton University Press, 1979.

————. "Wittgenstein, Heidegger, and the Reification of Language." In *Essays on Heidegger and Others: Philosophical Papers* Vol. 2. Cambridge: Cambridge University Press, 1991. 50–65.

Rosset, Clément. *Logique du pire*. Paris: Presses Universitaires de France, 1970.

Roudinesco, Elisabeth. *Jacques Lacan*. Trans. Barbara Bray. New York: Columbia University Press, 1997.

Rougemont, Denis de. *Love in the Western World*. Trans. Montgomery Belgion. Princeton, N.J.: Princeton University Press, 1983.

Rousseau, Jean-Jacques. *Essay on the Origin of Languages and Writings Related to Music*. Trans. John T. Scott. Hanover, N.H.: University Press of New England, 1998.

Ruether, Rosemary Radford. "Misogynism and Virginal Feminism in the Fathers of the Church." In *Woman in Western Thought*. Ed. Martha Lee Osborne. New York: Random House, 1979. 62–65.

Rüstow, Alexander. *Der Lügner, Theorie, Geschichte und Auflösung*. New York/London: Garland Publishing, 1987.

Sade, Marquis de. *The Complete Justine, Philosophy in the Bedroom, and Other Writings*. Ed. and trans. Richard Seaver and Austryn Wainhouse. New York: Grove Press, 1965.

Safranski, Rüdiger. *Das Böse oder das Drama der Freiheit*. Frankfurt: Fischer, 1999.

Sartre, Jean-Paul. *Being and Nothingness. A Phenomenological Essay on Ontology*. Trans. Hazel E. Barns. New York: Washington Square Press, 1956.

————. "Kierkegaard: The Singular Universal." In *Between Existentialism and Marxism*. Trans. John Matthews. London: NLB, 1974. 141–69.

Shepherdson, Charles. "The Intimate Alterity of the Real: A Response to Reader Commentary on 'History and the Real' (PMC v.5 n.2)." *Postmodern Culture* 6.3 (1996). Online at http://www.iath.virginia.edu/pmc/text-only/issue.996/

————. "Of Love and Beauty in Lacan's Antigone." *Umbr(a)* 1 (1999): 63–80.

————. *Vital Signs: Nature, Culture, Psychoanalysis*. New York/London: Routledge, 2000.

Silverman, Kaja. *Male Subjectivity at the Margins*. New York/London: Routledge, 1992.

Singleton, Charles. *Essay on the "Vita Nuova."* Cambridge: Harvard University Press, 1949.

Slipp, Samuel. *The Freudian Mystique: Freud, Women, and Feminism*. New York: New York University Press, 1993.

Sokal, Alan, and Jean Bricmont. *Fashionable Nonsense: Postmodern Intellectuals' Abuse of Science*. New York: Picador USA, 1998.

Soler, Colette. "The Curse on Sex." Trans. Sina Najafi and Marina Harss. In *Sexuation*. Ed. Renata Salecl. Durham, N.C./London: Duke University Press, 2000. 39–53.

Sophocles. *Antigone*. Trans. Declan Donellan. London: Oberon Books, 1999.

Spinoza, Baruch. *A Theologico-Political Treatise/A Political Treatise*. Trans. R. H. M. Elwes. New York: Dover, 1951.

Spivak, Gayatri Chakravorty. "Can the Subaltern Speak?" In *The Post-Colonial Studies Reader*. Eds. Bill Ashcroft, Gareth Griffiths, and Helen Tiffin. London: Routledge, 1995. 24–28.

Steakley, James. "*Per scientiam ad justitiam*: Magnus Hirschfeld and the Sexual Politics of Innate Homosexuality." In *Science and Homosexualities*. Ed. Vernon A. Rosario. New York: Routledge, 1997. 133–154.

Stern, David G. *Wittgenstein on Mind and Language*. New York/Oxford: Oxford University Press, 1995.

Suler, John R. *Psychoanalysis and Eastern Thought*. Albany: SUNY Press, 1993.

Tannen, Deborah. *You Just Don't Understand: Woman and Men in Conversation*. New York: Quill, 1990.

Taylor, Mark C. *Nots*. Chicago/London: University of Chicago Press, 1993.

Teresa, St. *Obras completas*. Eds. Efren de la Madre de Dios O. C. D. and Otger Steggimk O. Carm. Madrid: Biblioteca de Autores Cristianos, 1972.

Thornhill, Randy, and Craig T. Palmer. *A Natural History of Rape: Biological Bases of Sexual Coercion*. Cambridge, Mass.: MIT Press, 2000.

Vattimo, Gianni. *After Christianity*. Trans. Luca D'Isanto. New York: Columbia University Press, 2002.

Verhaeghe, Paul. *Does the Woman Exist? From Freud's Hysteric to Lacan's Feminine* Trans. Marc du Ry. New York: Other Press, 1999.

Vries, Hent de. *Philosophy and the Turn to Religion*. Baltimore: Johns Hopkins University Press, 1999.

Wallwork, Ernest. *Psychoanalysis and Ethics*. New Haven, Conn./London: Yale University Press, 1991.

Winkler, Isabella. *Quodlibet: The Affirmation of the Singular in Recent Continental Thought from Derrida to Deleuze*. Dissertation. State University of New York at Buffalo, 2003.

Wittgenstein, Ludwig. *The Blue and Brown Books*. New York: Blackwell, 1958.

———. "A Lecture on Ethics." *Philosophical Review* 74 (1965): 3–11.

———. *Philosophical Investigations*. Trans. G. E. M. Anscombe. Oxford: Blackwell, 1967.

Wittig, Monique. *The Straight Mind and Other Essays*. London/New York: Harvester Wheatsheaf, 1992.

Wood, David. "Thinking God in the Wake of Kierkegaard." In *Kierkegaard: A Critical Reader*. Eds. Jonathan Rée and Jane Chamberlain. Oxford/Maldon, Mass.: Blackwell Publishers, 1998. 53–74.

Ziarek, Ewa. *An Ethics of Dissensus: Postmodernity, Feminism, and the Politics of Radical Democracy.* Stanford, Calif.: Stanford University Press, 2001.

Ziarek, Krzysztof. "Love and the Debasement of Being: Irigaray's Revisions of Lacan and Heidegger." *Postmodern Culture* 10.1 (1999). Online at http://www. iath.virginia.edu/pmc/text-only/issue.999/

Žižek, Slavoj. *The Fragile Absolute—or, Why Is the Christian Legacy Worth Fighting For?* London/New York: Verso, 2000.

———. *The Indivisible Remainder.* London: Verso, 1996.

———. *Organs Without Bodies: Deleuze and Consequences.* London: Routledge, 2004.

———. *The Puppet and the Dwarf: The Perverse Core of Christianity.* Cambridge, Mass.: MIT Press, 2003.

———. *The Sublime Object of Ideology.* London: Verso, 1989.

———. *Tarrying with the Negative.* Durham, N.C.: Duke University Press, 1993.

———. *The Ticklish Subject: The Absent Center of Political Ontology.* London: Verso, 1999.

Zupancic, Alenka. *Ethics of the Real: Kant, Lacan.* London: Verso, 2000.

Index of Authors